Emilio Fernández

Manchester University Press

Spanish and Latin American Filmmakers

Series editors:
Núria Triana Toribio, University of Manchester
Andy Willis, University of Salford

Spanish and Latin American Filmmakers offers a focus on new, and reclaims previously neglected, filmmakers, and considers established figures from new and different perspectives. Each volume places its subjects in a variety of critical and production contexts.

The series sees filmmakers as more than just auteurs, thus offering an insight into the work and contexts of producers, writers, actors, production companies and studios. The studies in this series take into account the recent changes in Spanish and Latin American film studies, such as the new emphasis on popular cinema, the influence of cultural studies in the analysis of films and of the film cultures produced within the Spanish-speaking industries.

Emilio Fernández

Pictures in the margins

Dolores Tierney

Manchester University Press
Manchester and New York
distributed exclusively in the USA by Palgrave

Copyright © Dolores Tierney 2007

The right of Dolores Tierney to be identified as the author of this work has been asserted by her in accordance with the Copyright, Designs and Patents Act 1988.

Published by Manchester University Press
Oxford Road, Manchester M13 9NR, UK
and Room 400, 175 Fifth Avenue, New York, NY 10010, USA
www.manchesteruniversitypress.co.uk

Distributed in the United States exclusively by
Palgrave Macmillan, 175 Fifth Avenue,
New York, NY 10010, USA

Distributed in Canada exclusively by
UBC Press, University of British Columbia, 2029 West Mall,
Vancouver, BC, Canada V6T 1Z2

British Library Cataloguing-in-Publication Data is available

Library of Congress Cataloging-in-Publication Data is available

ISBN 978 0 7190 8844 5 paperback

First published by Manchester University Press in hardback 2007

This paperback edition first published 2012

The publisher has no responsibility for the persistence or accuracy of URLs for any external or third-party internet websites referred to in this book, and does not guarantee that any content on such websites is, or will remain, accurate or appropriate.

Printed by Lightning Source

For Nancy

Contents

	List of figures	*page* viii
	Preface	ix
	Introduction	1
1	'Poor reception' and the popular: the history of classical Mexican cinema and its scholarship	17
2	'El Indio' Fernández, Mexico's marginalized golden boy and national auteur	48
3	Calendar María: hybridity, *indigenismo* and the discourse of whitening	73
4	Gender, sexuality and the Revolution in *Enamorada*	104
5	Gender, sexuality and the Revolution in *Salón México*, *Las abandonadas* and *Víctimas del pecado*	121
6	Progress, modernity and Fernández' 'antimodernist utopia': *Río Escondido*	144
	Epilogue: Mexican cinema and Emilio Fernández post the Golden Age – from golden boy to 'the man in black'	160
	Filmography	172
	Bibliography	179
	Index	190

List of figures

2.1	Fernández as Zirahuén in *Janitzio*	61
3.1	*María Candelaria*: María Candelaria is sick	89
3.2	*María Candelaria*: 'Look the Virgin is crying'	92
3.3	*María Candelaria*: The Virgin is crying	93
3.4	*María Candelaria*: María is crying	93
3.5	Pedro Armendáriz as Kino in *La perla*	99
4.1	Eyes that look knowingly... connoting defiance rather than submission	111
4.2	*Enamorada*: José Juan rubs his cheek fetishistically	114
4.3	*Enamorada*: Beatriz and José Juan violence as romantic interest	115
4.4	*Enamorada*: Beatriz and José Juan leaving a world where they do not belong	118
6.1	*Río Escondido*: National Palace Mural *maestras rurales*	147
6.2	*Río Escondido*: National Palace Mural *campesinos* held at gunpoint	147
6.3	*Río Escondido*: Engraving of *cacique* issuing orders	149
6.4	*Río Escondido*: Engraving of Raised Torch	152

Preface

It is necessary to look behind the stereotypical figure [of Emilio Fernández] which the films of Sam Peckinpah helped to fix when 'El Indio' developed his career as an actor: the brutish womanizing sadist ... or the vindictive patriarch. (King, 2000: 48)

The image of Emilio Fernández (1904–86) the most successful director of classical Mexican cinema, as he appears on the cover of this book, in black *charro* (Mexican cowboy) costume with cartridge belts worn crossed on his chest, is an overdetermined image. It simultaneously channels the Mexican revolution (1910–1920) (he is pictured as Colonel Zeta from the revolutionary epic *La cucaracha* [Ismael Rodríguez, 1958]) and the Mexican national character i.e. the (gun-toting) *macho*. 'Lo macho' and the revolution are also recurrent themes within auteurist accounts of Fernández' work and also part of his myth. He is even rumored to be an ex-villista general (Monsiváis, 1992: 29). Fernández most famous films are often obscured by this very powerful image of Fernández the revolutionary Mexican *macho*.

Taking a cue from John King, *Emilio Fernández: Pictures in the Margins* seeks to look behind the stereotypical figure of Fernández as it has been established in Mexican film scholarship and beyond the clichés of the Mexican revolution and national character through which he and his films are so often represented. This book offers an account of Fernández' career and textual analyses of his most famous films (*María Candelaria, Maclovia, La perla, Enamorada, Salón México, Víctimas del pecado, Las abandonadas* and *Río Escondido*). However, rather than offering a classic auteur study this book interrogates the construction of Fernández as both a national and nationalist auteur. It also challenges auteurist readings of his films in order to make new arguments about the significance of Fernández and his work.

Classical Mexican cinema, it has been proposed, represents a successful attempt by the state to establish a position of ideological dominance, to forward a paradoxically conservative vision of the post-Revolutionary Mexican nation. Fernández is conceived as the director who best embodies this aspect of classical Mexican cinema. In criticism, his films affirm conservative values; machismo, patriarchy and hegemonic cultural nationalism. This book argues that Fernández's oeuvre is not the coherent depiction of the institutionalized Revolution's cultural nationalism that traditional scholarship perceives it to be, but instead a fissured, contradictory text. This book proposes radical new readings of Fernández' 1940s films which reveal the gaps and silences in hegemonic cultural nationalism. It takes issue with the representations of gender, racial ideology, national identity and nationalism. Through close textual analysis, post-colonial and transnational approaches, it reveals fissures and alterity in the films that suggest more subversive readings of Fernández's films than those permitted by institutionalized cultural nationalism.

At the same time, this book aims to question Mexico's festishization of its own position on the peripheries of the global cultural economy and the similar fetishization of Fernández' marginalization as a mixed-race (part white and part indigenous) director. This book argues that, as *Pictures in the margins*, classical Mexican cinema and specifically Fernández films are not transparent reflections of dominant post-Revolutionary Mexican culture but annotations and reinscriptions of the particularities of Mexican society in the post-Revolutionary era.

This project would not have been possible without leave from Sussex University and the help of many people. I thank all those at the Filmoteca of the Universidad Nacional Autónoma in Mexico City, especially Iván Trojillo and Antonia Rojas. I also thank the Mexican historian Julia Tuñón, the foremost Fernández scholar from whom I have drawn great inspiration for this book and with whose work I respectfully engage. I am also grateful to Adela Fernández, Emilio's daughter, who offered me hospitality and many great insights into the man himself at his *Casa Fuerte* in Mexico City.

I thank the many people who read and offered comments and feedback on parts of the manuscript particularly; Ana López, Charles Ramírez Berg, Andrew Syder, Beth Roberts, Robert Irwin, Sergio de la Mora, John King, Misha McClaird, Katie Grant, Gabriela Alemán, Jackie Stacey, and Winston Wheeler Dixon. I thank the series editors Andy Willis and Núria Triana Toribio and also Matthew Frost at Manchester University Press.

Many of the final revisions to this book were made in the aftermath of Hurricane Katrina, during a four-month exile from New Orleans. I would like to thank those who offered help, materials and shelter during these months, particularly Robbie Robb, Ernesto Acevedo-Muñoz, Sergio de la Mora (again), Marcie and Jason Wessels and the Communication Chair and his Assistant at the University of California San Diego Robert Horowitz and Judy Wertin.

I thank my mother for all her support and Eddie Besancon my husband for his patience and enduring love and for accompanying me during many nights and weekends of revisions and rewritings.

Introduction

During the 1940s the 'Golden Age' of Mexican cinema (1935–55) reached its zenith. This was a time of immense expansion and popularity in the Mexican film industry, when it came to enjoy dominance over Latin American and other Spanish-language markets comparable to the world dominance of Hollywood.[1] The name 'Golden' which refers to this period of filmmaking clearly refers to this hegemony as well as to the cinema's gilded, idealized representations of Mexican nationalism, an amorphous concept otherwise known as *lo mexicano* (Mexicanness).

For seven years, from 1943 until 1950, Emilio Fernández (1904–86) was regarded as one of the foremost purveyors of 'Mexicanness,' as one of the most important filmmakers of the Mexican film industry (along with his contemporaries Julio Bracho, Alejandro Galindo, Fernando de Fuentes, Ismael Rodríguez and Roberto Gavaldón), and as one of the most famous filmmakers in the Western World. His distinctive, 'authentically Mexican' visual style – developed over an extensive collaboration with photographer Gabriel Figueroa of thirteen years and twenty-two films – was praised for bringing international attention and prestige to the Mexican film industry, including praise from the French critic George Sadoul. His *María Candelaria* (1943), starring Dolores Del Rio[2] and Pedro Armendáriz, won the top prize at the first Cannes Film Festival in 1946.[3] At the height of his career in the 1940s he was loved by audiences and critics alike, not only for bringing international attention and artistic glory to the Mexican motion-picture industry but also for defining a school of Mexican film. Indeed, he underscored and in some ways initiated this approach to his work by repeatedly claiming '¡El cine mexicano soy yo!' (Tuñón, 1993: 160) (I am Mexican cinema). Also influential in his popular success was the fact that his vision of Mexico was very much in tune with the post-Revolutionary (capitalized to emphasize the historical revolution's institutionalization within Government)[4] nationalist rhetoric of Presidents Manuel Ávila Camacho (1940–46) and Miguel Alemán (1946–52): a dignifying of an essential and eternal Mexican identity.

Fernández' subsequent celebrity and consequent canonization in Mexico as part of the national patrimony – along with Figueroa – have created a frustrating situation for academics seeking to analyze Fernández' films. Hailed in film lore as a national icon, Fernández has achieved a standing as the originator of a specifically Mexican national cinema. But this is an appraisal that lacks a serious or rigorous analytical base (De la Vega Alfaro, 1995: 87). Fernández' specifically Mexican cinema is often reduced to a string of stylistic clichés: 'low angle shots' and 'fluffy Figueroan skies' (Wu, 2000: 177) which often derail formal analysis of his films. One such derailment has been the conflation of Fernández' oeuvre with the post-Revolutionary cultural political project of *forjando patria* (nation building) and modernization (Rozado, 1991: 19). This conflation triggers certain readings of Fernández' canonical texts (*María Candelaria, Enamorada, Río Escondido, Salón Mexico, La perla, Víctimas del pecado, Maclovia, Las abandonadas*)[5] which are mirrored in readings of all 1940s Mexican films that participated in and created the national film industry. These readings reiterate (rather than analyzing) how films like *Nosotros los pobres* (We the poor, Ismael Rodríguez, 1947) facilitated the project of cultural nationalism. In such readings 1940s Mexican films became the forum for renegotiating collective values and beliefs, creating a sense of 'national identity' or '*mexicanidad*' in the urban and also the rural masses displaced to the cities by the revolution. This is the myth of Mexican cinema in the 1940s.

It is common for readings of culture in the period *following* the mythical age of the 1940s and early 1950s – the 1960s through to the early 1980s – to highlight the cracks and fissures which signal the crisis of social cohesion and compare it with the 'harmonious' 'reciprocity' between society and culture of the Golden Age. Eric Zolov makes such a reading via popular (and specifically rock) music (1999) as does Charles Ramírez Berg via cinema (1992). This myth that Fernández and Golden Age cinema unproblematically represented national self-image has passed into Mexican film lore and become institutionalized. Hence the majority of readings of this period in Mexican cinema elide

Introduction

what can be seen as obvious contradictions of Fernández' films and Mexican post-Revolutionary society.

One such contradiction is that Fernández is famed for presenting an eternal, essential and antimodernist Mexico at a time when, under the presidencies of Ávila Camacho and Alemán, the country was going through rapid modernization (Rozado, 1991: 10–61; Tuñón, 1993: 165). This suggests that rather than embodying 'authentic Mexican identity' Fernández was out of touch with contemporary political imperatives. That he was 'out of touch' has been used as a reason to explain why, from 1950 onward, audiences and critics grew tired of Fernández' films, which seemed to repeat the same images and formulae with increasingly bombastic Revolutionary discourses (Tuñón, 2000: 27). In this line of argument Fernández' eternal Mexico of abnegated women (*mujeres abnegadas*), *machos* and noble indigenous people (*indígenas*) gradually became more and more foreign to a Mexico of social construction and progress. Sadly, in his twilight years of the late 1970s and early 1980s this great auteur was reduced to lingering around the Churubusco Studios in Mexico City, hoping to find financial backing for his film ideas.

This book attempts to develop ways of reading Fernández' films that will go beyond the myth of the 'Golden Age' and the clichés around Fernández that it produces, and explore the contradictions of post-Revolutionary representation as manifested in Fernández' canonical 1940s films: *María Candelaria, Víctimas del pecado, Las abandonadas, La perla, Enamorada, Río Escondido, Maclovia* and *Salón Mexico*.

Another important aim of this book is to explore transnational influences that shape Fernández' work, influences obscured by the focus on Fernández' films as 'authentic Mexican films' (Berg, 1992: 5). For example, Fernández along with many other Mexican film pioneers like Roberto Gavaldón, Chano Urueta, René Cardona, Tito Davison, Ismael Rodríguez and Gilberto Martínez Solares spent several years in Hollywood during the early sound era, working as an extra or as technical crew (García Riera, 1993a: 27–31).[6] And yet there are no existing studies which sufficiently acknowledge the intersection of the transnational with the local, or the national in Fernández' work.[7] Furthermore, Fernández' status as a national auteur was initially based in large part on the paradoxical approbation from abroad of French critics Sadoul, Raymond Borde and others. This is signalled by the way importance is conferred on his cinema precisely because it was recognized by the European critics. (Tuñón, 2000: 13) This study seeks to redress some of the imbalances of Fernández criticism caused by bounded nationalism and his auteur status by seeking to highlight the many transnational forces that shape and determine his films. At the same time, this book acknowledges how the events of the Mexican revolution impacted on the country's film industry and the ideological development of nationalism. The revolution of 1910–20 brought an end to the 30-year dictatorship of Porfirio Díaz. Sparked by an armed revolt led by Francisco Madero, a politician who represented urban middle-class disenchantment (and a call for 'universal suffrage, no reelection'), the revolution was fought simultaneously in rural uprisings on issues of land and social reform. These were led by the charismatic Francisco (Pancho) Villa in the north and Emiliano Zapata in the south. However, Madero supporters (including Villa and Mexico City's middle classes) soon felt betrayed when, newly elected as president, Madero made concessions to the old (Porfirian) regime and failed to implement social and land reforms. Madero was assassinated in 1913 and the country fell into a civil war with Villa and Zapata siding with different generals in the army. By 1920, the 'armed phase' of the revolution was over, and three of its major figures (Villa, Madero and the army general Venustiano Carranza who was elected president in 1917) assassinated. (Zapata also would be assassinated in 1923.) However, the revolution led to changes in Mexico's 'governmental' 'legal and 'economic systems.' A new constitution was promulgated in 1917. The revolution also led to a 'tremendous' shift in 'national consciousness' (O'Malley, 1986: 3). Twenty years later, Mexico's emergent film industry – and Fernández in particular – benefited from huge Government sponsorship designed to freeze and institutionalize an ideological image of the country and its revolution.

Fernández' work is popularly perceived from both inside and outside Mexican culture as the 'Mexicanist cinematic text,' offering a representation of *mexicanidad* as an unproblematic extension of this post-Revolutionary cultural nationalism (Berg, 1992: 5). Cultural nationalism emerged in the 1920s as an organizing motif for a country devastated by revolutionary turmoil (Joseph et al., 2001: 7). As a political project it was about redefining/consolidating national identity through indigenism, education and the notion of the fatherland: 'develop[ing] a system of values around which a society [could] unite and establish a collective livelihood' (Tuñón, 1993: 161).

This book takes note of current tendencies in film studies and postcolonial theory to look for the excesses, instabilities and incoherencies in texts, which challenge such totalizing projects of hegemony or cultural reification as 'cultural nationalism' or '*mexicanidad.*' The book also takes note of how the quest for *mexicanidad* has been critiqued in Mexico as an elaborate game played by intellectuals to maintain dominant power structures and to mask more serious problems (Berg, 1992: 5). Hence, against the aesthetic coherence and moral intentionality that is said to embody Fernández' authorial vision, this book charts the elements within Fernández films which suggest fewer mainstream pleasures and work counter to the mainstream ideologies they supposedly advocate.

The issue of ideology in relation to the study of nationhood and gender is central to this book as well as the ideologies of reading texts. Implicit in the book's approach is an awareness of the problems inherent in assumptions about how prescribed meanings are actually distributed and decoded into a set of texts (Hall, 1999). It asks how conventional (auteurist or nationalist) readings of Fernández' work themselves emblematize the process of political and cultural institutionalization in Mexico – what Stuart Hall might call the 'mapping of meaning,' which seeks to displace, recuperate or simply oppress all attempts to construct difference within a totalizing ideology.

For instance, whereas auteur theory in its *Cahiers du cinéma* phase was focused on dislocating the individual directors (Howard Hawks, John Ford, Alfred Hitchcock) from the dehumanizing studio system, in orthodox approaches to Fernández the auteur theory has been used to illustrate how his films were a part of the 'system,' consolidating Mexico's nationalist project within Mexico's state-funded fledgling studio system. This book incorporates André Bazin's critique of traditional auteurist studies (which argues that it is impossible to isolate the auteur in cinema separate from notions of nation, genre and industry) and takes what has been offered as an alternative to auteurism. Hence, rather than seeking to construct continuity and coherence across a body of work in the manner of a traditional auteur study, this book takes a director centered approach, acknowledging Fernández as an orchestrating figure yet reading each film as an individual text.

The book also takes into consideration genre manipulations which suggest readings beyond and above the narrative. For example, Fernández is often read in relation to the melodrama from a position which considers melodrama to be a totalizing force imposing moral certainties in a disrupted (post-Revolutionary) moral universe

(Monsiváis, 1995a: 147). Taking into consideration feminist and poststructuralist reevaluations of the Hollywood melodrama, which suggest that the genre implies its own contradictions, this book looks at how genre-based readings of Fernández' films expose the possibility of finding resistance to dominant perspectives and how his films often borrow from a wide range of other genres in addition to the melodrama – the action adventure film and the screwball comedy – in order to do this. This book also examines not just Mexican cinema's genre borrowings from Hollywood but also how these Hollywood genres are mediated by and tailored to Mexican concerns. For example, chapter 4 examines how the opposing genres of melodrama and action adventure work in relation to the idea of gender in Fernandez's *Enamorada* (Woman in Love, 1946). Hence the concept of genre – as a signifying system and as a form of dynamic interaction between filmmaker and audience – becomes a part of the post-Revolutionary renegotiation of gendered national identity.

As well as offering a genre-based study of Fernández' work this book also uses close textual analysis to reveal contradictions of each film's explicit ideologies. Mexican scholarship on classical Mexican cinema tends to avoid mise-en-scène analysis because it is feared such an approach would reveal Mexican cinema as 'underdeveloped' and challenge the official narrative of Mexico's progress into modernity from the 1940s onward. This book, through mise-en-scène analysis reveals that classical Mexican cinema can in fact support such detailed textual analysis and that textual analysis can actually reveal the polysemic discourses (rather than monological cultural nationalism) at work in Fernández' oeuvre.

Chapter 1 is a both a history of Mexican cinema from its arrival until the late 1940s and a review of the way it has been studied. It examines how some Mexican analyses of classical Mexican cinema privilege the subjects of cultural practices (the Mexican audience) and ignore the film texts themselves. It suggests that addressing the site of production of meaning (i.e., the films) provides the potential for 'other' readings within these texts.

The chapter begins with a brief history of cinema in Mexico from its arrival in 1896 up to and including the 1940s. The chapter then examines the State's relationship to popular culture (and particularly cinema) in Mexico in the 1940s in terms of the consolidation of the post-Revolutionary nationalist project. The chapter then looks at

Introduction

different critical templates for interpreting this relationship through competing definitions of the 'popular' in popular culture, noting the history of the term's particular use in relation to Latin American culture. The chapter shows how changes in the use of the term 'popular culture' are mirrored in the emergence of a different conception of the popular classes which results in a particular reading protocol in the study of Mexican cinema – i.e., a focus on the audience. The chapter suggests that this reading protocol is cyclical and ultimately contradictory in the project of finding the 'other' in Mexican cinema. By presupposing the existence of a cohesive Mexican subject/audience that can be identified and studied, this cultural-studies reading protocol ends up reaffirming that which cultural studies usually wants to question, the homogeneity of the nation. After a survey of some US studies of classical Mexican cinema which diverge from Mexican analyses by making space for the 'other' through genre and textual analyses, the chapter concludes by outlining how a textual approach, which builds on the advances made by Euro-American studies, might provide an account of Fernández' oeuvre as contradictory, non-homogeneous and evident of a fissured cultural nationalism.

Chapter 2 unpicks the complex figure of Fernández the auteur by arguing against the auteurist analyses of his life and work. It begins by looking at Fernández' role within the project of Mexican cultural nationalism, mapping how – in the critical analysis of his work, by both Mexican and non-Mexican academics – the construction of Fernández as auteur and '*indio*' (Indian) intersects with the processes of institutionalization involved in 'nation' and 'national culture.' It also looks at how this institutionalization is still evident in 1980s accounts, where Fernandez' perceived marginalization as a mixed-race director (part indigenous and part white in a Mexican context) is fetishized as part of a Mexican cultural criticism's fetishization of the country's position on the peripheries of the global cultural economy. It goes on to examine what is at stake when the proponents of Mexican national cinema (Tuñón, Monsiváis, Berg) promote 'El Indio' as auteur, particularly given the neocolonialist implications of the use of the (European) auteurist paradigm in Mexico. The chapter also incorporates a critique of traditional auteurist studies and the way in which these studies often sequester the meaning of a film by reading it only in terms of certain discourses – in this case conservative Mexican nationalism. This chapter justifies the book's resistance to auteurism and its resistance to the other significant totalizing discourse in classical Mexican cinema: nationalism.

Chapters 3, 4, 5 and 6 analyze Fernández' films. Chapter 3 examines how Octavio Paz' concept of hybridity mediates Mexico's post-Revolutionary discourse of *indigenismo* (indigenism) in its cinematic form. It traces the emergence of the cultural movement of indigenism from the Mexican muralists (Diego Rivera, David Alfaro Siquieros and José Clemente Orozco) in the 1920s through the Soviet director Sergei Eisenstein in the early 1930s, to Fernández in the 1940s. The chapter also looks specifically at how the concept of the foreign (*malinchismo*) which is also figured as a 'positive, valorisation of whiteness,' threatens the 'purity' of an idealized indigenous Mexican (Lomitz Adler, 1992: 276). This chapter examines the contradictions of indigenism as they are revealed in Fernández' indigenist films *María Candelaria* (1943), *Maclovia* (1948) and *La perla* (1945). In the case of *María Candelaria* it argues that the representation of the indigenous subject is predicated on a pre- as well as post-Revolutionary racial ideology that comes not just from a residual European influence but also from Hollywood.

Chapters 4 and 5 analyse the concept of gender in Fernández and how it pertains to Revolutionary discourses. Both chapters look at how Fernández' films deal with the Revolution's renegotiation of gender identity. With *Enamorada*, chapter 4 argues that Fernández and the Revolution's explicit gender discourses of 'lo macho', and female submission are often undermined by the melodramatic mise-en-scène and borrowings from the Hollywood screwball comedy. With *Salón Mexico* chapter 5 argues that Fernández' Revolutionary moral and ideological discourse of female sacrifice and patriarchal orthodoxy is undermined by an emotional and visual investment in the interests of the Other. For instance, while *Salón México* is read as a depiction of '*el México que debe ser*' (Mexico as it should be), the dominant, textual analysis illustrates how the camera work displays a greater pleasure in depicting '*el México que no debe ser*' (Mexico as it shouldn't be) – the forbidden Other (García Riera, 1993d: 264). The chapter also attempts to read Fernández' other 'women's films' *Las abandonadas* (1944) and *Víctimas del pecado* (1950) against the grain of cultural nationalism and patriarchal orthodoxy.

Chapter 6 looks at *Río Escondido*, the apotheosis of Fernández' nationalist style. It questions *Río Escondido*'s perceived consonance with conservative, Government ideology: specifically the tensions between Government discourses of progress and modernity and the film's representation of an underdeveloped Mexico. At the same time, the chapter challenges the idea that this film (along with all Fernández' films) represent an 'antimodernist utopia' and suggests instead that it is firmly rooted in the contemporary moment (and problems) of its production.

The Epilogue charts Fernández' career post the Golden Age, situating it alongside the developing industrial crisis in Mexican cinema and the Mexican state through the 1950s, 1960s and 1970s. It suggests that criticism continues to view and fetishize Fernández solely through the lens of cultural nationalism, producing readings of his films and life that reify him within dominant paradigms of Mexican identity. It concludes by suggesting Fernández' post-Golden Age films and career are ripe for reconsideration, and by evaluating how this textual reading of Fernández which problematizes cultural nationalism and auteurism suggests ways in which his films may be read in the future.

With its use of methodologies from Euro-American film studies, genre analysis, director-centered criticism and mise-en-scène analysis and by privileging transnational perspectives on Fernández the director, this book seeks to rescue Mexican cinema from potentially ghettoizing Third World or Third Cinema discourses where relationships between Mexico and Hollywood are figured solely in terms of imperialist domination. This book also problematizes the sociohistorical paradigms of nationalism and auteurism that have been used to approach his work.

Emilio Fernández and Mexican cinema in film studies

This book joins a healthy Mexican-cinema bibliography. In fact, Mexican cinema is now perhaps the most written about/documented of all Latin America's national cinemas in both English and Spanish. Such a vast bibliography is largely thanks to the archival, historical and cultural-studies work of many Mexican film researchers, archaeologists, historians and cultural historians which has in turn provided detailed resources for both Mexican film critics and Euro-American film critics. Writing on Mexican film is dominated by four big personalities: Aurelio de los Reyes, Emilio García Riera, Jorge Ayala Blanco and Carlos Monsiváis, with other writers often belonging to 'schools' represented by these personalities.

De los Reyes' work is often described as archaeological in its attempts to excavate the origins of Mexican cinema (Burton-Carvajal, 1998a: 19). The two volumes of his *Cine y sociedad en México: 1896–1930* (Cinema and Society in Mexico) (1996a) are fundamental in understanding the silent era in Mexico. He is the leading authority on Mexican silent film and offers 'the definitive social history the early years of the film medium' (Burton-Carvajal, 1998b: 235). He compensates for the loss of 90 percent of the early features and shorts with exhaustive archival research and by incorporating interviews, memoirs and period criticism (Miquel, 1998: 29). As such, apart from the subsequent compilations of this footage, including the work of Mexican film pioneers Salvador Toscano *Memorias de un mexicano* (1950, Carmen Toscano) and Jesús H. Abita *Epopeyas de la revolución* (1963), his volumes provide the only access to what would otherwise be a lost period in Mexico's film history. Other archival work also includes a volume on Dolores Del Rio, featuring an extensive selection of previously unpublished photographs (1996). His *Medio siglo de cine mexicano (1896–1947)* (Half a century of Mexican cinema 1896–1947, 1987) offers a briefer, but no less invaluable history of Mexican cinema.

García Riera's monumental, part factual and part critical, *Historia documental del cine mexicano* (Documental History of Mexican Cinema) collection is indispensable to the study of Mexican cinema. First published between 1969 and 1974, each of seventeen volumes has been republished in an updated and corrected form between 1993 and 1997. Each volume spans several years in Mexican film production, offering credits, synopses, contemporary critical evaluations and García Riera's own comments on every feature film made between 1926 and 1976. Every year of production is prefaced by an essay which introduces important events impacting on the film industry (e.g. the founding of the Banco Cinematográfico in 1942) and book-ended with overviews on the transnational work of Mexican actors outside Mexico. García Riera has also written a more concise history of Mexican cinema (1985), which offers a panoramic history of periods, genres, directors and trends from 1895 to 1982. The institution he presided over, the Centro de Investigación y Estudios Cinematográficos (Center for Cinematographic Research and Education, CIEC) at the Universidad of Guadalajara, is accountable for many other publications on Mexican cinema by diligent researchers and film historians who follow his precise 'collection of information' methodology. These include a collection of eleven monographs on individual directors including Bracho (1986), Juan Orol (1987) and Fernández (1987). (Mostly written by García Riera himself and by Eduardo de la Vega Alfaro, director of research at the CIEC, these are by no means auteur studies, and they involve mostly reviews of the different directors' films, written in similar collection-of-information style to that of the *Historia Documental* series). There are also several book-length interviews with filmmakers, among them Arturo Ripstein (1988) and Figueroa (1993).

Ayala Blanco, who teaches at the Centro de Estudios Cinematográficos at the UNAM (Universidad Autónoma de México) in Mexico City, focuses on specific periods in the production of sound cinema in Mexico from 1931 to 1967 (1993), through 1968–1972 (1974), and 1973–1985 (1986), and the 1990s (1991; 1994) up to the present day (2004). But the work of Ayala Blanco, De los Reyes and García Riera, and of their 'disciples,' as detailed as it is, has left substantial gaps, some of which have been filled by Monsiváis' very different style of film scholarship.

Monsiváis, Mexico's foremost cultural critic, has written widely on literature, journalism and photography as well as on cinema. He is the coauthor, along with Carlos Bonfil, of *A través del espejo, el cine mexicano y su público* (Through the looking glass, Mexican cinema and its audience, 1994a), as well as numerous articles and forewords on Mexican cinema in different journals and anthologies including De los Reyes' *Dolores Del Río*. Three of his *crónicas* (essay-chronicles) on cinema also feature in an English language collection of his work (1997) and his work on different film stars (María Félix, Dolores Del Rio) appears in different collections of his journalist essay-pieces (1995b), (1988a) and (2000). In Monsiváis' writing, cinema features as just one expression of an urban or national culture along with dance, mystic cults, pop stars, wrestling, comic books and the Virgin of Guadalupe. His work on cinema is thus part of a larger cultural-studies perspective that bears resemblance to US and European cultural studies. It has been noted that his work and its focus on micro-cultures, the minutiae of urban life and the 'scraps, patches and rags of daily life' out of which a mass society makes durable art, shares similarities with the work of Walter Benjamin, Raymond Williams and Homi Bhabha (Eagan, 2001: 36). This perhaps explains why Monsiváis is the cultural theorist most cited by US and European scholars in their work on Mexico. Most interestingly for the purpose of this study is his interest in dislodging local characteristics such as the macho from any essentializing definition of *mexicanidad*. Monsiváis' work is about finding cracks in monolithic 'national identity' (Eagan, 2001: 38, 42).

Given that Fernández is *the* critically avowed auteur of classical Mexican cinema, it is somewhat of a surprise that out of these four personalities only García Riera has written a book-length single-director study of him (1987). He offers his typical sociohistorical account of Fernández' career through a mixture of contemporary critical and journalistic accounts of the director's films and his own critical comments. The few studies of Fernández that do exist in book-length form predictably offer differing kinds of auteur criticism – a director-as-personality/biographical approach (Tuñón, 1988), a biographical account by his daughter Adela Fernández (1986), an anecdotal biographical study of his life and films (Taibo, 1986) and an analysis of the depiction of female characters in his oeuvre, (Tuñón, 2000). There is also a sociological study of his films (Rozado, 1991).

English-language publications on Fernández' films so far have been limited to book chapters or articles. For example, Charles Ramírez Berg makes a structuralist director-as-signature examination of the Fernández/Figueroa style (1994) rather than the personality/flesh-and-blood approach to Fernández of Mexican accounts. Other articles or book chapters on individual films, some of which do not follow auteurist logic, have appeared in monographs (Noble, 2005) or in major journals (Noble, 2001; Tierney, 1997, 2003; Feder, 2001; Podalsky, 1993a). Armes (1987) picks Fernández out as one of several noteworthy Third World auteurs in a list that includes Luis Buñuel and Satyajit Ray. *Pictures in the Margins* examines how, in relation to Fernández, the focus on the auteur in both English- and Spanish-language texts is problematic. It shows how the construction of Fernandez as an auteur or conservative straw man against which the new Mexican cinemas of the 1960s and 1970s (Berg, 1992), or the countercurrents of classical cinema – Luis Buñuel (Acevedo-Muñoz, 2003), and Matilde Landeta (Dever, 2003) – can be read, only confirms how his films serve the processes of conservative cultural nationalism while neglecting the many other important areas of meaning addressed in his films, such as gender, race and nationality.[8]

Mexican cinema was once marginalized in Latin American film scholarship 'because it was dissociated from the principle cinematic trends of the continent' – i.e., the explicitly anti-imperialist, often militantly political New Latin American Cinema movement of the 1960s and 1970s (Barnard, 1998: 255; López, 1994: 7). However,

Introduction

Mexican film publications are currently enjoying a boom in the US and the UK, reflecting growing academic interest in Mexican cinema. Recent publications include anthology-based surveys (Paranaguá, 1995; Hershfield and Maciel, 1999); the depiction of women in classical cinema (Hershfield, 1996); contemporary women filmmakers (Rashkin, 2001); Buñuel (Acevedo-Muñoz, 2003); individual 'modern classics' such as *Amores perros* (Smith; 2003); Mexican celluloid nationalism from 'Golden Age' Mexico to contemporary Los Angeles (Dever, 2003); monographs on Mexican national cinema (Noble, 2005) and an analysis of Mexican masculinities and sexualities (De la Mora, 2006). These newer publications follow in the footsteps of two existing monographs on Mexican cinema (Berg, 1992; Mora, 1989). *Pictures in the Margins* groups itself with the work of De la Mora and Dever which departs from previous work on Mexican cinema in English and Spanish in the way it seeks to contest the ideological certainties of post-Revolutionary nationalism in Mexico. This book hence questions the existence of a 'harmonious' 'reciprocity' between society and film of the Golden Age emphasized by Mexican and American accounts of this era's cinema. Secondly, it challenges the contention of most literature on classical Mexican cinema – i.e., that Fernández and the Golden age cinema unproblematically represented Mexico's national self-image. Thirdly, it is the first English-language single-director study of a director from Mexico's classical era. (The case of Spanish-born Buñuel, whose films have been the subject of many monographs is slightly different.) Lastly, unlike many other English-language texts that explore classical Mexican cinema, this book is substantially informed by close textual analysis.

New perspectives: new directions in recent scholarship

While striking new ground in terms of single (Mexican) director studies, at the same time *Pictures in the Margins* allies itself with new directions currently being explored in English-language Latin American film scholarship – i.e. feminist, queer and postcolonial perspectives on the continent's classical cinemas that reveal these cinemas as other than ideologically conservative. López is key in this reevaluation, with several articles and essays on the melodrama that perform a feminist analysis of that narrative mode (1993a; 1991). López has in turn engendered further feminist analyses that seek to contest the certainties of monolithic female subjectivity.[9] Dever for example, also interested in the 'range of contradictory ideologies' operating in classical Mexican melodramas suggests that '[a]lthough [they] might appear to have represented an impenetrable monolithic unity, there were telling fissures in both structures' (2003: 13–14).There is also Berg's work on the use of female archetypes from the Golden Age to the early 1980s (1992). These gender studies complement the excellent work on the image of woman in film scholarship in Mexico by Tuñón and Patricia Torres San Martín.[10] More recently, Rashkin (2001) and Dever (2003) offer analyses of Mexican women's filmmaking from the 1930s (Adela Sequeyro and Matilde Landeta) onward – Maryse Sistach, Busi Cortés, Guita Schyfter, María Novaro, Dana Rotberg and Marcela Fernández Violante. Furthermore, these new gender perspectives also include the study of masculinity. Following Berg's study of gender paradigms where masculinity embodies the State (1992), de la Mora examines how classical Mexican cinema developed strategies to veil the representation of homosexuality and the male body in particular around Mexico's other biggest *macho*, Pedro Infante (1999a, 1998). De la Mora (2006) builds on this research and explores how certain genres (the revolutionary melodrama, the musical comedy 'buddy movie', the *cabaretera* (cabaret/brothel melodrama)) challenge gendered and sexual forms of national identification.

The other 'new direction' in Latin American film scholarship is represented by Seth Fein who has published widely on the industrial transnationality of Golden Age Mexican cinema and as such is one of several scholars to retheorize how we look at national cinemas in Latin America (1998, 1999). López has also brought a transnational focus to Golden Age Mexican cinema by detailing its continental appeal and personnel (1994). Both Fein and López note how Mexican cinema embodied economic and cultural transnationality even at the height of its classical 'nationalist' era, and how the focus on nation obscures these important intercontinental forces. This transnational approach to national cinemas includes López' work on the transnational migration of film-industry personnel. López examines the cases of the Mexican actress Del Rio (1998) and the Argentine filmmaker Carlos Hugo Christensen (2000a). Also exemplary of this new approach is Berg's reconsideration of the advent of a unique 'classical' narrative style in Mexican cinema through analysis of Enrique Rosas' *El automóvil gris* (1919). Rather than promoting the film as a pure national product, 'Berg explores the diverse international influences – Italian melodramas, French crime serials and the Hollywood narrative paradigm – incorporated into Mexico's long emphasis on documentary production' (Noriega, 2000: xv).

Pictures in the Margins takes as a starting point recent scholarship's transcultural and transnational perspectives to understand Fernández who, not unlike Del Rio and Christensen, also embodies a 'travelling' identity. Although there have been several books and articles on Fernández as auteur (Berg 1994; Tuñón 2000; Taibo 1986) and nationalist director (Tuñón, 1993), there have been no monographic studies in English that analyze Emilio Fernández' films as transnational and potentially nonconservative texts. This study attempts to fill that gap.

Notes

1 This was hegemony more in scale than in terms of exhibition and production. As Paulo Antonio Paranaguá points out: '[e]ven during the heyday of the Mexican film industry, we must recall, the production figures could not rival the number of U.S. films distributed there; foreign hegemony over the Mexican market was in fact never really imperilled' (1998: 33 my translation). Ana López supports Paranaguá's argument. She argues that, although Mexican cinema was undoubtedly more dominant in Spanish-language film markets than any other, Hollywood still retained a 76 percent of exhibition in both Mexico and Latin America through the 1930s and 1940s (2000b: 428). The Mexican/US market share of 1943, the year known as Mexican cinema's 'Gran Año' (great year), was as follows: in 1943 Mexico's 57 feature films represented a 14 percent share of the market (vs. Hollywood's 76 per cent). This share was roughly maintained throughout the war with Mexico's share rising to 18 per cent in 1944 (but only because of Europe's declining imports) and settling at 18 per cent in 1945 (García Riera, 1998: 121).
2 Dolores Del Rio dropped the accent from her last name (Del Río) when she became a Hollywood starlet in the 1920s and continued to sign her name in this fashion for the rest of her career. To acknowledge the transnationality that her passage through Hollywood suggests I maintain this spelling of her name.
3 As Julia Tuñón suggests, the prize was actually much more 'commemorative' that anything else. *María Candelaria* shared the prize with eleven other films (2000: 13).
4 Revolution (and variants 'Revolutionary,' 'post-Revolutionary') is capitalized to refer to; the State sponsored ideological vision of society and culture and the institutionalized discourse of the Revolution. The word revolution (and variants) is written in small case to refer to the historical revolution (1910–20) e.g. 'pre-revolutionary power structures.'

5 Throughout this book I will cite film titles in the original Spanish followed by the established translation. Similarly, when citing critical material in Spanish I have chosen to provide the Spanish followed by my own English-language translation.

6 Fernández was an extra in Hollywood between 1926 and 1933. But, as García Riera points out, it is difficult to know on what projects he worked because Fernández is often given to self-invention. The list of films he worked on varies but includes *Ramona* (Edwin Carewe, 1928), *Beau Geste* (Herbert Brenon, 1926) The *Gaucho* (F. Richard Jones 1927), *Drums of Love* (D. W. Griffith, 1928), *Tempest* (Sam Taylor, 1928) *In Old Arizona* (Raoul Walsh and Irving Cummings, 1928) *The Virginian* (Victor Fleming, 1929) and *The Girl of the Rio* (Herbert Brenon, 1932). Fernández was apparently also one of the dancers in the number 'La carioca' dancing behind Fred Astaire and Ginger Rodgers in *Flying Down to Rio* (Thornton Freeland, 1933) (García Riera, 1987: 16).

7 While Berg's (1994) essay goes further than any other in exploring textual elements of Fernández' films in relation to Sergei Eisenstein's influence, there is no cross-film analysis of just exactly how Fernández is influenced by Eisenstein and John Ford in particular.

8 Dever (2003) constructs Fernández and his work as the embodiment of male-centered cultural nationalism. She does this in order to posit Matilde Landeta's heroines (from *La negra Angustias* [The Black Angustias, 1949], and *Lola Casanova* 1948) as exceptional, which they are, but Dever's strategy results in a downplaying of Fernández' equally exceptional heroines: Violeta in *Víctimas del pecado*, Rosaura in *Día Escondido* and Beatriz in *Enamorada*.

9 For example, Joanne Hershfield (1996) looks at classical cinema's construction of woman. Jean Franco (1989) also does woman-centered readings of Luis Buñuel's *Los olvidados* (1950) and Fernández' *Enamorada* (1946).

10 The participation of women in Mexico's 'Golden Age' of cinema and before is a topic only just beginning to be published in the work of several film historians, although there are numerable Masters and Ph.D theses on the topic (Torres San Martín, 1998: 41). Patricia Torres San Martín, who works at the CIEC, has coauthored the first major study of Adela Sequeyro, a pioneer woman director, producer and scriptwriter from Mexico's pre-industrial cinema (1997). She has also published on Matilde Landeta and Adela Sequeyro in Spanish and English anthologies (1998, 1999). The thematic treatment of women in Golden Age cinema has been tackled by the historian Julia Tuñón in two excellent recent volumes, (1997, 2000), which offer analyses of how female characters in films relate to societal mores and also to the authorial vision of Fernández himself.

1

'Poor reception' and the popular: the history of classical Mexican cinema and its scholarship

This chapter looks at how classical Mexican cinema has been studied. It examines how Mexican analyses of classical Mexican cinema privilege the subjects of cultural practices and consequently disadvantage the film texts themselves. It challenges local nontextual perspectives which characterize Mexican cinema as 'underdeveloped' and suggests a means of reading against an approach that continually reasserts subalternity in the face of the colonizing culture (Hollywood). This chapter also explores how this local approach fails to address the site of production of meaning (the practices of coding) and the potential for 'other' ideologies and 'other' readings within these texts.

The chapter begins with a history of cinema in Mexico up to and including the 1940s. It goes on to examine the state's relationship to popular culture (and particularly cinema) in Mexico in the 1940s in terms of a consolidation of the post-Revolutionary nationalist project. It then looks at different critical templates for interpreting this relationship through competing definitions of the 'popular,' noting the history of its particular use in relation to Latin American culture. It suggests that changes in the use of the term 'popular culture' are mirrored in the emergence of a different conception of the popular classes which results in a particular reading protocol in the study of Mexican cinema. The chapter also suggests that this reading protocol is cyclical and ultimately contradictory in the project of finding the 'other' in Mexican cinema. By presupposing the existence of a cohesive Mexican subject that can be identified and studied, this cultural-studies reading protocol ends up reaffirming that which cultural studies usually wants to question: the homogeneity of the nation. After a survey of US studies of classical Mexican cinema which diverge from Mexican analyses by making space for the 'other' through genre and textual analyses, it concludes by outlining how a textual approach, building on the advances made by US studies of Mexican cinema, might provide an account of Emilio Fernández' oeuvre as contradictory, non homogeneous and evident of a fissured cultural nationalism.

Beginnings: importation, exhibition and attraction

The history of cinema in Mexico begins only months after its commercial introduction in Paris in December 1895. Following the established routes of transatlantic commerce, two Lumière projectionist-operators – Gabriel Veyre and C.F. Bon – arrive in Mexico City in August 1896 and exhibit the *cinématographe* to an audience astounded by images of what is for them a still inaccessible modernity. Within days of this first exhibition of moving images in Mexico City (in a program that included Lumière *actualités, Le repas du bébé* and *Sortie d'Usine*), the two cameramen are filming views of the city to project to Mexican audiences (De los Reyes, 1995: 63). Their first subject is the dictator General Porfirio Díaz who is filmed walking with his family in Mexico City's Chapultepec Park. What these beginnings suggest is how, from its inception, Mexican cinema is allied with the State and with those in power, and offers Mexicans a view of (and a means of imagining) the nation, for which Díaz metaphorically stands. State involvement and imagining the nation are two important characteristics which continue to shape the Mexican cinema through its early, preindustrial and industrial stages.

Although these beginnings might also suggest a simple case of neocolonial dependency 'typical of Latin America's position in the global capitalist system' by which the imperialist nation (France) takes control of the less powerful nation, there is a rapid shift from importation to adoption and then adaptation, albeit initially on a small scale (López, 2000: 48). Within less than a year from the cinema's arrival, in July 1897, Mexican entrepreneurs begin using foreign technology to exhibit moving images at makeshift exhibition sites in major cities, while 'curious individuals' from provincial cities begin ordering projectors (De los Reyes, 1995: 63). Within three years, in 1899, itinerant exhibitors begin supplementing the repertoire of European and North American views by filming the places they visit. Again, this ensures spectators are offered not just the attractions of 'accessible globality' (i.e. the sophisticated dress of Parisian factory workers) but also the attractions of 'nationness,' seeing either themselves or people like themselves on screen (López, 2000: 52). For example, in order to bolster audience numbers, on arriving in a new town, exhibitors would often announce to townspeople, an upcoming filming. These same townspeople would then appear in huge numbers, first to be filmed and then to watch the resulting views (De los Reyes, 1995: 64).

Thus, with an itinerant mode of exhibition, the need to guarantee audience appeal and also the positivist spirit of the era, early filmmaking in Mexico develops to favor documentary and mistrust fiction.[1] From 1900 to 1910, Mexican pioneers Salvador Toscano and the Alva brothers (Eduardo, Guillermo and Salvador) compete to reproduce the extraordinary current events of Díaz's political tours and meetings, *Viaje a Yucatán* (Trip to the Yucatan, Toscano, 1906), and *La entrevista Díaz-Taft* (The Díaz-Taft meeting, Avla Bros, 1909) as well as images of Mexico's incipient modernity – i.e., the images of the inauguration of a dam in *Memorias de un mexicano*.[2] They are influenced by foreign models, developing films that follow chronological sequence like the primitive narrative structure of French filmmaker George Méliès' *Cendrillon* (1899), yet adapt them (rather than simply adopting them) to local circumstances (the desire to capture objectively current events and daily life) in the ongoing development of a national style.

De los Reyes pinpoints 1910 as a significant moment in Mexican film history at which a national style, a kind of newsreel that documents the everyday, the extraordinary (including catastrophes), and the modern, begins to come together (De los Reyes, 1995: 68). This is of course contemporaneous with the resignation of the dictator Díaz and the beginning of events which would later be called the Mexican revolution. The developing national aesthetic was therefore propitious to recording these events and in part explains why Mexico's chronology of film development differs from that in the rest of the world.[3] The battles, uprisings and meetings of the revolution provide not just wonderful material for the continuation of the already established parameters of a national style but potentially the first films shaped by audience demand. The success of the Alva brothers *Insurrección de México* (Insurrection in Mexico, 1911) 'demonstrate[s] that audiences are avid for news of revolution' (López, 2000: 66). Toscano, the Alva brothers and others follow the battles and film the unfolding events of the Revolution in chronological order in order to inform the public.[4] It is the first major war to be captured in its entirety on film from beginning to end.[5] However, objectivity is not necessarily the ruling sensibility at work in the reproduction of the events of the revolution.

The Mutual Film Company gets General Pancho Villa to wear a uniform and sign a contract in which he agrees to attack and execute only when conditions are favorable to the camera (López, 2000: 68). Villa is the first of many important figures to recognize the importance to the revolution of representation.

Victoriano Huerta's takeover in 1913 and his imposition of censorship have important repercussions on the 'objectivity' of the revolutionary documentary, forcing it to assume the perspective of those in power – i.e., the federalist bias of *Sangre hermana* (Brother's Blood, 1914) (López, 2000: 68). Restrictions imposed by Venustiano Carranza's government, and dwindling popularity with audiences, bring about the end of the revolutionary documentary in 1916. Filmmakers are now fixed on making narrative films or *films d'art* using as models the French, Italian and US films which had previously catered to the Mexican audience's desire for fiction. For De los Reyes this produces films that are essentially copies of foreign films, such as *La luz* (The light, Ezequiel Carrasco, 1917), a copy of Piero Fosco's *Il Fuoco* (Italy, 1915), and marks an end (for the time being) of the development of a national style.

However, in the period 1917–21, the most prolific of the silent era, several films are made which do suggest adaptation rather than straightforward adoption of foreign models. *El automóvil gris* (The grey car, Enrique Rosas, 1919), for example, aptly illustrates the synthesis of Mexico's documentary style (in terms of a fidelity to chronology of events and accuracy to facts), Italian tradition (in terms of period detail and mobile camera), French crime serials and the emerging Hollywood paradigm (in terms of goal-driven protagonist(s), causal narrative, editing and shooting) (Berg, 2000: 4). Originally a twelve-part serial, *El automóvil gris* recreates the real-life story of a group of thieves who in 1915 used army uniforms, official documents and a grey Fiat (the car of the title) to fool their way into and then steal from upper-class households in Mexico City – this crime is also taken up in Fernández' *Las abandonadas* (The abandoned women, 1944). *El automóvil gris* includes actual footage, shot by Rosas, of the execution of some of the culprits. De los Reyes argues that this film represents the culmination of the national style (De los Reyes, 1995: 65). In *El automóvil gris*, Mexican cinema both approximates and yet also continues to differentiate itself from the Hollywood product now flooding its market by promoting the 'attractions of nationness' just like the early *actualités* giving Mexicans an image of themselves and current events. Even, non-current-event based films like *Santa* (Luis G. Peredo, 1918), an adaptation of the novel by Federico Gamboa (1903), includes narratively unmotivated extended sequences of Mexico City, specifically of Reforma (one of the Capital's large avenues) and the statue of the Angel de la Independencia, seemingly still invested in showing views of the nation as modern and impressive.

The advent of sound

From 1920 onward, while the US consolidated its cinematic presence in Mexico and the rest of the world, Mexican silent cinema does not fare well and falls into disarray. During the Álvaro Obregón regime (1920–24) there is limited state interest in cinema as an educational tool through revived interest in the objective possibilities of the medium. However, this does not stretch to the promotion or sponsoring of narrative films (De los Reyes, 1995: 76). It is not until the advent of sound cinema in the late 1920s that Mexico receives state support in the form of protectionist trade barriers and gets an opportunity to 'face up' to its North American competitors (López, 2000: 425). At the same time, in order to maintain its non-English-language markets, including Latin America, Hollywood begins production of foreign-language cinema including a Hispanic cinema. These films were often foreign-language versions of big Hollywood films. The method of production was to produce an exact copy of a film with, in the case of the Hispanic cinema, Spanish dialogue. Hence a Hispanic production like *Dracula* (George Melford, 1931) was made at night on the same sets as Tod Browning's classic of the same name, only with a Spanish-speaking cast including Lupita Tovar (Mexican) and Carlos Villarías (Spanish). However, these films failed, not necessarily for reasons of quality (Melford's version is arguably scarier than Browning's) but partly because of the lack of respect shown for linguistic differences between different nationalities of Spanish speakers (Spence and Stam, 1999: 248). Such a lack of respect meant productions that strained the limits of plausibility – e.g. placing a Spaniard, an Argentinean and a Mexican within the same family. The failure of Hollywood's Hispanic cinema opened a window of opportunity for Mexico and other countries to 'compete with Hollywood on its own terms.' (López, 2000b: 425) The first major film to be made with direct sound was another version of *Santa* (Antonio Moreno, 1931). This film illustrates the inventiveness of the Mexican cinema which up till this point had been dependent on the US for equipment and raw film stock. It was made using a sound system developed by two Mexican engineers resident in Los Angeles, Joselito and Roberto Rodríguez and with a cast (Lupita Tovar and Donald Reed) and crew who returned from Hollywood, where they were acting and working (some in Hollywood's Hispanic cinema), to make the film. This pattern of border crossings and migration back and forth is key in understanding the transnationality of the Mexican cinema in terms of personnel, equipment and style, and continues to be a feature through the preindustrial, industrial and postindustrial era of the beginnings of the twenty-first century.[6] Also significant about *Santa* is its use of music. When Hollywood's temporary inability to deal with language issues gave them a window of opportunity, the national cinemas of Latin America sought to differentiate themselves from the homogenized Hispanic cinema through the exploitation of national musical forms. In *Santa*, the heavily featured *boleros* of Agustín Lara, particularly the eponymously titled 'Santa,' played an important part in establishing the film's urban milieu and also in suggesting a modern sensibility.

In this experimental preindustrial period when Mexican filmmakers sought ways of defining their films against a foreign product, *Santa* was extremely influential. As a brothel melodrama (and based on one of Mexico's foundational fictions)[7] it grew into a recognizable national form which gave rise to several films in the same period: *La mujer del puerto* (The woman of the port, Arcady Boytler, 1934) and the experimental *La mancha de sangre* (The blood stain, 1937) by the avant-garde painter Adolfo Best Maguard, and years later a distinct genre, the *cabaretera* (cabaret/brothel melodrama). *Santa* also established the close connections between cinema and popular music which was to be the most important feature of Mexican national cinema. The films made during this era of national experimentation fall into two distinct categories: a Lázaro Cárdenas (1934–1940)-inspired liberal nationalist trend which allows for a critical exploration of the revolution such as Fernando de Fuentes' Revolutionary trilogy, *¡Vámonos con Pancho Villa!* (Let's Go With Pancho Villa! 1935), *El compadre Mendoza* (The Godfather Mendoza, 1933), and *El prisionero trece* (Prisoner 13, 1933) and also accounts of unionization in *Redes* (Nets, Paul Strand, Fred Zinneman and Emilio Gómez Muriel, 1934); and a conservative nationalist trend which attempts to integrate the *charro/hacendado* (cowboy/ranch owner) class into the new Revolutionary family. Out of the latter trend developed the *comedia ranchera* (rural comedy) genre which often elides the revolution altogether as well as the contemporaneous issue of agrarian reform to show happy, singing *peones* (peasants) working for their *amos* (bosses) in feudal bliss. Any conflicts are usually romantic and class-based rather than social, and are resolved by means of *intermedios cantados* (sung interludes/ exchanges).[8]

1938-42: An industry is born

As with *Santa* and the *bolero*, the success of the *comedia ranchera* is based on popular forms, specifically the *ranchera* song and other more local popular forms, such as the *jarabe tapatío*, a dance performed in *Allá en el Rancho Grande* (Over on Rancho Grande, Fernando de Fuentes 1936) by Emilio Fernández in his pre-directing days. This film is extraordinarily successful both in Mexico and Latin America. It becomes the prototype that establishes an international market for the *comedia ranchera* and consequently a hugely increased production (of films following the same formula) allowing Mexican cinema to finally take on the status of a film industry (López, 2000b 427). From the year of *Allá en el Rancho Grande* onward, Mexican cinema expanded to function on an industrial basis with increased production (25 films in 1936 to 57 films in 1937), national forms and genres, and even a star system. *Allá en el Rancho Grande* is often cited as beginning Mexican Cinema's 'Golden Age,' a period in which the newly formed industry achieved unrivalled dominance in the Spanish-language film market (see Introduction). It was aided in part by the fact that its two competitors, Argentina and Spain, were both undergoing reduced production. In Spain, cinema was crippled by the bloody civil war, while in Argentina in the late 1930s the number of productions was falling and would fall even further at the outbreak of the Second World War when, due to its status as a neutral country, the US would not provide it with raw film stock (Paranaguá, 1995: 9). However, in 1939, protectionist measures set in place by the Cárdenas government, in which at least one Mexican film should be exhibited per month, did not stop Mexican productions falling off either, as the *comedia ranchera* formula had now saturated the foreign markets, and as the country had slipped into economic crisis after the nationalization of foreign oil interests (García Riera, 1993c: 89).

The beginning of Ávila Camacho's presidential term in 1940 marked the start of a period which would technically and ideologically favor the

Mexican film industry, both as a result of extensive Government patronage of the arts and also the *entendimiento* (understanding) between Mexico and the US. This *entendimiento* was in part an extension of US Good Neighborism. In the early 1930s the Good Neighbor Policy had sought to restore the domestic US economy after the 1928 crash and following depression, by fostering exports to Latin America. During the Second World War, Good Neighbor policies sought to expand Latin American domestic film markets favorable to the Hollywood product.

1942–48: From 'collaboration' to 'containment'

At the outbreak of the Second World War, the Office of the Coordinator for Inter-American Affairs took over the handling of the Good Neighbor policy as the issue of hemispheric unity with Latin America became a question of political importance (López, 1993a: 67–70). At the same time, the film industry in Mexico becomes a key player in reconciling this apparent disjunction between the nationalist rhetoric of the Ávila Camacho state and its simultaneous turn away from the highly nationalist progressive reformism of Cárdenas toward a more development-oriented modernizing conservatism that included an alliance with the US. According to Seth Fein: '[r]egarding narrative content and ideology, much Golden Age Mexican Cinema (across genres) sought to resolve or distract from the contradictions between official rhetoric and actual practices of the post-Revolutionary state as it made its rightward turn in the 1940s' (1998: 105). Hence, the nationalist cinema of the Golden Age, and more specifically the Fernández films with which it is most famously identified, becomes 'a nationalist veneer in an age of Transnationalism' (Fein, 1998: 105; 2001: 163).

As part of the US Government's wartime propaganda efforts, the Mexican film industry received unprecedented help from Hollywood. This help came in the form of technical (equipment), financial and artistic (technical personnel were sent to train technicians) support but was not necessarily given freely by the Hollywood studios, who resented being forced (by the State department interested in fostering inter-American relations and pro-US propaganda) to support a competitor national film industry, especially when that industry was having such success in the Spanish language market of Latin America, the US and Spain (Peredo Castro, 2004: 125). This transnational collaboration is largely credited with modernizing the Mexican film industry and making possible the high technical quality of Fernández-Figueroa's films, particularly *Río Escondido* which was filmed at Azteca Studios with CLASA Films a 'chief recipient of war time U.S. assistance' (Fein: 1999: 123, 126). The period favored by the transnational collaboration between the Mexican and US film industry 1942–48 was arguably when Fernández makes his 'best' films and receives the greatest praise both at home and abroad. At the height of this technical development, in 1946, the Mexican industry fittingly founded its own Motion Picture Academy (la Academia Mexicana de Ciencias y Artes Cinematográficas) and began the annual distribution of the *Ariel* awards (Oscar equivalent) of which Fernández' films were the greatest recipients. In 1947 *Enamorada* won eight *Arieles*, in 1948, *La perla* won five *Arieles*, and in 1949 *Río Escondido* won nine and *Maclovia* two (García Riera, 1993c: 223–224; 1993d: 13, 109; 1987: 130). Fernández and Figueroa were similarly lauded abroad. *María Candelaria* won at the Cannes Film Festival in 1946 and Figueroa won a prize as photographer on *La perla* at the Venice Film Festival in 1947 (García Riera, 1987: 88).

But even before the Second World War had ended, the US was 'planning to contain Mexican production' and recoup the hegemony in Spanish-language markets threatened by a strong Mexican film industry (Fein 1999: 134, 138–140). Once the war was over, Hollywood – free from State Department controls – could pursue tactics which would constrain further development of the Mexican industry particularly in terms of its market reach abroad. These tactics included the practice of block booking (i.e., US major distributors forcing Mexican exhibitors to take all their films in order to get hold of profitable A-list films), reducing screen time available to Mexican cinema; threatened retaliation (limiting of the lucrative US market for Mexican films) for any protectionist measures such as screen quotas for national films; limitations on the supply of virgin stock (still controlled by the US until the late 1940s); and securing preferential treatment for Hollywood films in other Spanish-language markets (Fein, 1999: 145). Hence, the transnational forces that in part facilitated Fernández' and Mexican cinema's great success in the 1940s were the same forces that limited further success in the postwar period through the imposition of conditions unfavorable to the Mexican industry.

State and culture

Although in the 1940s the cinema was the privileged medium of cultural nationalism, it had not figured in José Vasconcelos' – minister of education under Obregón (1920–24) – original plan for national regeneration through culture. Indeed Vasconcelos had believed the cinema to be an inherently North American medium, 'impossible to develop as a national form' (De La Vega Alfaro, 1995: 79).

In the wake of the armed stage of the revolution (1910–20) and the cultural and political uncertainty it left behind, Vasconcelos imagined the role of culture as one of regenerating, redefining and reeducating a new Mexican nation (Monsiváis, 1976: 345). Thus, in the 1920s, Vasconcelos facilitated the diffusion and promotion of education and the arts through literacy programs, state sponsoring of artists and commissioning of murals to be painted on public buildings. His recognition of the pedagogical value of culture in building the post-Revolutionary state and consolidating the nation sowed seeds which, although not immediately fruitful in Government policy, were to bear fruit in the administration of Ávila Camacho (Miller, 1998: 14). Vasconcelos' sponsoring of the arts established the principle of state support of culture, central to the policies of Ávila Camacho.

In the 1930s, Cárdenas' reformist ideology had also extended to culture as a means of incorporating the masses into the nation, reaching those in the remotest regions of Mexico through his famous radio broadcasts (ibid.: 15–17). There was also state support for those films which provided a view of the nation in keeping with the liberal projects of *cardenismo*: agrarian reform, labor reform, socialist education, and incorporation of the *indígena* (indigenous people) within the bounds of the nation state. Hence both *Redes*, a film about a fishermen's strike, and *¡Vámonos con Pancho Villa!*, a critical, realist examination of the revolution, received help from the state. Specifically, Cárdenas provided the funds for the building of the CLASA studios where *¡Vámonos con Pancho Villa!* was made, and also donated army regiments to act as extras and even a train (King, 2000: 45).

Mexico's revolution was one of the defining moments of the twentieth century. The very nature of Mexican identity, guaranteed during the *Porfiriato* (the period of Porfirio Díaz' dictatorship, 1876–1910) by the family, village, religion and region, was seriously disrupted by the revolution. When Ávila Camacho came to power in 1940, Mexico was a secular state with a fast-growing urban population where 'this disintegration of the old way of life was both a problem and an opportunity for the state' (Miller, 1998: 28). For the Ávila Camacho state, the Vasconcelista idea of building through culture presented itself as a chance to construct a new and truly post-Revolutionary state, in which the fissures caused by the revolution could be mended and the country united. The administration of Ávila Camacho invested in the creation and promotion of a national culture more aggressively than any other state in the Western Hemisphere. From 1940 to 1946, the administration supported a national ballet, a national symphony orchestra, a national school system, and a continuing mural tradition (ibid.: 3). And even though Vasconcelos had not foreseen its potential as an instrument of nation building, the cinema was also funded as a major part of Ávila Camacho's cultural nationalism. In 1942, the Government was instrumental in setting up the Banco Cinematográfico, 'a loan granting organization created by the state to consolidate the development of the industry' with the precise aim of helping a film industry which would promote a positive and unified image of Mexico (De la Vega Alfaro, 1995: 85). Fernández benefited from such a pro-cinema nationalist policy, making his first successful films with funding from the Banco Cinematográfico in 1943, *Flor Silvestre* and *María Candelaria* (García Riera, 1993c: 7–12).

This account of the relationship between state and culture under the cultural nationalism of Ávila Camacho, in which mass culture functions as a means of uniting a disunited nation, is the traditional 'Revolution to Evolution' narrative of orthodox Mexican cultural history. It considers culture as effecting the necessary (and welcome) post-Revolutionary (metaphysical and institutional) reconstruction and modernization of the Mexican nation. The relationship between state and culture is characterized as fortuitous for a nation in search of identity *and* a state willing to provide such an identity in search of a nation.

Straightforward historical analyses like this one, however, fail to explore the workings of culture or the institutional power relations which created such a situation of hegemony. They also typically fail to explore questions of difference in terms of conflict with the state. In one such orthodox reading, Michael Nelson Miller mentions how difference or dissent itself becomes part of the state, arguing that there was not only room for dissent – the communist politics of many prominent artists patronized by the state such as Diego Rivera and Frida Kahlo – but it was encouraged as evidence of a healthy state

(1998: 108–109). Straightforward historical analyses also unproblematically link mass culture and popular culture, without considering how the two are historically constituted in Mexico and without considering how modernization, as part of Ávila Camacho's and subsequent Mexican president Miguel Alemán's nation-building project, impacted on popular culture.

More recently, revisionist cultural histories of post-1940 Mexico, rather than bolstering the idea of state power and its narrative of a modernizing 'Revolution to Evolution', actually address the fragmentation of these absolutes and invert the slogan of cultural nationalism so that it reads 'Revolution to Demolition' instead. One such history is a collection edited by Joseph et al. (2001) exemplary of a more cultural-studies approach to Mexican history. Each essay reexplores the dimensions of cultural nationalism through a different micro-narrative: illustrated magazines (Mraz), cooking (Pilcher), *rocanrol* (Martínez), and television coverage of *lucha libre* (Levi).

In their introduction the editors point out how the cultural history of post-Revolutionary Mexico has most often been examined in terms of a 'bounded nationalism' celebrated for its authenticity and idiosyncrasy and epitomized by the amorphous concept of *lo mexicano* (The Mexican way) (Joseph et al. 2001: 7). *Lo mexicano* is embodied politically by a one-party state orchestrated by the Institutional Revolutionary Party (PRI), and by the sense of the new 'Revolutionary Family' of which every Mexican in every region or class is told he or she is a part. What the collection attempts to do is to resist the mythology of *lo mexicano* as the only means by which this culture can be read and 'examine [instead] the intersection of local, national, and transnational realms' (ibid.: 7).

The importance of the transnational within the national

As we have already seen, the consolidation of the Mexican motion picture industry in 1938 with the continental success of *Allá en el Rancho Grande* (1936) and resultant *comedia ranchera* genre meant that the cinema became highly important to the populist nationalist project. Mexican cultural criticism commonly notes how the circulation of Mexican ways of speaking, styles and customs through popular Mexican cinema helped foster, through a sense of appropriation and recognition, a feeling of belonging to the nation (Monsiváis 1994a: 73; Martín Barbero, 1998: 177–81). Within a (Michel) de Certeauian perspective, Mexican cinema thus becomes an expression of popular nationalism. However, it is also important to relativize this cultural-studies perspective of a domestic cinema's national representativeness. Despite the extent of Mexican cinema's relative popularity in Mexico and the rest of Latin America and its circulation of local 'images, voices, songs and history,' Hollywood cinema never lost its hegemony over the domestic and Latin American market. In the 1930s, 76 percent of feature films premiered in Mexico's capital were US-made, and a roughly similar percentage was maintained throughout the Golden Age (López, 2000b: 428). So we can presume that audiences' viewing habits were very much molded by US fare and equally that a film industry which sought to be popular at the box office would need to take this into consideration when making its own films. Indeed, an expected Hollywood influence can be surmised not just from distribution and viewing figures but also in terms of technical history. As with the production of *Santa* (1931), many of the pioneers of Mexico's film history learned their trade in Hollywood as actors, extras and technicians (García Riera, 1993a: 27–31). Gabriel Figueroa, prior to his work with Fernández, also spent time in Hollywood as a pupil of Gregg Toland, Orson Welles' cinematographer on *Citizen Kane* (1941). Toland's influence is often traced in Figueroa's work to his characteristic low angle shots and deep focus photography (Berg, 1994: 17). Hence, as López suggests, it is important to consider the influence of Hollywood – the non-local – in this construction of national identity: not, as often happens in criticism, in terms of cultural colonization (imperfect imitation) but in terms of transnationalism and cultural flows (López, 2000b: 433). Taking a cue from López, my approach to Fernández looks not at generic borrowings either as derivative or as something which endangers a truly national cinema, but at how certain Hollywood genres (the screwball, the 'women's film') are not only mediated by but also tailored to local concerns.

Notes on constructing the 'popular' in Latin America

The approaches to 'popular culture' in Latin American theoretical discourses have largely blossomed out of British cultural studies. The work of Néstor García Canclini, Jesús Martín Barbero and Monsiváis can be identified within the British tradition because, as with British Cultural Studies, their work is characterized by a particular response to industrial capitalism and in particular the effects of the culture industries in transforming the texture of everyday life (O'Connor, 1991: 61). The uneven development of postwar Britain that gives rise to the seminal text of British cultural studies, *The Uses of Literacy* (Hoggart, 1957), continues to be a feature in Latin America. However, despite these affinities with British cultural studies, to speak about classical Mexican cinema as 'popular culture' is also to use a term which has specific resonances in Latin America. In cultural studies the term popular culture has been used in a variety of different ways which are useful to examine in relation to Latin American cultural analyses.

The Frankfurt School paradigm which dismisses popular (mass) culture against an implicit model of individualizing, original, structurally complex high culture, held a certain currency in Latin America in the 1960s and 1970s, particularly in relation to the practices and theories of the militant New Latin American Cinema movements. The Frankfurt School's model of capitalism's manipulation and domination of popular classes was useful in critiques both of the mass media as a tool of social control (i.e., substituting and eliminating popular tradition) and also of US cultural imperialism. Hence the classical Latin American cinemas and particularly the melodramas of Mexico and Argentina were dismissed as complicit with bourgeois ideology and the controlling forces of imperialism. In an important essay Cuban critics Enrique Colina and Daniel Díaz Torres accuse the Mexican middle-class filmmaking bourgeoisie of hijacking the ideals of the revolution which threatened its class privilege and producing instead a reactionary cinema (Colina and Diaz Torres, 1972: 16). More recently, the political and social processes of the 1970s and 1980s – authoritarian regimes, the fights for freedom in Central America, emigrations in huge numbers of intellectuals – have led to a different perspective on and relationship toward popular culture itself (Martín Barbero, 1998: 10). Martín Barbero argues that although at one point Latin American criticism was implicated in the Frankfurt School, this model had eventually to be superseded as it did not allow for certain elements of Latin American reality (ibid.: 48–9).

There has also been a change of perspective toward mass culture in relation to the 'popular.' The founding works of cultural studies, attacked mass culture as detrimental to an organic culture that grows out of working-class life – day trips, devotion to 'our mam', the emotional (comm)unity of club singing (Hoggart, 1957: 38, 121, 128–9). But these attacks disappeared once mass culture was conceived of as

The popular in classical Mexican cinema

a site for marginal/minority discourse and cultural studies began to celebrate commercial mass culture and not consider it as a site for automatic denial of difference or homogenization (During, 1999: 14–17). Similarly, Martín Barbero develops the idea that mass culture rather than being radically different and threatening to the popular has historically sprung *from* the popular in Latin America. In support of this argument, Martín Barbero traces a genealogy of melodrama from the nineteenth-century *folletín* (serial novel) through to the industrially produced film melodramas of Mexico and Argentina of the 1940s and 1950s and beyond to contemporary *telenovelas* (Latin American soap operas) (1995: 277–81).

Martín Barbero's perspective, that mass culture is not necessarily antithetical to the popular, and that classical Mexican cinema can be considered *both* mass and popular culture, also brings with it a new perspective on the popular classes. To Latin American cultural studies Martín Barbero has introduced the notion of *mediations*, that is, local traditions, habits, and practices of interpretation and communication which allow for the possibility of the popular classes having a both active and critical relationship toward mass culture. This neatly discards the deeply unsocialist Frankfurt School notion of the working class as passive 'cultural dopes' and, borrows more from Hall's and De Certeau's models. Both theorists characterize popular culture as a fragmented (rather than an authentic or an 'organic') culture of the popular (working) classes which is contained by but also resists mass/dominant culture (Hall, 1981: 228). De Certeau characterizes the process of resistance as *bricolage*, the artisan-like inventiveness by which the consumer traces out trajectories or meanings other than those intended by functionalist rationality (1988: 29–32). Hall's, de Certeau's and Martín Barbero's ideas of both an active and critical relationship toward mass culture – mediations – takes into account the changed perception of the popular classes from Latin America's recent history of dictatorship, where the popular classes proved to have a radical and productive, rather than passive, relationship toward dominant/mass culture. This change in perspective has also been noted on an intercontinental level. Global perspectives, namely those of Arjun Appadurai, have allowed academics to note how the popular classes of neocolonized or decolonized countries are also active and critical subjects of an imperialist mass culture and work to produce new, contestatory and specifically local 'codes of reception' of this culture rather than just passively imitate it (Appadurai, 1996: 32).

López, for example, has noted how early Latin American *cinéastes* sought to 'indigenize' the film vistas that came to them from Europe and the US by producing their own specifically Latin American styles and views (2001: 52). *El automóvil gris* figures as one such example of the indigenization of foreign forms, in this case the French crime serial and the nascent Hollywood narrative form.

In accordance with this change in perspective, Martín Barbero defines the relationship between state and culture in Mexican cultural nationalism in the classical era as both an authentic search for identity on the part of the Mexican peoples themselves *and* an ideological imposition by the state. Similarly, although, in more folkloric cultural studies approaches, the processes of modernity which are part of Mexican cultural nationalism (such as the development of electronic mass media) might be considered as eroding authentic popular traditions, for García Canclini the two cannot be considered antagonistically in Latin America. He argues that the development of modern communications as part of the process of constructing the nation states includes the massification of popular culture. Quoting both Martín Barbero and Monsiváis, García Canclini charts the use of the mass media – radio and cinema – in the populist politics of nation building (1995: 184–5). All three theorists argue that, rather than the ideological or industrial content in culture, what is most important is the sense of appropriation and recognition in the masses to which this culture is directed. In relation to the question of cultural difference, Martín Barbero argues that in Mexico it is both displaced and projected onto the nation as national heritage, e.g. the state patronage of communist artists, or it is folklorized and offered as a curiosity (1998: 178–9). In either scenario, difference is integrated into the state.

Monsiváis similarly defines this relationship between culture and state in terms of populist manipulation as a process by which the state sought to impose an idea of the nation through mass culture. Yet, like Martín Barbero, he also frames this in Gramscian terms, as hegemony, acknowledging the part played by the masses in their own willingness to be interpolated as part of the nation: 'The surrender to the new medium is *almost* unconditional' (Monsiváis, 1995a: 147).

In their analysis of the mass media, Monsiváis and Martín Barbero both agree that in Mexico the cinema was *the* most nationalist expression and the best example of mass culture acting as a conduit for popular culture (Martín Barbero, 1998: 180). In the following quotation we see how cinema acts to mediate between tradition and modernity while at the same time functioning as part of a totalitarian state. In the sense that Monsiváis' work also refers to culture as an industry within a totalitarian state, it often resemble the ideas of Adorno and Horkheimer:

> Our national cinema offers itself as a unifying space where the deep convictions of the audience coexist with the beliefs imposed by modernity. It must be conceded: *the strong State is the owner of all revolutionary representation.* It heads the educational system and determines the levels of political, economic and social interpretation . . . what The People may do in their spare time is the preserve of the cultural industry. *That is why the cinema is a crucial element in the process of national integration.* Its importance increases because of its status as intermediary between a victorious state and the masses, who lacking any democratic tradition find their sentimental education their most visible source of unity. If political life is denied them, let the laughter ring out and the tears flow instead. *If Good Society excludes us, let film, radio, comic books forge a society that will accept us.* (Monsiváis, 1985: 239, my emphasis)

This sense that the state controls all areas of representation, to create the idea (rather than the reality) of a unified Mexico, is often emblematized in conventional readings of Fernández' work. Fernández' oeuvre is popularly perceived within Mexican culture as forming 'the Mexicanist cinematic text,' as an unproblematic extension of cultural nationalism, consolidating national identity through indigenism education and the fatherland: 'develop[ing] a system of values around which a society [could] unite and establish a collective livelihood' (Tuñón, 1993: 161, 162, 164). Monsiváis describes Fernández' cinema as a fabricated representation of a 'codifiable . . . Mexicanness.' Monsiváis also describes Fernández' work as the apex of cultural nationalism, yet he is the only critic to show awareness of what is not explored in conventional readings of Fernández' work; the disjunction between Fernández' films and the project of modernization which is also a part of the nationalist project:

> Mexican cinema's cultural nationalism derives from its epic repertoire of imitations of Eisenstein and the Hollywood Western . . . *The result is the Fabricated Nation where we hide from the Real Nation. Emilio 'El Indio' Fernández is the pinnacle of this cinematic nationalism. He believes in the existence of a perfectly codifiable mexicanidad (Mexicanness): a lost paradise where tragedy reigns, where landscapes and musical numbers wreak sentimental havoc, where cowed women and very manly men unite in classic couples.* For several years, his lyric power . . . managed to make

these 'atavistic catharses' credible. The film going public (and the foreign film critics) were convinced: that's how Mexicans are, that's how they experience their surroundings, that's how they love, that's how they face their destiny. (Monsiváis, 1985: 242, my emphasis)

As Monsiváis points out, the images around which Fernández constructed his idea of the nation were not those of reality, nor indeed those of the modernizing *avilacamachista* (from Ávila Camacho) or *alemanista* (from Alemán) State, but, instead, those of the part Eisenstein-inspired, part Hollywood-inspired folkloric Mexican landscape.[9] We see this particularly in his rural dramas, *María Candelaria* (1943), *Flor Silvestre* (1943), and *Maclovia* (1948). Despite not offering a 'real' picture of the nation, these are the films which Mexican criticism proposes as examples of how Fernández embodies the themes of cultural nationalism and national identity. They are seen to actively promote the essence of the nation as the noble *indígena* (*María Candelaria*) or the self-abnegating teacher (*Río Escondido*).

These readings of Fernández by Tuñón, Monsiváis and others illustrate cultural nationalism as a process of institutionalization which seeks to displace, recuperate or simply oppress all attempts to construct difference within a totalizing ideology. It is generally accepted in Mexican cinema scholarship that the rest of classical Mexican cinema also acted as both an extension and a tool of the dominant ideology of homogeneity and national unity.

Monsiváis and others reiterate that the vast majority of classical Mexican cinema illustrated and provided a set of moral rules by which to bring the 'other' – the popular classes, marginal social types such as the *pelado* (an urban country bumpkin epitomized by Cantinflas (Mario Moreno) in *Ahí está el detalle* (That's the Point! Juan Bustillo Oro, 1940)) and the *pachuco* (an urban hipster epitomized by Tin Tan (Germán Valdés) in *El rey del barrio* (King of the Neighborhood, Gilberto Martínez Solares, 1950)), the effeminate man (the actor Joaquín Pardavé), the homosexual or *marimacha* (like Angustias in *La negra Angustias*, The Black Angustias, Matilde Landeta, 1949) the indigenous, the fallen woman – within the boundaries of acceptable national identity. Exemplary of this opinion of cinema providing a 'set of rules,' Julia Tuñón states: 'En la primera mirada que busca a las mujeres de celuloide se encuentra que el cine mexicano muestra el código de la conducta debida a un sistema de ideas estructurado y consciente que la ideología dominante plantea para la sociedad en su conjunto' (In one's first look at celluloid women one finds that Mexican cinema displays a code of conduct based on a system of ideas structured by and conscious of that which dominant ideology proposes for society as a whole) (Tuñón, 1997: 283). However, there are of course exceptions to this strict control of behavior and all areas of representation. In his analysis of Cantinflas, Monsiváis identifies a social defiance and marginal voice in the popular comedian's depiction of the *pelado* (1997: 103). Monsiváis argues that in his film roles, particularly *Ahí está el detalle*, Cantinflas rehabilitates the *pelado*, a figure Samuel Ramos in *El perfil del hombre y de la cultura en Mexico* (Profile of Man and Culture in Mexico) associates with representing all that is backward and primitive in Mexican society, to produce a more palatable figure that does not threaten the wealthy and yet with whom the popular classes can still identify (Ramos, 1972 [1936]: 59; Monsiváis, 1997: 103). However, to a certain extent the resistance that Cantinflas represents is a limited one. Cantinflas is also recuperated by dominant culture. Monsiváis points out how his *pelado*, rehabilitated as the diminutive *peladito*, reifies the paternalist dominant perspective by depicting the poor as essentially 'inoffensive' (1997: 99).

US analyses of classical Mexican cinema diverge from Mexican studies in their analysis of elements resistant to dominant ideology. It is largely thanks to the critical reevaluation of melodrama as a significant form with radical potential in US film studies that classical Mexican cinema has received so much attention over the last decade (Peter Brooks, Thomas Elsaesser, Christine Gledhill). In such texts as López' 'Tears and Desire: Women and melodrama in the "old" Mexican cinema' (1993a), US scholars like her have started to examine the popular appeal and resistive possibilities of melodrama from classical Mexican cinema.

Mexican analyses of Fernández' oeuvre have not yet taken into consideration these theoretical perspectives which suggest that totalizing projects of hegemony or cultural reification as 'cultural nationalism' create unity by forgetting or excluding others (Bhabha, 1994: 297). Hence, against the transparent moral intentionality that is said to characterize most of Fernández' work, later chapters in this book chart the elements within the texts which work counter to mainstream pleasures and the dominant ideologies that they supposedly advocate.

Rather than looking at the texts as a site of potential subversion, the study of classical Mexican cinema has been influenced by the belief in an active, critical subject. This has resulted in a move toward reception – or mediations in Martín Barbero's terms – as a reading protocol in the study of classical Mexican cinema. Hence when Tuñón suggests that there are 'other' elements working against the dominant in classical Mexican cinema, them at the level of reception she situates and in the form of 'unconscious feelings.' Continuing on from the previous quotation, Tuñón states:

> Sin embargo, al escudriñar más se observa que también transmite elementos de la mentalidad de ese mundo de ideas y representaciones, en gran medida inconscientes que atañen a los sentimientos, valores, afectos, emociones, las partes menos controladas por sus sujetos que se traducen en comportamientos, prácticas, hábitos, actitudes, rechazos y aceptaciones. (1997: 283)

> (However, on further scrutiny, one notices that [The Mexican Cinema] also transmits (largely unconsciously) certain aspects of the mentality of this world of ideas and representations that relate to feelings, values, emotions – all that which is least controlled by the subject but which translate into behaviors, practices, habits, attitudes, rejection and acceptances.)

The consensus among Tuñón and other academics of classical Mexican cinema is that it was a strongly Catholic and conservative cinema which nevertheless allowed for a certain transgression of the status quo but only at the levels of sensibility and reception, particularly in the *cabaretera* melodrama and particularly in relation to ideas of gender. The idea is that this transgression is always recuperated by the dominant order because it is only temporary or located at the level of sensibility.

In general, classical Mexican cinema is considered in terms of its practical use to a nation in search of an identity. Consider for example Monsiváis' illustration (quoted by Martín Barbero) of how the urban working classes use/experience Mexican cinema:

> El público mexicano . . . no resintieron al cine como fenómeno específico artístico o industrial. La razón generativa del éxito fue estructural, vital; en el cine este público vio la posibilidad de experimentar, de adoptar nuevos hábitos y de ver reiterados (*y dramatizados con las voces que le gustaría tener y oír*) códigos y costumbres. No se accedió al cine a soñar: se fue a aprender. A través de los estilos de los artistas o de los géneros de moda el público se fue reconociendo y transformando, se apaciguó se resignó y se encumbró secretamente. (Monsiváis, 1994b: 181)

> (The Mexican audiences did not experience the cinema as a specifically artistic or industrial phenomenon. The reason for [the cinema's] success was structural and vital; in the cinema the audience saw the potential for

experiencing and adopting new habits and to see reiterated (and dramatized in the voices that they would like to have and to listen to) codes and customs. [The audience] did not go to the cinema to dream: they went to learn. Through the actors' style and different fashions the audiences both recognized and transformed themselves, they were pacified, resigned and secretly encumbered.)

Mexican cinema according to Monsiváis thus becomes a way of 'imagining the nation,' (Anderson, 1991) a way of experiencing and adopting those habits and practices, moral codes and customs which make one a national subject. However, Tuñón, Monsiváis and Martín Barbero are simplifying this period of Mexican cinema, dividing it along regular cultural-studies lines: the 'dominant classes' and 'the people' who make their own meanings within and *sometimes* against the culture provided for them (Morris, 1990: 23). In the case of Mexican cinema the popular classes both 'recognize' themselves in film as national subjects and learn how to be national subjects from films. But how productive is it to reiterate the basic de Certeauian argument of containment and resistance? Does this affirmative approach end up simply celebrating the status quo?

Meaghan Morris has suggested that studies which divide themselves along these regular cultural-studies lines oversimplify the field of popular culture, recycling a basic (imaginary) pop-theory article. In this 'imaginary' pop-theory article, an illustration of how 'the people' make their own meanings is provided by the 'enabling' thesis of contemporary cultural studies, which state that:

> Consumers are not 'cultural dopes' but active, critical users of mass culture; consumption practices cannot be derived from or reduced to a mirror of production; consumer practice is 'far more than just economic activity: *it is also about dreams and consolation, communication and confrontation, image and identity. Like sexuality it consists of a multiplicity of fragmented and contradictory discourses.*' (Morris, 1990: 21–2, my emphasis)[10]

Morris' description of the cultural-studies clichés produced by the 'enabling' thesis of contemporary cultural studies is very similar to many reception-based readings of classical Mexican cinema. In particular it resembles Monsiváis' analyses of the cinema audience: 'In overcrowded conditions of poverty, what is most private is the flow of fantasy, the relationship between what is lived and what is dreamed, individually and collectively, the string of tragicomic stories that make up genuine identity and privacy' (Monsiváis, 1995a: 151).

To further her argument Morris goes on to analyze John Fiske's cultural studies analysis and encouragement of 'cultural democracy' – i.e., finding out what the people say and think about their culture. Morris says that this produces a concept of the people as 'the most creative energies and functions of critical reading [against the hegemonic force of the dominant classes]' (1990: 23). This in turn leads inevitably to a conception of 'the people' as 'both a source of authority for a text and a figure of its own critical activity' (ibid.). This idea of 'the people' as remaking the materials of culture is one shared by Monsiváis and Martín Barbero. However, as Morris points out, the argument that the audience determines the meaning ends up being both circular and 'narcissistic' in structure – i.e., repetitive (ibid.).

Although Monsiváis and Martín Barbero's argument that the people remake the culture may be repetitive, we should acknowledge that the idea of resistance to and appropriation of Mexican classical cinema represents progress from the Frankfurt School view of 'old' melodrama as purely ideological manipulation, as circulated by the critics Colina and Díaz Torres in the 1970s. However, this reading (that Mexican spectators are interpolated by hegemonic images of national identity and unity) still allows little space for other readings which go against the status quo.

By suggesting that one nation exists or can be imagined through film, Monsiváis and Martín Barbero thus assume the unity and homogeneity of the audience. This contradicts Monsiváis' other work on popular and urban culture other than film in which he constantly seeks to deconstruct the monoliths of Mexican identity. While Monsiváis and Martín Barbero's methodology shows cultural studies' increasing focus on the (complexity of) reception of the texts the question – 'how are texts read?' replacing 'what do texts mean?' – these critics diverge from classic cultural-studies approaches in two crucial aspects. Unlike most cultural studies, Monsiváis and Martín Barbero do not question the unity of the text or the unity of the subject, or how readings of the texts might vary according to social categories, class, religion or epochs. By doing this they support a position which cultural studies traditionally seeks to undermine – that meaning is monolithic and that the subject is unified. Monsiváis and Martín Barbero also diverge from current Latin American approaches to identity politics. Indeed, many scholars have recently criticized monological discourses and strategies of nation building in Latin America, instead favoring the conceptualization of Latin American identities in terms of plurality, hybridity and heterogeneity (Chanady, 1994). One possible approach for this study, therefore, could be to problematize this position by examining the various counterinterpretations the consuming public has made of the products of cultural nationalism. Instead, however, the following chapters take into consideration how the *texts* themselves embody the disunity and contradiction that fractures the national unifying project in a way which avoids the narcissistic cycle of reception analysis.

One reason why the reception-based reading strategy is so popular is that it supports the orthodox narrative of post-Revolutionary society: that cinema facilitated and also reflected the modernizing process of the institutionalized Revolution from the 1940s onward. Furthermore, it complements cultural, sociological and historical readings of film which also support the 'Revolution to Evolution' narrative. Textual analysis, on the other hand, is pushed aside as a reading strategy because it risks challenging the notion of Mexico's progress into modernity from the 1940s onward.

Mexico in the shadow of Hollywood

As Paranaguá points out, Mexico's national cinema, like the rest of the national cinemas in Latin America, is victim to the idea of its own poverty/underdevelopment in the face of Hollywood (1995: 8). This sense of striving for and not achieving the industrial development of its near neighbor to the north translates in film scholarship into the assertion of technical inferiority and a refusal to examine film texts textually. For example, *Mexican Cinema*, an anthology of Mexican film scholarship by Mexican scholars, contains no textual analysis at all – except for a non-Mexican (Paranaguá's) analysis of *El compadre Mendoza* (Paranaguá, 1995: 3). On why textual approaches to Mexican cinema are so rarely made, Monsiváis suggests that: 'The study of Mexican cinema should be of some use although almost everyone insists (with good reason) that its interest is more sociological than aesthetic' (1985: 236). In another article he writes:

> la historia del cine mexicano ha sido la acumulación de *basura estética*, el desperdicio de la voracidad económica, la defensa de los intereses más reaccionarios, la despolitización, el sexismo. Por lo mismo, el examen de esta cinematografía nos familiariza – de un modo u otro – con los procedimientos de la ideología dominante, que han *modelado la cultura popular y han ofrecido a la vez la interpretación del mundo y un catálogo de conductas 'socialmente adecuadas'* y también nos demuestra que a

pesar de todo, en una etapa, esa cultura popular manipulada supo describir enriquecedoramente la realidad.

(The history of Mexican cinema amounts to an aesthetic rubbish tip; to the waste of economic voracity, to the defense of the most reactionary interests, to depoliticization and sexism. For this very reason, the study of this cinema gives us a means of entry into the workings of the dominant ideology that has modelled popular culture and offered an interpretation of the world and a way of behaving that is 'socially adequate' and which shows us that, despite everything, at a certain moment, this manipulated popular culture was able to richly describe reality.) (Monsiváis, 1976: 435–6)

Monsiváis and Martín Barbero (who draws from Monsiváis) focus on the cinema as a document of socio-historical significance – i.e., how dominant ideology molds and controls popular culture while simultaneously 'richly describ[ing] reality'. However, at the same time as pointing out its value as a sociological source they dismiss it as reactionary, escapist and sexist '*basura estética*' (aesthetic rubbish).

It is this perception of aesthetic inferiority that has characterized the majority of Mexican film analyses of Mexican cinema, resulting in a rejection of the texts themselves as unworthy of study beyond narrative and thematic analyses. Tuñón prefaces her study of the representation of women in classical Mexican cinema (1997) by quoting Monsiváis' comment above about '*basura estética*.' This perceived underdevelopment in Mexican cinema is measured in relation to Hollywood. Monsiváis talks about how Mexican cinema's aspiration to copy is thwarted by its own lack of resources:

[T]he Mexican film industry believed that mere imitation was suicidal (among other reasons because of the *lack of financial resources*). It was preferable to have intensely local faces, landscapes, and ways of speaking and being within Hollywood-derived cinematic structures. Once the familiar landscapes and sounds were recognized, the audience happily accepted the mechanics of emotional blackmail, the endlessly repeated formulas and *the lack of resources which is a sign of poverty* as well as an invitation to fantasy. (1995c: 117)

Monsiváis focuses on the poverty and imitation of Mexican cinema and how again it does not measure up to Hollywood:

In extremely precarious, badly lit studios with deficient sound equipment, it makes no sense to try to compete with Hollywood. To captivate an illiterate public all that is needed is to give them scenes and situations that

The popular in classical Mexican cinema

they perceive as very much their own. All it takes is 'nationalizing' Hollywood's formulae. (1985: 236)

To a certain degree Monsiváis' comments echo those of Vasconcelos, whose perception of cinema was that it could only be developed with limited technical artistry. Such comments, even from those who seek to praise Mexican culture, embody Mexico's inherent problem of neocolonialism/cultural colonization as figured by Paz, Ramos and other Mexican intellectuals. Paz writes:

> Es cierto que Nueva España, al fin y al cabo sociedad satélite, no creó un arte, un pensamiento, un mito o formas, de vida originales . . . También es cierto que la superioridad técnica del mundo colonial y la introducción de formas culturales más ricas y complejas que las mesoamericanas, no bastan para justificar una época.
>
> (It is certain that New Spain [Mexico], ultimately a satellite society, did not create an original art form, tradition of thought, myth or form . . . It is also true that the technical superiority of the colonial world and the introduction of cultural forms that were much richer and more complex than those of Mesoamerica, was not enough to justify an era.) (1997: 113)

Ramos connects this perceived inferiority complex in Mexico as a nation to La Malinche and her betrayal of the indigenous culture. By sleeping with the Spanish Conquistador Hernán Cortés she left Mexico open to the invasion of foreign powers and to the debasement of its own culture/society. Hence, the assumption is that due to its condition as a colonized society – first by Spain and then culturally and economically by the US – Mexico is incapable of originality in art and is condemned instead to a dependent culture which will always be a poor reproduction of the colonizing culture. This is the sentiment that is continually repeated throughout analyses of classical Mexican cinema by Mexican critics.

There is a fundamental problem with the analyses of popular classical Mexican cinema by Tuñón and others which take on this cultural-studies perspective and make classical Mexican cinema speak with the voice of the 'other.' It is a problem which, rather than revindicating the 'other,' results in the reification of the sense of inferiority of Mexico's own status as 'other' within a global cultural economy. By favoring reception-based socio-historical approaches over aesthetic approaches as a reading protocol for Mexican classical cinema, these critics frame Mexico as a dependent society within an imperialist cultural system and reify the idea of a Mexican popular cinema as a homogenizing, force of '*unidad nacional*' (national unity).

Of course when Tuñón and Monsiváis talk about '*basura estética*' they are not referring to the 'quality' films of Fernández (or other Golden Age auteurs Galindo, Bracho, De Fuentes, etc.) which were technically highly acclaimed, but to the vast majority of Mexican films made during the late 1940s and 1950s which are referred to as '*churros*' (García Riera, 1987: 127). *Churro*, a cheap, machine-produced sugary dough, refers in Mexican film parlance to films made at great speed and little cost. However, in contemporary film scholarship, when the distinctions between Hollywood categories of A and B films have largely been devalued – mainly because many 'B' films (*Detour* 1945 Edgar G. Ulmer and *Cat People* 1942, Jacques Tourneur) have since received artistic recognition – to maintain a similar distinction in Mexican film production seems equally unproductive. And yet the idea of technical inferiority taken from the *churro* production strategy is maintained as a reason for not textually analyzing any classical Mexican cinema.

This problem of neocolonialism and the inferiority complex which it creates seems somewhat anachronistic in cinema, given that the New Latin America Cinemas of the 1960s and 1970s have already sought to challenge the basis of this complex.[11] These movements, although not homogeneous, sought to work through the same problematic of underdeveloped national cinemas in several ways. Julio García Espinosa's thesis, 'For an Imperfect Cinema,' (1997 [1969]) for example, advocates making a virtue out of poverty. García Espinosa argues that, rather than striving for the lavish production values of the US, the filmmaker should instead concentrate on a message of anti-imperialist resistance. Furthermore, Roger Bartra offers a deconstruction of this 'philosophy of Mexicanness' and argues that this sense of inferiority, rather than being a part of the national psyche, is no more than the cultural projection of the aspiring Europeanized intellectuals' own sense of inferiority onto the *pueblo* (1996: 92).

As well as our rejecting the imperialist model, it is also important for us to remember that economic impoverishment which inevitably hinders all neocolonial societies does not necessarily produce a cinema of 'lesser quality'. The early Soviet cinema, for example, under strict financial limitations, managed to produce some of the most technically exquisite films. In 1945 Welles wrote a commentary on the different styles of Soviet and American movies. He argued that Soviet montage had developed out of economic necessity: '[b]ecause of the inferiority of Russian film stock, lenses, and other equipment, the camera must assert itself by what it selects and by the manner of selection' (Naremore, 1993: 1). Meanwhile, the more lavishly appointed, technically advanced Hollywood cinema had developed a 'merchant's eye,' devoting itself to 'star-hogging close-ups' and to 'lovingly evaluative texture, the screen being filled as a window is dressed in a swank department store' (Naremore, 1993: 1). Indeed, more recently, financial limitations have come to be considered in themselves a positive virtue in the Danish Dogme 95 school which eschews the high-budget, technical wizardry of contemporary mainstream filmmaking to 'return' to a purer (cheaper) form of cinema, as evident in films like *The Idiots* (Lars Von Trier 1998).

With the lessons learned by the New Cinema movements in Latin America and also the precedent set by Soviet cinema, surely continuing to measure Mexican cinema as technically poor in relation to a Hollywood model is to continue to interiorize the allegedly Mexican inferiority complex.

Exemplary of a post-New Latin American cinema approach and a cultural-studies revindication of Mexican cinema as a national cinema, recent US accounts of early Mexican cinema, while acknowledging the US and European influences, refuse to posit Hollywood as a formal ideal to which Mexican cinema must aspire. While recognizing a certain amount of imitation, critics emphasize that this takes place as part of a dialogue with local creativity and innovation (López 2000a: 52; Berg, 2000: 11). It is also important to acknowledge that within another cultural system, the Spanish-language film market (including Spain, Latin America and the Spanish-language cinemas in the US), Mexico also exerted an imperialist hegemony during the classical period, creating a cinema with relative dominance (López, 1994: 7).

Encoding/Decoding

In 'Encoding/Decoding,' Hall asks how we go about reading ideological discourse into a set of texts. He argues that, although social practices as a transformation of the discourses of media apparatuses are important, so too are the practices of coding in the understanding of how texts produce meaning (1999: 508). This is an argument consistent with my concerns about Mexican analyses of classical Mexican cinema which focus on social practices and neglect the text as the site of the production of meaning. Hall argues that communication is never transparent or 'determined' and that the way texts are read or decoded does not follow inevitably from the way they are produced or encoded: 'it is always possible to classify an event within more than one mapping' (1999: 513). Hall offers several possible decoding positions/mappings: dominant-hegemonic, negotiated and oppositional.

In the first position, the dominant-hegemonic position, the viewer takes the connoted meaning 'full and straight,' decoding the message in the same terms of the code in which it has been encoded. Hence, Monsiváis', Tuñón's and Martín Barbero's reading of Fernández' work as 'the Mexicanist cinematic text' would be made from the dominant hegemonic position – cultural nationalism – operating inside the dominant code. Hall would call this a case of 'perfectly transparent communication' (1999: 515).

In the second position, the negotiated position, the viewer understands the connoted meaning in relation to the *global*, or overall reach of the dominant discourse, and yet also simultaneously makes a reading which is more personal and local to their own needs and desires.

> Decoding within the *negotiated version* contains a mixture of adaptive and oppositional elements: it acknowledges the legitimacy of the hegemonic definitions to make the grand significations (abstract), while, at a more restricted, situational level, it makes its own ground rules – it operates with exceptions to the rule. (Hall, 1999: 516)

So when López, in her reading of *cabareteras* (cabaret/brothel melodramas), suggests that classical Mexican cinema's 'teaching people how to behave' was not a simple case of a lesson 'imposed' from above, this would be consistent with a negotiated position. She suggests that, rather than providing a uniform model of how to behave, '[t]hese films addressed pressing contradictions and desires within Mexican society. And even when their narrative work suggests utter complicity with the work of the law, the emotional excesses set loose and the multiple desires detonated are not easily recuperated' (1993a: 153). In keeping with Hall's model of how the negotiated position works, López signals an awareness of the dominant code under which these films are encoded when she asserts that 'narrative work [in these films] suggests utter complicity with the work of the law' – in this case, patriarchy as part of a male-oriented cultural nationalism (ibid.). López then decodes these texts within the more restricted code, a feminist-oriented analysis of the films' melodramatic features. Thanks to feminist and post-structuralist analysis, melodrama as a genre has been revalued in terms of how its excessive nature, rather than upholding dominant ideology, actually questions this ideology.

In the third position, the oppositional code, Hall argues: '[i]t is possible for a viewer perfectly to understand both the literal and the connotative inflection given by a discourse but to decode the message in a *globally* contrary way. He or she detotalises the message in the preferred code in order to retotalise the message within some alternative framework of reference' (1999: 517). When we operate within an oppositional mode we read one code as another. Hence we can read calls for 'national unity' within the texts of Mexican mass culture, not within the dominant hegemonic code in which it was encoded – cultural nationalism – but within an oppositional code as 'government interest.' This polysemy questions the success of any totalizing ideology such as cultural nationalism and gives rise to the 'others' and 'other' readings it would repress. Following Hall's model that a text can be decoded in multiple numbers of reading positions we can acknowledge the potentiality for the presence of a number of different 'other' readings in the texts of Fernández' oeuvre.

Notes

1 Positivism was a nineteenth-century philosophy originated by the French philosopher Auguste Comte. It played a part in a number of different nation-building projects in nineteenth-century Latin America, Mexico and Brazil in particular. Positivism basically holds a belief in the possibilities of rational 'scientific' thought to order and tame the chaos of the nation and set it on the road to modernity.

2 *Memorias de un mexicano* is a compilation of Salvador Toscano's films put together by his daughter Carmen Toscano in the 1950s. A similar compilation of Jesús H. Abita's early films (*Epopeyas de la revolución*) was put together by Gustavo Carrero in 1963. For an illuminating analysis of *Memorias de un mexicano* see Noble, *Mexican National Cinema* (2005: 48–94).

3 The spirit of Positivism together with the arrival of the revolution conspire to create a prolonged period of 'primitive mode of production' in Mexico (Burch, 1990: 220). In the US, the primitive mode of production (tableau shots, non-narrative spectacle, views, exteriority and emblematic shots or apotheosis) begins to be displaced by the nascent narrative mode (story told through image, analytical editing, continuity of space through eye-line match, shot/reverse shot and screen direction) evident in *The Great Train Robbery* (Edwin Porter) as early as 1903 (ibid.: 220, 224). In Mexico the

primitive style suits Positivism and the objective recording of the events of the revolution. Storytelling and classicism do not begin to emerge in Mexican cinema until the film d'art of 1916, and is concretized in films such as Santa (Luis G. Peredo, 1918) and El automóvil gris (Enrique Rosas, 1919) (Berg, 2000: 5).

4   In fact, as Zuzana Pick points out, 'Mexican revolutionary leaders granted access and integrated photographers and cameramen into their armies to record their campaigns.' (2006: 1) Pioneer filmmaker Jesús Ábita accompanied Álvaro Obregón's Constitutional Army (ibid.: 7) This 'embedding' of cinematographers and photographers allowed various military and political leaders to promote their own agendas (ibid.: 3).

5   The Spanish-American War of 1898 was the first major conflict to be filmed. However, due to the problematic filming conditions (i.e., battles taking place at sea or at night), as well as the staging difficulties of battle scenes because of new long-range weapons and less hand-to-hand combat, half of the films of the Spanish American War are staged reconstructions. While the static cameras could pick up 'human' yet banal events such as US troops disembarking, more 'action'-related events – such as battles or ambushes – had to be staged for the camera, often in West Orange, New Jersey where Thomas Edison had his studios. For this reason, films of the conflict are sometimes looked at suspiciously in terms of their historiographic significance, but what is not in doubt are the ideological implications of the filming of the war in terms of cultural production. For more on the films of the Spanish-American War see Charles Musser's *The Emergence of Cinema: The American Screen to 1907* (1990: 261) or Michael Chanan's *Cuban Cinema* (2004).

6   Actors (Salma Hayek) and more significantly directors Alfonso Cuarón (*Sólo con tu pareja* (1991) *Great Expectations* (1998), *A Little Princess* (1995), *Y tu mamá también* (2001), *Harry Potter and the Prisoner of Azkaban* (2004), *Children of Men* (2006)); Alejandro González Iñárritu (*Amores Perros* (2000), *21 Grams* (2003), *Babel* (2006)); and Guillermo del Toro (*Cronos* (1993), *Mimic* (1997), *El Espinazo del Diablo* (2001) *Blade II* (2002), *Hellboy* (2004), *El laberinto del fauno* (2006)) all shuffle between Mexico City and Los Angeles and between Hollywood (or Indiewood) and Mexican Cinema projects. See Juan Carlos Vargas' 'Mexican post-industrial cinema (1990–2002) in *El ojo que piensa* online magazine (2002).

7   Here I take note of Debra A. Castillo's reference to *Santa* as a key text in the development of Mexican National identity (1998: 37). At the same time I acknowledge that *Santa* is not a 'foundational fiction' in the same way as Doris Sommer (1991) uses the term to refer to 'national romances' that narrate the nation through a central couple. In fact, *Santa* is the story of a failed romance (between the prostitute and her admirer Hipólito), and of a failure to establish the sanctioned couple.

8 We can also read *Allá en el Rancho Grande* as part of a reaction against the Agrarian Reform Act (put into practice in the year of the film's making by the Government of Lázaro Cárdenas) and its 'controversial process of dividing up the land' (De la Vega Alfaro, 2003: 29).

9 In 1930 Sergei Eisenstein came to Mexico and filmed a number of scenes of the country in what was to be a documentary/narrative film. Eisenstein was never able to complete his film, but it was edited and released some years later as *¡Que viva México!* The film is perceived to have had an enormous influence on the development of a 'photogenic' nationalism and particularly on Figueroa's work.

10 Morris is citing firstly Stuart Hall (1981) and then secondly Mica Nava (1987).

11 Furthermore, Berg's analysis of classical Mexican cinema emphasizes its 'craftmanship' in comparison to the relative absence of craftsmanship in the 1960s (1992: 31).

2

'El Indio' Fernández, Mexico's marginalized golden boy and national auteur

Fernández has generated a considerable amount of interest, both in Mexico and abroad, in the form of book-length studies or articles. Most, as we would expect from studies on an individual director, offer differing forms of auteur criticism. There are several director-as-personality/biographical approaches to his work including: a long interview with Fernández (Tuñón, 1988); a biographical account by his daughter Adela Fernández (1986); and a sarcastic, anecdotal biographical study of his life and films by Paco Ignacio Taibo (1986). There are also several structuralist director-as-signature approaches, which focus on the director less as a flesh-and-blood individual and more as a core of structures and repetitions; these include an analysis of the depiction of female characters in his oeuvre (Tuñón, 2000) and an examination of the Fernández/Figueroa style by Berg (1994). There is a sociological study of his films by Alejandro Rozado (1991). García Riera offers his typical socio-historical account of Fernández' career through a mixture of contemporary critical and journalistic accounts of Fernández films as well as his own critical comments (1987). Roy Armes picks him out as one of several noteworthy Third World auteurs in a list that includes Luis Buñuel and Satyajit Ray (1987: 72).

These different accounts depict Fernández as one of Mexico's most celebrated and maligned auteurs, with an expansive and paradoxical persona, far in excess of his role behind the camera. They suggest that, famous for his violent and explosive personality (he shot a man dead in a shoot-out) and for his telling of tall tales (such as claiming that he taught Rudolf Valentino to tango), he is a complex figure who defies confinement within a single paradigm (Monsiváis, 1992: 39).[1] He was a revolutionary, a legend, a patriarch, a director, an actor, a raconteur and much, much more besides. And yet in Mexico, despite the assertion that he defies confinement, he is always referred to by his *apodo* (nickname) '*El Indio*' (the Indian), which refers to his mixed-racial heritage. His father was 'white'/Creole and his mother was a Kikapú Indian. This nickname, '*El Indio*,' features prominently in the titles and texts of the many biographical studies of his films by Taibo, Tuñón, Monsiváis and others. In a country where it is an insult to call someone '*indio*,' the use of this *apodo* is highly charged, as it implies a certain depiction of him different to that usually made of the auteur, where nicknames can often suggest familiarity or even heightened individuality – such as 'Hitch' for Alfred Hitchcock or 'Titón' for Tomás Gutiérrez Alea.[2] By referring to him as '*El Indio*' Fernández or even just '*El Indio*,' he becomes not only an auteur (filmmaker with a personal vision and of exceptional talent) but also an anthropological subject in what was, until Vicente Fox's PAN (National Action Party) election victory which ended the 70-year rule of the Institutional Revolutionary Party (PRI) in 2000, Mexico's ongoing institutionalization of the Revolution and its racial ideology.

While the auteur theory throughout the 1950s, 1960s and 1970s acted as a means to revise film history and challenge the idea that the director was a functionary of a dehumanizing, formulaic, profit-hungry studio system in old Hollywood (Schatz, 1988: 5–6) or, in Marxist terms, a worker of the base reproducing the superstructure of American ideology, in Mexico, in the case of Fernández, the auteur theory is part of the system, supporting and upholding a state-controlled idea of the nation. The auteur theory in Mexico diverges from the theory's counterideological origins and illustrates how the films Fernández was making were a part of the 'system,' consolidating the nationalist project while he was working for Mexico's fledgling studio system.

This chapter begins by looking at Fernández' role within the system, mapping how, in the critical analysis of his work, by both local and nonlocal academics, the construction of Fernández as auteur and '*indio*' intersects with the processes of institutionalization involved in 'nation' and 'national culture.' It also looks at how this institutionalization is still evident in the 1980s accounts of him written coincidentally at the same time as the biggest upsurge in the production of Mexican culture studies – Guillermo Bonfil's *Mexico profundo* and Bartra's *La jaula de la melancolía* – since it was initiated by Ramos in the 1930s and climaxed in the 1950s with Paz' *El laberinto de la soledad* (Labyrinth of Solitude) (Lomitz Adler, 1992: 247). It goes on to examine what is at stake when the proponents of Mexican national cinema promote Fernández as auteur, particularly given the neo-colonialist implications of the use of the auteurist paradigm in Mexico. Taking a cue from theorists who seek to resist the totalizing effects of auteur criticism, it incorporates a critique of the way traditional auteurist studies violate the organic totality of the text by reading it only in terms of certain discourses. This chapter therefore justifies why this book resists any totalizing discourse – nationalism or auteurism – and takes a director-centered approach, acknowledging Fernández as an orchestrating figure yet reading each film as an individual text, rather than seeking to construct continuity and coherence across the body of his work in the manner of a traditional auteurist study.

'El Indio' Fernández: national cinema and the auteur

Since its heyday in the late 1950s and 1960s, auteurism has been displaced by successive waves of radical theory: first in the 1970s by Sausserian linguistics, Lacanian psychoanalysis and Althusserian Marxism, and then in the 1980s by film theorists (like Monsiváis and Martín Barbero) skeptical of authoritarian models of communication who turned instead to Gramsci, De Certeau, and British cultural studies, and the possibility of resistance against these models to be found there and in reception theories (Naremore, 1990: 14).

Furthermore, auteurism has had a rather mixed reception among Latin American filmmakers and theorists. While Brazilian filmmaker/critic Glauber Rocha wrote in 1963 that 'if commercial cinema is the tradition, auteur cinema is the revolution' (Miller and Stam, 2000: 5), auteurism itself was specifically rejected by other New Cinema filmmaker/theorists who considered it to be complicit with bourgeois cinema and its cult of the individual. Cuban filmmaker/critic García Espinosa argues that the category of the individual artist (filmmaker/auteur) becomes defunct in a revolutionary society in which the goal is for everyone to be creators of a popular art (1997 [1969]: 76). Argentine filmmakers/theorists Octavio Getino and Fernando Solanas reject along with 'Hollywood' cinema the author's cinema as equally trapped inside a capitalist system of production, that allows only personal, but not political aesthetic freedom (1997 [1970]: 42).

Furthermore, for our study, which has positioned itself as similarly resistant to authoritarian models such as monolithic Mexican cultural nationalism, it must therefore appear like theoretical backtracking to be approaching our project via the work of an individual director. However, our seemingly 'auteurist' approach is validated by the fact that, before we can displace the hegemonic auteur figure weighing down on the text, we need first to look at the (nationalist) assumptions which have historically put him at the center of these films. Hence we will look at how the figure of Fernández as auteur emerges in Mexican national cinema, and how he and his work become representative of national culture.

It must also seem theoretically suspect to be dealing with (the similarly authoritarian model of) national cinema when, like auteurism, the concept of national cinema has equally been displaced by contemporary critical theories' emphases on globalization, transculturation and geoaesthetic areas with a broader scope beyond the nation (García Canclini, 1997: 227). Furthermore, cultural studies also teaches us to be suspicious of any particularisms like 'national culture' that rely on processes of hegemony and homogenization and the attempt to contain or prevent the potential proliferation of meanings other than those assigned by national orthodoxy – i.e., those of the counterculture (Higson, 1989: 37; Larsen, 1995: 119). However, within a world cultural-studies map, the cultures of the postcolonial nations and their marginal position in relation to the First World coincide with the 'counterculture' we wish to rescue from containment and homogenization, in this case Mexican national cinema and alternatives to Mexican cultural nationalism.

Therefore, as Larsen points out, in difference to First World cultural-studies' rejection of the category of national culture, the response of a Third World or postcolonial 'cultural studies' has been to deny that culture and nation can be disentangled (1995: 120). Indeed, along the same lines, independently of each other in the same year, both King and Noriega argue for the continued relevance of national categories in the analysis of cinema in Latin America despite the border crossings and global market that increasingly govern contemporary film production (Noriega, 2000: xi.). King argues that in the year 2000 the terrain on which Latin American filmmakers struggle to produce films has been and continues to be that of the nation (King, 2000: 253–5).

King's idea of the national as a site of struggle is an appropriate way of theorizing the insistent nationalism and 'resistance' to imperialist encroachment of Mexican classical cinema. Allegedly 'born' out of the armed phase of the revolution, the specific cultural history of twentieth-century Mexico – the ruling Institutional Revolutionary Party's treatment of national culture as a source of national unity and pride – signals the primacy of the concept of national cinema in a study of this kind *even if* we seek to challenge its homogeneity. From its inception in the 1930s with the production of *Redes* (Nets, Paul Strand, 1934) and *¡Vámonos con Pancho Villa!* (Let's go with Pancho Villa, Fernando de Fuentes, 1935), classical Mexican cinema was circumscribed by state cinema policies and national cultural characteristics. The shaping of a national identity through culture continued to be an important part of Government policy in the period 1940–60, but as Fein (2001: 160) and also Joseph et al. (2001: 11) point out, with a remarkably different focus from the early 1930s. From 1940 onward the perspective shifted from an inward-looking culture (focused on the folkloric aspects of Mexico) to one that looked outward, projecting these aspects of Mexican culture to the rest of the world. This cultural aperture is both a reflection and a product of the very different industrial and economic policies of the Mexican presidents from 1940 onward. Unlike Lázaro Cárdenas (1934–40), who set in place protectionist policies, for example nationalizing foreign oil interests, Manuel Ávila Camacho (1940–46) and Miguel Alemán (1946–52) encouraged policies that would foment commercial links with the US and other countries. This change in Government policy also effects a change in the way the filmmaker is perceived. 'Internationalist' government policy is reflected in contemporary local accounts of Fernández films and is also relevant to the roughly contemporaneous emergence of Fernández as Mexico's 'first' internationally known auteur. In other words, auteurism is what Fein refers to as a discursive practice to maintain nationalist ideological veneer in an era of transnationalization during the Second World War (2001: 163).

Higson argues that discussions of national cinema mobilize discourses of 'art,' 'culture,' 'quality' and 'national identity' (1989: 37). The concept of a national cinema is often put into play as 'a strategy of cultural and economic resistance; a means of asserting national autonomy in the face of (usually) Hollywood's international domination' (ibid.: 41). In 1940s Mexico this approach to national cinema translates into a vested interest in the presence of directors who are *auteurs* within the national cinema. The auteur figure implies the autonomous artist and provides a measure of independent quality in the national cinema. Following this reasoning, Fernández' internationally recognized 'nationalist cinema' becomes 'an international symbol of cultural prestige' and a sign of Mexico's own ability to assimilate the cultural values of the West – where the concept of filmmaking as an art form and the filmmaker as artist originally develops in its pre-*politique des auteurs* manifestation – and implicitly attain the level of development of the United States and Europe, the 'ultimate goal of progress' within the post-Revolutionary state (Fein, 1998: 105; Lomitz Adler, 1992: 278). We can link this desire for Western approval as evidence of what Monsiváis calls the Mexican elite's aspiration toward being a late-arriving, yet nonetheless worthy part of Western culture (1976: 308). Hence the presence of the auteur is both a sign of resistance to Western culture (Hollywood) – dignifying Mexico, its cultural production and its people in the face of pernicious stereotypes circulated by North American cinema (Tuñón, 1993: 161) – but also at the same time a sign of assimilation of Western cultural paradigms, which undermines this resistance.

In the nationalist construction of Fernández as an auteur he is credited with defining and thus representing a school of Mexican film. Fernández the auteur and the national cinema are conflated in his most often quoted pronouncement '¡El cine mexicano soy yo!' ('I am Mexican cinema') (Tuñón, 1993: 160). And he is also rumored to have famously defended this claim by brandishing a gun at a journalist who dared to refute it (Taibo, 1986: 155).

However, the process by which Fernández came to be conflated with the nationalist cinema does not take the route that Higson, Tuñón and other auteurist critics suggest. It initially depends on foreign approbation. At the premiere of *María Candelana* the film was received with boos and whistles by Mexican journalists. It was only the intervention of the Soviet Ambassador at the end of the film that silenced these catcalls (Garcia Riera, 1987: 48). But the film was generally well received by the public and Mexican critics. Only the poet Xavier Villarutia and muralist Rivera (who was actually Fernández' friend) rejected it (ibid.: 54). The film was further welcomed and appreciated in Mexico when it won at Cannes (1946), and received adulation from European critics (Taibo, 1986: 82–85). And it was only from this point onward that Fernández was acclaimed as a Mexican auteur by Mexican intellectuals (ibid.: 105). Significantly, in accounts of Fernández' work, his success is measured against recognition from a European institution, the Cannes Film Festival, and recognition from French critics such as Sadoul and Borde (Monsiváis, 1992: 33).

This suggests that the nature of authorship in Mexico exists in constant tension as both a signifier of anticolonial artistic production – assertion of autonomous artistry – but also as a marker of colonial approval sought after by the colonized cultural elite. Hence the signifiers of nation in a postcolonial society like Mexico are dependent on their recognition from colonial nation(s). Auteurism seeringly locks Mexico into a cycle of cultural dependency, which is largely why the 1960s New Cinemas in Latin America rejected it as a production strategy.

Furthermore, the nature of authorship in roughly contemporary European accounts of Fernández differs greatly to those written locally. At home some of Fernández' films are welcomed by leftist artists and writers (although Rivera called *María Candelaria* a *mamarracho* (an abomination)) for their revolutionary sentiments, while right-wing critics reject his dogmatism and radical revolutionary ideology (Tuñón, 2003: 49; García Riera, 1987: 54, 116–117). The basis for authorship (i.e., difference from the ordinary commercial fare) is that the films incorporate a socially significant message – the plight of the *maestros rurales* (rural teachers) and the literacy programs as in *Río Escondido* (1947) – and, at the same time, achieve aesthetic excellence. On the other hand, the basis for authorship in European accounts, such as Borde's interpretation of *Las abandonadas* (1944), *Salón México* (1949) and *Víctimas del pecado* (1950), is the expression of Fernández' own Romantic vision. For Borde: 'Fernández est donc un vrai romantique: le bonheur lui donne de l'angoisse. C'est dans le malheur, dans les fins douloureuses qui'il retrouve son équilibre' (Fernández is, therefore, a true romantic: happiness tortures him. It is only in misfortune and unhappy endings that he finds his equilibrium) (Borde, 1954: 17). Borde writes about Fernández as a (tortured) individual artist who wallows in misfortune and unhappy endings as if these were a personal preference, rather than the result of historically determined plots. Borde does not take into account the particular aesthetic traditions nor indeed the history that produced Fernández, nor the generic norms of the *cabareteras* (cabaret/brothel melodrama) nor indeed the team of talented individuals (Figueroa, writer Mauricio Magdaleno, editor Gloria Schoeman) who produced the films that bear Fernández' 'mark.' Borde's interpretation of Fernández corresponds more to the European Romantic idea circulated by those writers (including Borde) who wrote for *Cahiers du cinéma* and *Positif* in the 1950s. This results in the imposition of Euro-American paradigms and aesthetic theories upon non-European cultural practices, and in Borde's case in the marginalization of Mexico's specific sociocultural formations such as the codes of the Mexican national imaginary – i.e., *cabaretera* films as the product of social and political crisis and corruption – that Fernández worked in (Willemen, 1994: 211).

However, despite the drawbacks of Borde's analysis, it is potentially no less a distortion of the films themselves to be overly sensitive to national aesthetic traditions or the notion of collaborative authorship. Berg examines Fernández not as an individual auteur but as part of a team (which functions in the manner of auteur in terms of a certain coherency of style and vision). The Fernández/Figueroa style for Berg is 'the disavowal of Hollywood's influences and the quest for Mexican roots' (1994: 13). Berg ties Fernández into the national by tracing the development of a Fernández/Figueroa nationalist aesthetic through traditions of fine and popular Mexican art. He describes how Fernández and Figueroa created a non-Western – i.e., nonlinear, curved – perspective benefiting from both local (Dr Arlt, José Guadalupe Posada (popular art), David Alfaro Siqueiros (fine art)) and also nonlocal influences (Sergei Eisenstein, Gregg Toland and John Ford). The Fernández/Figueroa style is listed and distilled into the following elements: use of Posada's *calaveras* (skulls) and *magueyes* (via Eisenstein), Dr Arlt's 'curvilinear perspective,' Siqueiros' dramatic foreshortening, Eisentein's Hand Toland's low-angle and deep-focus photography – and dialectical use of diagonals in the composition (Berg, 1994: 14–18).

Berg's analysis of Fernández and Figueroa's style becomes a 'perfect' analysis of a Third World auteur, which according to Armes should show sensitivity to indigenous forms and yet also show awareness of the inevitable transnationalism of film style in Third World, postcolonial societies (Armes, 1987: 79). While the model of Third World authorship that Armes offers, which assigns Fernández the label of auteur for his 'sympathetic portrayals of the poor and oppressed in Mexico from the 1940s,' is arguably more accurate than Borde's European model, it is also somewhat anachronistic as a theoretical paradigm with which to approach Fernández (ibid.: 72). It anachronistically credits Fernández as making films in the 1940s with a late 1950s' radical Third World consciousness.

Berg's analysis is also exemplary of the structuralist approach to film auteurism as outlined by Peter Wollen (1970), which treats repeating patterns and recurrent structures as grounds for authorship. Perkins suggests Wollen makes a crucial error in creating such a model of authorship. This error, Perkins argues, is 'an exaggerated concern with the continuities and coherence across a body of a director's work' (1990: 57). The emphasis falls on repetition and, as Perkins suggests, leads to the kinds of analysis of films which obsessively look for structures across an oeuvre, and distort attempts at textual analysis.

While Berg's analysis of the Fernández/Figueroa style is groundbreaking in terms of its attention to tracing the often mentioned but rarely corroborated formal influences in their work, this analysis turns into the 'exaggerated concern for coherence' that Perkins warns against. For example, as one element of the Fernández/Figueroa nationalist cinematic style, Berg focuses on the use of diagonal lines and dialectical oppositions (light/dark, foreground/background, flatlands/mountains, the shore/the sea) within the composition of the image. On the drawing up of oppositions, Perkins warns: 'The mere presence of these "oppositions" in a film does not declare their pertinence' (1990: 59). Rather than read those images in terms of the relationships set up by the different elements within the frame, Berg reads them in terms of moral absolutes – 'that which needs to be overcome' – that he applies blanket-form across the Fernández/ Figueroa oeuvre. For example, near the beginning of *Río Escondido* the protagonists, Rosaura (María Félix) and Felipe (Fernando Fernández), trek to a remote village. At one point they are seen descending a hill which cuts the frame diagonally into landscape and sky, and dwarfs their tiny figures. Berg interprets this as 'foreshadow[ing] the oppressive, unbalanced social order [they are] entering' (Berg, 1994: 20), and indeed posits that in *all* Fernández/Figueroa films diagonals act as a motif which always represents disequilibria in the social order. While persuasive, this reading seems to miss out other evaluations of such a composition or even make significant a feature which may not be relevant to the film. While these features could be signifiers of 'extraordinary richness,' the use of diagonals could also be considered a commonplace of composition that wants to suggest the expansive space of rural Mexico (in the same way as the diagonal lines of the pavement suggest expansive space in the 'Singin' in the Rain' sequence from *Singin' in the Rain* (Stanley Donen, 1952)) or the struggle and hardship of the quest (as in the Western genre) and not necessarily pertinent to a broader social issue. However, once Berg establishes the use of the diagonal as a nationalist motif, further (potentially trasnational) evaluation of the composition is effectively annulled, not only in this but also in all the Fernández/Figueroa films. What further complicates and closes off Berg's analysis of the films is the fact that all 'recurring characteristics of style' become nationalist motifs – i.e., part of institutionalized cultural nationalism: muralism, *magueyes*, *indígenas* and *grabados*. The dialectics of diagonal composition would, following Berg's line of reasoning, reflect the institutionalized Revolution's (i.e., the Government's) alleged sympathy with '*los de abajo*' (the underclass) which seeks to uncover and redress the inequalities in society. The film becomes unreadable outside a matrix of auteurism and nationalism. These two discourses become indistinguishable and also self-perpetuating, and we end up again in a different kind of cyclical reading strategy not unlike that of audience reception examined in chapter one. Effectively, by assigning meaning according to greater narratives than those of the films themselves – auteurism and nationalism – Berg brings to the surface the values, assumptions and meanings that are most central to the belief in a 'true' Mexican nation, but these may also have the effect of silencing other values, alternative perspectives and competing bids for meaning. For example, examining the film in strict nationalist terms – i.e., solely in terms of their aesthetic differences to the Hollywood product – causes problems with the many Fernández films which borrow heavily (and significantly) from US generic formula, such as *Enamorada* (1946) and the screwball comedy. What is important to establish at this stage is an understanding of Fernández and his films that takes into account the cultural specificity of Mexico and the very different context for filmmaking that exists in Latin America, but which does so without overemphasizing potentially problematic elements of nationalism and ethnicity.

Authorizing and authenticating 'El Indio'

> Casi *desnudo* sobre una piragua, el indio Zirahuén comienza a mostrar al 'Indio' Fernández la punta del camino.
>
> (Almost naked in a canoe, the Indian Zirahuén begins to show the 'Indian' Fernández the way forward.) (Taibo, 1986: 58)
>
> When Zirahuén turns the canoe around, is he integrated into society or separated from himself? Was he individually marginalized although already part of a socially marginalized group? This tension reflects Emilio Fernández' own *personal problem*: he who looks from outside, who feels

excluded. We do not know whether this was a result of his own Indian blood (his mother was Kikapú), but he always defined himself in these terms. (Tuñón, 1995: 180)

In the indigenist drama *Janitzio* (Carlos Novaro, 1934), Fernández, in his pre-director days, plays Zirahuén who is betrothed to Erendida (María Teresa Orozco). They live on Janitzio, an island community isolated from society, which lives off the fish it catches and forbids its women to have sexual relations with outsiders. Manuel, a Creole speculator, comes to the island from the city and proceeds to lower the price at which the *indígenas* can sell their fish. When Zirahuén protests, Manuel has him incarcerated. Manuel offers Erendida Zirahuén's liberty in exchange for her sexual favors. Zirahuén gets out of prison and finds out that Erendida has given herself to Manuel. He kills Manuel and prepares to bring Erendida back to the village. However, he is torn between the demands of his own isolated community, which tell him he must kill Erendida as punishment for being with a 'foreigner,' and his desire to forgive and marry her, which is representative of assimilation into broader society. Ultimately, Zirahuén, chooses love over duty, or assimilation over the integrity of his community's values. The villagers, however, take the matter into their own hands and stone Erendida to death. This in turn precludes Zirahuén's assimilation. As a final gesture he picks up her dead body and walks with it into the lake to his own death.

Janitzio reflects the dominant discourse of post-Revolutionary Mexico in which the locus of authentic popular culture was ambivalently imagined to be the Indian, *campesino* sphere. Indigenous Mexicans were portrayed as 'backward' and 'suffering', like the villagers who stone Erendida to death, but also the repository of a 'rich and colorful cultural tradition' as in the film's extended fishing sequences, awaiting the 'modernizing' and 'civilizing efforts' of the *mestizo* national subject (Levi, 2001: 344; Lomitz-Adler, 1992: 2).

This discourse which attempted to construct 'pure,' originary notions of an 'authentic' national and popular culture in Mexico and elsewhere in Latin America, has largely been deconstructed and demystified by García Canclini and others who argue that the forces of urbanization, industrialization, massification and foreign influences make the preservation of these notions of 'purity' and 'authenticity' impossible (García Canclini, 1995: 4). Furthermore, deconstructive thinking encourages skepticism of the idea that a prelapsarian originary moment 'before' civilization ever existed. Nevertheless, relatively recent (Tuñón, 1986; Monsiváis, 1992) accounts of Fernández seem to repeat the discourse of authentic, national and popular culture by focusing on the filmmaker's ethnicity, (the fact that he was a *mestizo*, half Kikapú and half 'white,') as some kind of nationalist credential that legitimates and gives 'authenticity' to his work.

Both of the quotations that begin this section refer to Fernández' first major role in Mexican cinema, playing the character of Zirahuén in *Janitzio*, and erroneously construct it as a 'myth of origins' for Fernández as a filmmaker and auteur. Taibo suggests that Fernández is literally 'shown the way' – for the rest of his filmography – by this indigenist drama. (Out of the forty one films Fernández made, only two of them were remakes of *Janitzio*: *María Candelaria* and *Maclovia*.)

Similarly, Tuñón equates Zirahuén's isolation with Fernández' sense of his own social marginalization, because of his racial/social origins: 'I knew perfectly well that they would never give me the chance to direct. It was very difficult. They were already here: the intellectuals, the college graduates, the sons of millionaires' (Tuñón, 1995: 181). Tuñón argues that this sense of isolation becomes the primal drama reenacted throughout his oeuvre. Fernández' indigenist films *María Candelaria* (1943), *Maclovia* (1948) and *La perla* (1945) are read as isolationist fantasies; perceived as an extension of his own sense of exclusion, and yet desire to retreat, from society. Such critical readings reveal a slippage between the analysis of the character of Zirahuén and the actor/director Fernández. On the one hand auteurist accounts like those of Tuñón emphasize Fernández as the 'Indio,' who has a somewhat timeless (read 'backward') vision of the world and who experienced a great deal of discrimination (read 'suffering') in his career but is still the locus of the 'authentic' in classical Mexican cinema (Tuñón, 1993: 165). On the other, they emphasize his mixed racial heritage, constructing him as the *mestizo*, the true Mexican, who, in keeping with Revolutionary racial ideology represents the fruitful (artistic) coming together of Mexico's two heritages: indigenous and Spanish. Following this logic it is fitting that Mexico's 'first internationally renowned auteur' should be of marked mixed racial heritage.

However, paradoxically, while Fernández ethnicity is the basis for his 'authority' as a filmmaker in a nationalist cinema, Eurocentric notions within that nationalist tradition deauthorize him on the basis of his own ethnicity, placing him in a weak position. Fernández is put in the position of 'other' within his own country. Local critics like Taibo who criticize European critics for perceiving what their socialist vision wishes them to see – i.e., realism in *Flor Silvestre* – repeat these same Eurocentric pitfalls by seeing in Fernández the 'noble savage' (1986: 79–80).

In fact, the assumption that Fernández is 'ethnic' at all, whereas other classical Mexican auteurs (De Fuentes, Bracho, Galindo) are not, is ultimately based on the Eurocentric view that certain groups (Europeans) are not ethnic, whereas other groups (Asians, Native Americans, Africans, indigenous peoples) are (Shohat, 1991: 215; Dyer, 1997: 1). By making an issue out of Fernández' ethnicity he is being both praised (as an authentic Mexican) and marginalized. As 'El Indio,' an ethnic, he is not part of the dominant group which envisions itself as the 'universal' or the 'essential' and therefore somehow above or beyond ethnicity. This would be in direct contradistinction to institutionalized Revolutionary discourse and its envisaging of the *mestizo* as the 'essential' Mexican. We can interpret the fact that his ethnicity should even be an issue, i.e., the constant use of his nickname – despite the fact that it is used knowingly, affectionately or ironically within quotation marks – as evidence of a nevertheless peripheralizing strategy on the part of auteurist accounts. By restricting Fernández to his ethnicity, auteurism effectively becomes a ghettoizing discourse which considers ethnic and racial groups in isolation (Shohat, 1991: 216). Viewed from this position, *Janitzio*'s narrative of isolation and its perceived subsequent mirroring of Fernández' own social isolation is also emblematic of the marginalizing Eurocentric discourses that characterize Fernández as a director.

In the quotations at the beginning of this section Fernández is continually represented in terms of racially defined characteristics and qualities. The slippage between character and actor/director again causes Taibo to read Fernández in Eurocentric terms; he focuses on Zirahuén's nakedness thus defining Fernández in colonialist terms as body rather than mind (Figure 2.1). Taibo goes on to describe Fernández in terms of pure physicality, while hinting at the, equally colonialist, threat of Fernández' untamed sexuality: 'Alto, fuerte, moreno, de piel atezada y pelo negro, de aspecto rudo . . . Tipos así no sobraban en el cine mexicano . . . Pasea por los estudios su apostura, su raza y también su muy autoelogiada capacidad amatoria' (Tall, strong and dark, with a tanned complexion and black hair, he had a

2.1 Fernández as Zirahuén in *Janitzio*

rugged look... There weren't a lot of guys like that in Mexican Cinema ... He strides through the studio wearing his race and also his self-acclaimed abilities as a lover) (Taibo, 1986: 57). He also sees parts of Fernández as Zirahuén in the different roles he creates in his own films. Taibo says that the two protagonists in Fernández' *La red* (The Net, 1953) resemble Fernández/Zirahuén: 'Los dos personajes... se parecen algo a él mismo; son como el 'Indio' que fue en su primer film importante: *Janitzio*. Fuertes, machos corpulentos, gráciles, asperos. Y en los dos está Emilio en cuerpo y también en oscuros deseos.' (The two characters... are just like [Fernández] himself. They are like 'El Indio' as he was in his first important film: *Janitzio*. [They are] strong, macho, corpulent, rough. Fernández is in both of them, in body and in [their] dark desires.) (ibid.: 141).

What is initially striking about these images of Fernández is their deep ambivalence. His 'primitive nobility' and corporeality (fused in the author's mind with the fictional character Zirahuén) contain both a nostalgia for an innocence lost forever to the 'civilized' world, and the threat of civilization being overrun or undermined by the recurrence of savagery (which is always lurking just below the surface) or by an untutored sexuality threatening to 'break out.' Indeed, Taibo describes him as: 'ese ser ... salvaje, inculto y arbitrario' (a savage, uncouth and arbitrary being) (ibid.: 85). Furthermore, the title of Taibo's biography of Fernández *El Indio Fernández: El cine por mis pistolas* (The Indian Fernández: Cinema with my guns) suggests precisely the primitivist interrelationship of the director, his films and violence.[3] Taibo documents this savagery in his violent behavior toward journalists and his cast and crew. It is caricatured in the parts he plays in Mexican and US films – for example, the vicious patriarch he plays in Sam Peckinpah's *Bring Me the Head of Alfredo Garcia* (1974) who asks for the 'head' of his daughter's lover, or General Mapache in Pekinpah's *The Wild Bunch* (1969) who has Angel (Jaime Sanchez) dragged (almost to death) behind his Model T Ford car. We see that the figure of the *indígena* is one of desire and threat: desire for the noble savage, for retreat from civilization to the promise of harmony, and the threat of violence that could explode at any second. However, the threat of the noble savage is conveniently dispelled through the process of *mestizaje* (miscegenation). Gilbert Joseph et al. point out:

> Whereas once a minuscule and insecure cosmopolitan elite eschewed rural culture as barbaric and 'Indian,' now [1940–60] enlarged middle and upper classes flaunted their internationalism while simultaneously embracing a rural culture that had been conveniently mesticized and mainstreamed. Indeed, the post revolutionary discourse of the state identified a seemingly timeless rustic landscape as an important wellspring of Mexican cultural 'authenticity.' (2001: 11)

Both sides of Fernández, his artistry and his violent nature, are aspects of the 'good 'and the 'bad' sides of primitivism. In these images, 'primitivism' is defined by the fixed proximity of the individual – Fernández – to nature (Hall, 1990: 16). Adela Fernández quotes her father: 'Ser indio es ser uno con la naturaleza y con Dios; es palpar en la tierra, en el agua y en el aire las fuerzas divinas, y cada instante de la vida' (Being an Indian is like being one with nature and with God; it is like experiencing the divine forces at work in the earth, the water and the air and in every moment of life) (Fernández, 1986: 38).

However, such primitivist notions as displayed by Taibo and Tuñón are no strangers to Latin American national identities. The figure of the noble savage is in fact essential to the formation of Latin American nations (Franco, 1993: 81). The central texts of the Latin American genealogy, *La raza cósmica* (José Vasconcelos, 1999 [1925]) and *Nuestra America* (José Martí, 1977 [1891]), all depict the essential Latin American as a 'noble savage.'

On the other hand, Jean Franco points out that the figure of the noble savage has also been central to the imperialist project (ibid.). We note something of the imperialist project in terms of mapping and knowing the world in the way the auteurist accounts of Fernández (except for Berg's) tend to take the 'director as personality' approach to his films (à *la* Peter Bogdanovich), in contradistinction to the studies of other (white) classical Mexican directors (García Riera, 1987: 11) which do not treat the biography as the most important aspect of the filmmaker. The rationale given for focusing in Fernández case on his lifestory is his 'extraordinary' life, and that his life and his films are not just connected but symbiotically linked (Tuñón, 1995: 181) and that his films would not read so coherently unless read concurrently with his colorful life.[4] Biographical auteurist accounts such as these proliferated in the 1960s and take the route of interpreting films as simple reflections of the director's life, experiences and opinions. This is emblematized when Tuñón writes that those Fernández films in which *machos* (allegedly) dominate submissive *hembras*, *Enamorada* (1946), *Bugambilia* (1944) and *Las abandonadas* (1944) reflect Fernández' own treatment of women (Tuñón, 1993: 169).

¡Viva la revolución! Fernández' life story as nationalist *telos*

Although there is some confusion over the exact details of his life, the various accounts (Monsiváis, García Riera, Adela Fernández, Taibo) agree on some of the following: Fernández was born in 1904, son of an army captain, Emilio Fernández Snr. and his Kikapú wife, Sara Romo. At the age of 9 he allegedly caught his mother with another man, killed the man/both of them and escaped into/left with his father for the revolution fighting with both Venustiano Carranza and then Pancho Villa at some of the latter's most famous battles including Torreón. He entered military college at the age of 13 and remained in the army travelling with it to Argentina and Puerto Rico. In 1923 he fought on the side of Adolfo de la Huerta and was captured and imprisoned. He escaped and fled to the US three years later. In the US he worked at a number of jobs and travelled around the country. He went first to Chicago where he met and became friends with Rudolf Valentino, who remarked on his excellent ability to dance tango. He was allegedly forced to leave Chicago because he got into 'trouble' with Baby-Face Nelson, Al Capone's right-hand man. He then went to Hollywood, and worked as an extra with other Mexicans (Chano Urueta and Roberto Gavaldón) who, on their return to Mexico, would also enter the filmmaking business as producers, directors and actors (Taibo, 1986: 43–44). Symbolically, his rumoured to be impressive physique was one of the models on which the Oscar statuette was based in 1927 (García Riera, 1987: 16) – interestingly, making him a 'golden boy' of a different kind to that of Mexico's Golden Age years later. While in the film Mecca 'learning his trade,' he also met Dolores Del Rio. She was a star at the time and he was a humble extra on two of her movies – *Ramona* (1928) and *Flying Down to Rio* (1933). He also met the Nicaraguan nationalist Augusto César Sandino (1895–1934) who invited him to fight in the struggle against US intervention in Nicaragua. He met Adolfo de la Huerta, who had been the interim President of Mexico (1920), who told him to go back to Mexico and make films which were 'a greater weapon than any gun' in the struggle over Mexican nationalism – a surprisingly new cinema-like analogy and one that partly explains Taibo's biography title *El cine por mis pistolas* (Taibo, 1986: 29–31; Tuñón, 1988: 22). This avowed power of cinema (and, if we are to believe the auteurist apologists, a great deal of formal inspiration for his later films) was further confirmed by watching Sergei Eisenstein's incomplete masterpiece *¡Que viva México!* (1932) which was also circulating in Hollywood in 1933 (Taibo, 1986: 55). Nostalgic for his home/expatriated as part of Depression-era measures, he returned to Mexico in 1933 and went straight into the nascent Mexican film industry.

What we notice from this first part of Fernández' alleged biography culled from various accounts, is that up to his departure for the US it closely ties the auteur into the narrative of Mexican national identity and national culture. For even though Taibo refutes that Fernández ever fought in the revolution, he still maintains that the revolution marked him in a certain way (Taibo, 1986: 30). No matter how wary the biographical critics are of the details of his life story, Fernández is always classed as a product of the revolution, both racially and socially. Indeed, the story of his early life reads like a Mexican Forrest Gump

(*Forrest Gump*, Robert Zemeckis, 1994), embodying what it has been suggested are the myths of twentieth-century Mexican nationalism and national character – i.e., the revolution and the betrayal by the mother, engendering the inferiority complex and the Virgin/Whore duality in Mexican representations of the female.

The next part of his biography from his Hollywood sojourn onward becomes a quest for cinematic nationalism which, as he tells it and it is told, took him first to the US and Hollywood and then back to Mexico. The biography is constructed around a strong nationalist *telos*. Like Forrest Gump, Fernández meets with a number of prominent figures (in terms of both Latin American, Mexican and US film and history) and is involved in a staggering amount of historically significant events, all of which lead inexorably to the product of a 'Mexicanist' cinematic oeuvre.

The account continues with his first film in 1934, *Janitzio*, as Zirahuén, which, as we have already examined, according to most criticism casts the die in terms of his future film projects. Despite a series of secondary parts (*Adiós Nicanor* 1937; *Corazón bandolero* 1934; *El superloco* 1936: *El impostor* 1936; *Almas rebeldes* 1937) and rejected scripts, through the 1930s Fernández lives an artistically rich and colorful life along with the other pioneers of Mexican cinema. He perseveres in his endeavors to become a director and finally gets to direct a feature film in 1941 *La isla de pasión* (The Passionate Island). *La isla de pasión* is a nationalist narrative about the defence of an island. His second film, *Soy puro mexicano* (I'm a real Mexican, 1942), is similarly nationalist in terms of its topic. It is set during the Second World War and involves a bizarre plot in which a bandit (Pedro Armendáriz) defies the combined forces of the Axis, a German, an Italian and a Japanese man, hiding out in a Mexican hacienda and planning an invasion. Between 1943 and 1949, along with a team of actors (Del Rio, Pedro Armendáriz, María Félix, María Elena Marqués, Marga López, Columba Domínguez, Miguel Inclán, Carlos López Moctezuma, Roberto Cañedo), a technical crew (Gabriel Figueroa and Gloria Schoeman), a screenwriter (Mauricio Magdaleno) and musicians (Antonio Díaz Conde and Francisco Domínguez), he makes a cinema that is truly Mexican. The first significant film in this impressive oeuvre is *Flor Silvestre* (1943), which represents a stylistic and cultural departure from anything seen before in Mexican cinema. It represents the momentous beginning of the 'nationalist aesthetic.'

From his biography as it is recounted in auteurist accounts summarized above, a picture emerges of Fernández as the essential Mexican male displaying those personality traits which are common currency for Mexican masculinity: machismo, defensiveness, closedness (Lomitz Adler, 1992: 258). For Monsiváis, who is always somewhat ironic, Fernández is 'el macho colosal que representa física y simbólicamente a México, no un país sino la geografía marcada por estados de ánimo' (The colossal macho who physically and symbolically represents Mexico, not just as a country but as a place marked by certain moods) (Monsiváis, 1992: 35). However, it has been suggested that these characteristics, which supposedly make Fernández and the characters he creates the prototypical Mexican male, are no more than 'a stagnating pool of descriptions of national traits that were produced by the *pensadores* (thinkers Ramos, Alfonso Reyes and Paz) in the literature of national culture' (Lomitz Adler, 1992: 258). So, while Taibo and Tuñón question the veracity of Fernández' account and acknowledge 'El Indio's' own capacity for self-invention, following a certain Mexican script, they repeat this invention and reify Fernández and his films within this tradition of national stereotypes. The obsession with certain images and stereotypes leads to a kind of essentialism, reducing a complex figure to a set of reified formulae. Fernández is thus *Indio, bandido* (bandit), and *revolucionario* (revolutionary). These types are reflective of a Eurocentric perspective. This potentially explains Fernández' great success in US films playing these same types including General Mapache in *The Wild Bunch*. His off-screen persona easily transfers into Hollywood films where *bandido, indio* and *revolucionario* are the *lingua franca* for Mexican (Woll, 1980: 2).

The received version of his life story continues: after his own 'Golden Age' (1943–50), Fernández appropriately goes into decline along with the cinema he allegedly represented. Financial hardship forces the director into acting in other people's films (an activity he reportedly did not like), such as playing Coronel Zeta in Ismael Rodríguez' *La cucaracha* (1958), and making commercial films which have nothing to do with his own artistic vision (*Islas Marías*, 1950). The few films he does make which are considered 'part' of his aesthetic tradition in the 1950s (*Víctimas del pecado*, (Victims of sin), *Un día de vida* (One day of life), *La red* (The Net), *El impostor* (The Impostor)), 1960s (*Pueblito*) and 1970s (*La Choca, Zona roja, Erótica*) insistently repeat themes from an original model. His decline and stagnation are blamed on the repetition of the same images of nationalism that brought him great success during his most prestigious years. This reading is in part symptomatic of auteurist approaches which decide a paradigm of nationalist images (the themes of Fernández' cinematic nationalism, isolationism, indigenism, tragic love) and then examine films as they fit into that paradigm, discarding those films which do not fit the predetermined paradigm as anomalies – notably *Pepita Jiménez* (1945) and *Bugambilia* (1944).

The incredible burden of representation that is placed on Fernández as 'el macho colosal', representing not just the national cinema but also Mexico, ultimately brought about his downfall: 'a Emilio Fernández lo daña inmensamente, en su obra y su vida la seguridad de ser México, al pie de la letra, *sin fisuras*, el hombre hecho nación harto de las argucias de los picapleitos y ávido de no fallarle al instinto' (Emilio Fernández is immensely harmed by his own certainty that his life and his work embodies Mexico, to the letter. [The idea that he is] the man as nation, tired of the sophistry of the shysters and anxious to never fail [to live up to] his own instincts) (Monsiváis, 1992: 35). However, as Monsiváis suggests with the ironic tone and overinflated vocabulary which characterizes the majority of his writing about Fernández, neither Fernández nor his films represented an 'authentic' Mexico.

The *Testimonio*: authenticity undone

When Tuñón explains in the Forward to *En su propio espejo* how she met Fernández, what is initially striking is how much her perspective resembles that of the anthropologist and how her description of the man himself folkloricizes him as the 'subject:'

> El 7 de mayo me presenté en su casa, sin grabadora ... Llamó mi atención el delicado y recio gusto de la construcción, de los muebles; el *cuadro de los dos gallos* y sobre todo la fotografía *de un toro* que, luego supe, lo persigue en sus pesadillas. Recordé entonces la escena increíble de una corrida en el interior de su casa en *Soy puro mexicano*. Me apaciguó el miedo. De pronto su presencia me sacó de la abstracción: era un torso descomunal enfundado en *ropa militar* ... Empezó a hablar, a recordar ... Después de una hora me despedí con la pregunta de cuándo volvía. Para mi sorpresa me pidió que pronto, y grabamos juntos, a lo largo de un año, veinte sesiones de una entrevista que me permitió acercarme al conversador. Al Indio cuentero y cuentista, al hombre creador.
>
> (On 7 May, I presented myself at his house without a tape recorder ... I was struck by the delicate yet robust taste with which it was built and by

its furniture. [I was also struck by] a painting of some cocks and above all by a photograph of a bull that I later found out chases [Fernández] in his nightmares. I then remembered the incredible scene of a bull fight inside his house in *Soy puro mexicano*. My fear subsided ... Suddenly; the presence of his unnatural torso swathed in military clothing roused me from my musings ... He began to speak, to remember ... After an hour I said my goodbyes and asked when I might return. To my surprise he asked that I return soon and together over a year we recorded twenty sessions of an interview that allowed me to get closer to my interlocutor, closer to 'El Indio' the storyteller and teller of tales, and closer to the creative man.) (Tuñón, 1988: 11–12).

As well as her repeating of the primitivist tropes of physicality (i.e. his 'unnatural torso') and magicality (i.e. as 'story teller'), we also notice how in Tuñón's description Fernández is linked to the military (and hence to the revolution), to a masculinist nature (*los gallos* and *el toro*), to his films (*Soy puro mexicano* (1941), although he actually built the house after he made the film) and to Mexican nationalism. What is striking is that the long-interview-as-book that Tuñón presents to us resembles the testimonial particularly in terms of the conception of the testimonial endeavor as one of transcription and transparency, 'traté de ser únicamente la vocera de Emilio Fernández, de no inmiscuirme en sus opiniones' (I tried to be the spokesperson for Fernandez, to not involve myself in his opinions) (ibid.: 9). However, the testimonial work also refers by definition to a first-person narration by members of the underprivileged sectors of society who relate their experiences, usually to a writer, journalist or ethnographer (Shea, 1993: 139). Although Fernández is not underprivileged, his ethnic status and the way Tuñón presents herself as his *vocera* (spokesperson) sets up unequal power relations between herself and Fernández. As a result she appears as the writer/journalist (anthropologist) and he the 'native informant.' However, the optimism and faith of the 1980s in the political potential of transparent self-representation offered by the *testimonio* – which is reflected in the title and introduction to *En su propio espejo* (In His Own Mirror) written in 1986, published in 1988 – proves to be somewhat of a fallacy in the discourse of the late 1990s onward. In a post-Rigoberta Menchú/Elisabeth Burgos era, postcolonial approaches conclude that the *testimonio* has become emblematic of the impossibility of authenticity or transparency in the anthropological endeavor (Spivak, 1995). As evident from Ruth Behar's *Translated Woman* (1993), rather than letting the subaltern speak, the testimonial genre gets caught in a process of self-representation, not of the subject but of the compiler/editor/ transcriber/anthropologist him/herself.

Rather than a coherent, 'authentic' representation of the essential Mexican, the *mestizo*, the *testimonio* genre presents Fernández as a fissured personality (which Monsiváis has hinted at by ironically calling him 'el hombre *sin fisuras*' (the man without fissures)). Tuñón's testimonial interview reveals Fernández as a hybrid, incoherent figure with a number of traits which problematize his presentation as the essential Mexican.

An example of how Fernández is incoherent as a personality is the improbable biography that Taibo, Adela Fernández, Tuñón and García Riera all agree is full of dubious facts. Although they question the veracity of the stories or narratives he tells of his life, they do not question the substance of these narratives and therefore implicitly let them stand as narratives that they use to construct him as an emblematically national figure.[5] For example, Taibo says that, although it is likely Fernández did not experience the historical revolution as closely as he professes, he was nevertheless firmly marked by it (1986: 30). It is as if the auteurists are prepared to accept Fernández' mythomania as long as it coincides with the mythos of post-Revolutionary national identity. Meanwhile, those elements that do not coincide with the mythos of post-Revolutionary national identity they carefully elide.

For example, while some critics mention the fact that Fernández' high, watery voice was so incongruous with his dominating persona that it had to be dubbed (by Narciso Busquets) whenever he appeared in film, no critics explore why, within a Mexican context, the 'macho' image should be so important nor indeed how the disjunction between image and voice might problematize any discourse that essentialized Fernández as the 'macho colosal' (Taibo, 1986: 162; Tuñón, 1988: 11; García Riera, 1987: 251).

Adela Fernández reads her father's fictitious biography in a different yet nonetheless equally essentializing and mythologizing manner. She links her father's generous mixing of fantasy and reality first to the Mexican tradition of the *cuentero*, (storyteller) saying that her father is inspired by the greatness of his '*antepasados*' (ancestors), and then to the 'mundo mágico' (magical world) of the Kikapú people, which she argues is also responsible for the creative spirit which brought him such acclaim (1986: 23, 26). While she does not attempt to pretend the

Kikapú live untouched by modern society or totally separate to it, she does conflate culture and nature by assigning a variety of her father's (and paternal grandmother's) personality traits – hermeticism, stoicism, mixing of fantasy and reality – to be part of an essential ethnic identity rather than culturally determined (1986: 37).[6]

What makes things even more problematic in terms of the truth versus fabrication dichotomy is that, as Taibo points out, many of Fernández' stories about his early life are impossible to confirm and some which seem to be implausible (that the Oscar statuette is modelled on his body) turn out to be true (García Riera, 1987: 16).

Further evidence of the incoherency of Fernández as an individual within a (officially at least) racially democratic Revolution is his professed admiration of Adolf Hitler and fascism (Tuñón, 1988: 36). Tuñón seems again to downplay this part of his personality, which, like his voice, would be incongruous to the essential Mexican *mestizo* that Fernández represents. Note in the following quotation her paraphrasing within square brackets which serve to mitigate Fernández' incendiary statements by emphasizing military discipline rather than genocidal anti-Semitism:

> Yo soy militar . . . y siempre lo he sido. Yo soy germanófilo de hueso colorado en el sentido militar . . . Ahora bien . . . [la disciplina alemana] es lo mejor. Es la única cosa que puede hacer un gran ejército. Su opinión ante la figura de Adolfo Hitler era también ambivalente: lo odiaba y lo admiraba muchísimo . . . como militar [le parecía supremo] qué magnetismo tendrá un hombre para tener, hacer todas las, las masas todo ahí se entrega.
>
> (I am a military man and I have always been one. I am a germanophile in the military sense. Above all [German discipline] is the best. It is the only thing that can make an army great. His opinion of the figure of Adolf Hitler was also ambivalent; he hated yet admired him a lot . . . as a military man [to him, he seemed supreme] what kind of magnetism must such a man have had to have made so many people hand themselves over to him.) (1988: 36)

With Tuñón's numerous interjections, explanations and paraphrasing in square brackets it becomes difficult to disentangle Fernández' own words (italicized in Tuñón's text) from the rest of the text. The biography of the (always classed as) European (though actually Mexican in citizenship) auteur Luis Buñuel, *Mi último suspiro* (*My Last Sigh*) (1996), also produced with another party, Jean-Claude Carrière, as with Tuñón in *En su proprio espejo*, is significantly ghostwritten so that

Buñuel appears to speak with agency ('I') rather than mediated through the gaze and interjections of another. Fernández, the 'native informant,' gets not even the illusion of autonomy and agency that Buñuel is afforded, but instead the paraphrasing and elision of his words. Furthermore, Fernández' anti-Semitic rantings (in letters and interviews published in the 1950s and 1960s), against those in the film industry who supposedly conspired against him, are significantly elided (García Riera, 1987: 241). It becomes difficult to reconcile Fernández' own racial heritage which is celebrated in Tuñón's interview with a political ideology based in the supposed racial superiority of the Aryan race (Taibo, 1986: 150). This is further complicated by the fact that in the late 1970s/early 1980s Fernández' virulent anti-Semitism brought public opposition to naming the Cinemateca Nacional after him (Paranaguá, 1995: 6). Not mentioning any of this represents therefore an important gap or silence in the construction of him as a 'nationalist' auteur.

It has been suggested that auteurism, like pre-García Canclini anthropological discourses in Latin America, is a search for/ festishization of an imagined purity of spirit or core of meanings and a guarantor of authenticity and authority (Andrew, 2000: 21). Bazin suggests that such a search for purity is out of place in what is an essentially 'impure medium' (Andrew, 2000: 21), and also argues that auteurism must be complemented by other approaches – technological, historical, sociological (Stam, 2000: 2). This chapter has questioned those auteurist readings of Fernández which, by seeking to construct him as a flesh-and-blood individual who gives meaning and coherence to a unified oeuvre, fall into the trap of the 'cult of personality.' This chapter has also problematized the structuralist auteurist strategies which introduce the figure of the auteur as text made by his films finding relevance in repetition and structure – i.e., what Fernández did often, rather than in what he did well (Berg, 1994). This chapter has suggested that the reading of Fernández' films as texts of Mexican cultural nationalism depend more on the figure of Fernández as he has been constructed as an auteur than on the texts themselves. Following this, if the figure of the author can be found to be noncoherent then the texts themselves become free and open to a polysemy of ideas and readings.

How then do we look for alternatives to these two approaches, without reifying the figure of Fernández within any tradition that we seek to challenge? A Mexico-specific reading of the figure of the auteur offers a potential way forward. This would be an auteur who, like the revolution and Revolutionary culture, embodied a sense of the 'popular': i.e., the specific construction of a cinema that would be artistic and yet appeal at the same time to the masses. Such an auteur would be in direct contrast to European notions of the auteur which are more elite than they are popular.

Notes

1 In 1976 in Torreón, Coahuila province, Fernández shot and killed a man. After initially fleeing the country, he returned to face justice and was sentenced to four and a half years in prison. He was released on bail and later pardoned.
2 Adela Fernández' quotes her father: 'Me apodaron *el Indio* como queriéndome estigmatizar, pero gracias al sobrenombre yo no perdí un minuto de conciencia de que soy indio, y ha sido en mis raíces culturales donde he econtrado grandes valores.' (They nicknamed me 'Indian' to ostracize me, but thanks to the nickname I never forgot for one moment that I am an Indian, and it's in my roots that I have found my greatest values) (Fernández, 1986: 38).
3 Furthermore, in the title of Taibo's biography, the words '*por mis pistolas*' are paralleled by the Mexican saying supposed to emphasize bravery and cheek '*por mis huevos*' (with my balls).
4 However, with Fernández, his life story is not just the key to understanding his films, but recounted more as if it were another of his films, a continuation of the creative spirit that infused his oeuvre. Monsiváis calls it the *materia prima* of a film script (1992: 29) while Taibo refers to it as his 'película personal' ('his own personal film') (1986: 47).
5 Some indication of how these local critics do not question these greater narratives of Mexican identity is that non-local accounts of his life, which inevitably use these local accounts as sources, reproduce these narratives and do not even question the unlikely fact that he killed a man and fought in the revolution although only aged 9 (López, 2000b: 560.)
6 It is significant that Adela Fernández has also written several interesting anthropological collections on pre-Hispanic cultures in Mexico: *Diccionario de voces nahuas* (1985), *Así vivieron las Mayas* (1983), *Dioses prehispánicos de México: mitos y deidades del panteón náhuatl* (1983), and *Mayas: vida, cultura y arte a través de un personaje de su tiempo* (1983).

3

Calendar María: hybridity, *indigenismo* and the discourse of whitening

As Octavio Paz avows, the Mexican subject is a hybrid subject, radically divided by the encounter with Spain. This hybridity is viewed as both positive and negative. On the one hand, in the discourse of *mestizaje*, hybridity figures as a fruitful coming-together of two separate cultures, the Spanish culture and the indigenous culture. On the other hand, in the complex of *malinchismo* (from La Malinche, a derogatory name for Conquistador Cortés' captive mistress Doña María who supposedly betrayed her people to the foreigner), hybridity is vilified as the threat of the other polluting an essential *mexicanidad*.[1] Hence, in Mexican movies of the 1940s, Tin Tan (Germán Valdés), the *pachuco*, the urban wise guy from the North (the border between Mexico and the United States), is perceived as corrupting the Mexican language with his Spanglish, his 'guachadors' (watchmen) and his North American ways.[2]

This chapter examines how the concept of hybridity mediates the post-Revolutionary discourse of *indigenismo* (indigenism) in its cinematic form. It looks specifically at how *malinchismo*, which is also figured as a 'positive, valorisation of whiteness,' threatens the 'purity' of an essential Mexican (Lomitz Adler, 1992: 276) in *María Candelaria* (1943), Fernández' most famous indigenist film.

Indigenismo argues that the roots of modern Mexican identity lie in the cultural legacy of its pre-Colombian Indian cultures. In the immediate post-Revolutionary period (1920–40), *indigenismo* provided Mexico with a 'myth of origins' which conveniently elided its colonial past and provided a notion of national identity and a racial ideology that broke free from the European-dependent culture of the *Porfiriato* (1876–1910) (Monsiváis, 1976: 307). However, it has been widely noted that *indigenismo* was only ever the 'fantasy of origin and identity' of the ruling classes, and that the political and cultural discourse of *indigenismo* only paid lip-service to an imaginary pre-Colombian Mexican past, while ignoring the more contemporary representative of that history, the underclass of unassimilated Indians separated from the rest of the nation by skin color, geography, language and low social status (Berg, 1992: 137). The *indígena* has received scant attention in Mexican cinema, and what little treatment there has been often reflects the fantasy of otherness, painting the *indígena* as an exceptional other while suppressing the reasons for his social marginalization, backwardness and exploitation (ibid.: 138; Huaco-Nuzum, 1992: 128; Ayala Blanco, 1993: 145).

Fernández has often been portrayed as both the filmic savior and representational jailer of Mexico's Indian underclass. His indigenist films *María Candelaria*, *Maclovia* (1948), and *La perla* (1945) and their several precursors *Janitzio* (Carlos Novaro, 1934) and *Redes* (Paul Strand, 1934) are alternately praised for representing indigenous people in a 'positive' light (Berg, 1992: 137) or criticized for creating stereotypes that imprison the *indígena* within archetypes, preventing further development in their representation (Ayala Blanco, 1993: 212; García Riera 1993c: 69).

Similarly, most Mexican and US studies of the portrayal of the *indígena* in Fernández' work alternate between these positive and negative evaluations. On the one hand, Hershfield criticizes Fernández and Mexican cinema in general for reproducing the stereotypes of the indigenist muralist Rivera which portray Indians as 'pure and simple, like children who had to be led to social (and revolutionary) consciousness by the intellectual *mestizo* elite' (Hershfield, 1999: 86). Likewise, Tuñón accuses Fernández of erasing differences and creating homogeneous (read stereotypical) *indígenas* (1995: 187).[3] On the other hand, Mora says that *María Candelaria*'s positive presentation of *indígenas* retains a 'simplicity and lyrical beauty that can . . . be appreciated over [fifty]-five years later' (1989: 65).

As these analyses suggest, a difficulty in analyzing the representation of racial difference is that arguments are based on 'positive' or 'negative' representation. When critics write of a 'positive' representation of difference, they mean it in terms of realism: that a positive representation is authentic, and a negative representation is inauthentic. For example, Carmen Huaco-Nuzum reads 'white' actress Del Rio's[4] interpretation of an *indígena* in *María Candelaria* as a masquerade (1992: 129). Similarly, De los Reyes adds that, rather than represent an 'authentic' indigenous female, her portrayal invented a 'mask' (1988: 196–197). In addition to embodying a biological understanding of race that presupposes it as a static category, the authentic-versus-inauthentic approach to *indigenismo* presents certain critical problems to understanding the representation of difference in classical Mexican cinema. Rather than sustaining *indigenismo* as a monological conception of national identity, which can be authentically represented, it is critically important to recognize cultural hybridity and cultural heterogeneity in the analysis of how difference is represented (Chanady, 1994). Thus, rather than focusing on positive or negative stereotypes, following Bhabha's suggestions the point of intervention should shift from 'a ready recognition of images as positive or negative, to an understanding of the process of subjectification made possible through stereotypical discourse' (Bhabha, 1994: 67). In the case of the cinema, and specifically Fernández' indigenist films, to understand the processes of subjectification it is imperative to take into consideration 'the specific cinematic dimensions of the film' (Spence and Stam 1999: 236).

This chapter looks at the contradictions of indigenism in Fernández' often cited as exemplary *María Candelaria*, suggesting that rather than presenting a pure, originary notion of the *indígena* as traditional scholarship asserts, the film's representation of the *indígena* embodies a hybrid incoherent identity. The chapter also argues that the representation of *indigenismo* in *María Candelaria* is predicated on a pre-Revolutionary racial ideology that comes not just from a residual European influence but also from Fernández' borrowings from Hollywood. This chapter also looks at the contradictions of indigenism in Fernández' two other Golden Age indigenist films *Maclovia* and *La perla* (The Pearl). At the same time, mindful of the pitfalls of auteurism, analysis of *Maclovia* and *La perla* seeks to eschew the logic of necessary coherency between these films and *María Candelaria*.

Indigenismo: its history in representation

Indigenismo a late nineteenth-/early twentieth-century Latin American movement, advocated assimilating the indigenous populations within nation states (Dawson, 1998: 279). *Indigenismo* or 'the discourse of the autochthonous' was pan-Latin American in scope and is often considered the foundation of an emergent anti-imperialist, Latin

Americanism (J. Ramos, 2001: 250). In Mexico, after the revolution, indigenism was institutionalized as a program of reconstruction – offering a way of improving Mexico's self-image by positively reassessing its other (O'Malley, 1986: 119).

One of the central texts of the discourse of the autochthonous, José Vasconcelos' *La raza cósmica* (The Cosmic Race, 1925), offers a utopian vision of a fifth or cosmic race which would be an ideal mix of the all the best qualities of the existent 'four' races. The problem with *La raza cósmica* is that the condition of racial utopia that it envisions is not racial harmony between races but the effective annihilation of those features considered 'degenerate' in 'darker' races through mixing with 'lighter' races. For example, in the following excerpt the sentence construction leads us to read 'lower examples' as black and 'superior examples' as potentially 'white': 'Los tipos bajos de la especie serán absorbidos por el tipo superior. De esta suerte podría redimirse, por ejemplo, el negro, y poco a poco, por extinción voluntaría, las estirpes más feas irán cediendo el paso a las más hermosas.' (The lower examples of the species will be absorbed by the superior examples. In this way the Negro could be redeemed and, gradually through voluntary extinction, the uglier pedigrees will give way to the fairer pedigrees.) (1999: 43). Therefore, although the aspiration is not explicitly toward being 'white,' *La raza cósmica* predicts that 'el negro' (which the sentence construction leads us to read as 'one of the "uglier pedigrees"') will disappear or be redeemed (which itself implies moral connotations equating blackness with sin) or be whitened-out through racial mixing. Elsewhere Vasconcelos states that, although the cosmic race will not be 'precisamente blanco' (precisely white), it will be closer to the more industrious people 'of the Northern Hemisphere' (which again connotes 'whiteness') than to the other races (1999: 36, 43). Hence, despite Vasconcelos' 'fierce anti-Positivism,' his fifth or cosmic race is nevertheless figured in terms as equally racist as is Positivism.

1920s *Indigenismo* in murals
Despite his somewhat suspect vision of racial harmony, Vasconcelos plays an important part in making *indigenismo* a powerful reforming voice in the development of a nationalist culture in Mexico.[5] *Indigenismo* envisioned a specifically Mexican style that would reflect Mexican themes, popular art and the autonomy of the nation. Conceived as the promotion of a popular 'native style' over an elitist

'European style' in all artistic mediums, it represented a foundational aesthetic that would express the autonomy of the 'new' Mexican nation. Rivera's and Orozco's murals commissioned by Vasconcelos – then Minister at the Department of Education (Secretaría de Educación Pública or SEP) in General Álvaro Obregón's revolutionary government (1920–24) – largely defined that aesthetic. These murals covered the walls of the SEP, and eventually (being not finished until the 1940s) the National Palace as well as other public buildings – (literally) magnifying and elevating the indigenous element within Mexico's history. These public art works provided a suitable means of nationalist cultural expression responding to both *indigenista* and Revolutionary objectives to create and define a sense of '*mexicanidad*' around which a nation could unite.

To a certain extent, indigenist cultural production in the 1920s was far in advance of Government policy. The massive institutional reorganization of education, which began in 1921 under Vasconcelos, followed policies which considered indigenous assimilation to mean solely the imposition of Spanish culture on the indigenous population. Like the sentiments expressed in *La raza cósmica*, the 'socialist education' policies which the SEP teachers followed were more concerned with hispanizing (or, within Vasconcelos' cosmic logic the 'whitening out' of) the indigenous peoples rather than making any accommodation for indigenous languages or customs (Miller, 1998: 48).

1930s *Indigenismo* in cinema: the beginnings of a Mexican school

Like the muralists who strove to reflect notions of a 'pure' and essential Mexican national identity – but were, in the case of Rivera at least, actually channelling and adapting two decades of training in European painting styles – (Wolfe, 2000: 115, 120) the origins of a Mexican cinema school, and the idea of a 'truly' national style, ironically reflect the processes of cultural hybridization and transculturation proper to the diffusion of cinema worldwide. In 1930 Sergei Eisenstein, the Soviet filmmaker acclaimed for *Strike* (1925) and *Battleship Potemkin* (1925), came to Mexico with his cameraman Edouard Tissé and filmed a number of scenes of the country in what was to be a documentary/narrative film. His desire to film the *indígena* coincided with the cultural *indigenismo* of the muralists who acted as his guides to Mexico. Eisenstein was never able to complete his film, but an apocryphal version was edited and released some years later as *¡Que* *viva México!* (Long live Mexico, 1932). In *¡Que viva México!* Eisenstein successfully realized the dual ideals of *indigenismo*, the respectful depiction of *indígena*s and their everyday lives and surroundings in a style that incorporated elements of popular Mexican art. His static shots of José Guadalupe Posada's engravings, maguey plants and vast Mexican skies were influential in developing cinematic indigenism, bridging the gap between the plastic arts and cinema.

However, scholars have questioned *indigenismo*'s cinematic beginnings, arguing that rather than reflecting an anti-Imperialist desire for cultural autonomy, Eisenstein's work inscribes Mexico within European primitivism (Podalsky, 1993b: 26). For example, in the opening section of the film we are presented with half naked virgins, spied on by monkeys and smiling coyly at the camera. This seems more like a primitivist 'cinema of attractions' for a European audience than a revolutionary dignifying of Mexico's indigenous population. Following this it could be argued that, to a certain extent, Eisenstein's influence on cinematic cultural nationalism was contradictory, in that it placed later Mexican filmmakers who copied his style, specifically Fernández, in the position of the colonial voyeur (Podalsky, 1993b: 31).

Two films made in 1934 draw from Eisenstein's legacy and reflect Government indigenist policy (which despite the rhetoric of the 1920s was only beginning to address the 'problem' of Mexico's indigenous population with the election of Cárdenas to the presidency in 1934): *Redes* (Nets) and *Janitzio*. *Redes*, which was funded by the SEP, tells the story of a group of fisherman who revolt against their exploitative *patrón* (boss). The social content of the film – its defense of the fisherman's worker's rights and its dignifying of rural life – is evidence of its strong nationalist impulse and its affinity with the policies of the Cárdenas' presidency in which it was completed. However, De los Reyes explains how this film is also evident of cultural hybridism, first in terms of its 'foreign' influence (Eisenstein) and secondly in terms of the multiple nationalities of the personnel who played a part in its production: it was directed by an American photographer (Strand), a Viennese director (Fred Zinneman) and a Mexican editor (Emilio Gómez Muriel).

Janitzio, the second film in this developing history of cinematic indigenism, is also perceived as being constructed 'under the shadow' of Eisenstein (De los Reyes, 1988: 189). *Janitzio* does display, however, nationalist sensibilities, in the way it filters the concerns of the *vasconcelista* aesthetic of '*redención del indígena*' (indigenous redemption) through an Eisensteinian lens (ibid.). As we have seen in analysis of the film in chapter two, *Janitzio* takes up an obviously *indigenista* position through its explicit denouncing of the abuses of the 'white man' against the indigenous people. However, De los Reyes argues that this is really just a pretext to capture the folkloric qualities of the Tarascos, the indigenous group whose village is the focus of the film (ibid.). Indeed, the way the diegesis embeds the activities of the Tarascos does suggest that this is a folkloric (interested in exploiting the picturesque quality of the Tarascos) rather than an indigenist film (concerned with a socially meaningful depiction). There are several sequences where plot development or behavior is explained for a diegetic white audience (who stand in for a nondiegetic white audience) in the manner of an anthropological study. For example, near the beginning of the film, we are offered vistas of fishing and daily life in semi-documentary mode. Several 'white' people arrive on the island and, when there is a commotion, it is Don Pablo the 'white' shop-owner on the island who explains to Manuel the new arrival (who stands in for the nondiegetic white audience because he too does not understand these seemingly impenetrable ways) that the right to fish in this lake was given to the people of Janitzio by the Tarasco emperors long before Mexico was conquered by the Spanish. Hence, although folkloric in certain aspects, the film does succeed in following the indigenist practice of making the explicit link between contemporary Mexico and its pre-Colombian past.

However, although *Janitzio* is meant to reflect contemporary cardenist attitudes toward the defense of the indigenous people, it is set in the pre-revolutionary period (1909). The purpose of such a displacement would seem to be to suggest that the racist attitudes toward the *indígena* depicted in the film belong to the pre-revolutionary moment and have been successfully eradicated by the revolution. This move avoids any challenge to the achievements of post-Revolutionary governments in terms of reform or of suggesting that their policies of *indigenismo* have failed. However, the result of such a displacement is to distance the subject matter from contemporary Mexico and suggest that it bears no relevance to actual events. This is in direct contradistinction to the modernizing intentions of *indigenismo* – i.e., to incorporate indigenous populations within the Mexican nation. This chapter looks at how this aspect contradicts the explicit role of *indigenismo* in cultural nationalism in Fernández' remakes of this story, *María Candelaria* and *Maclovia*.

Janitzio and films that follow it, such as *La noche de los Mayas* (The Night of the Mayas, Urueta, 1939), seem to show a desire for an approximation and an understanding of the *indígena* and their cultures. However, rather than reflecting an indigenist sensibility, *La noche de los Mayas* suggests that this desire for approximation is not based on incorporation but is instead a partially anthropological, partially colonial endeavor. Notably the story concerns a group of 'explorers' who come across a Mayan tribe and stay to study their 'ways.' The explorers' safari jackets and white hats construct a colonial iconography reminiscent of early 1930s 'colonialist' Hollywood films like *Trader Horn* (W.S. Van Dyke 1931), where the explorer/scientist figure is a key trope (Dyer, 1997: 37). The film's colonial iconography outweighs its attempt to represent Mayan culture in an indigenist light.

1940s: Emilio Fernández' representation of racial difference in *María Candelaria*

It is Fernández who is credited with transcending the 1930s Eisensteinian and anthropological portrayals of the *indígena* to provide the kind of representation that would make possible the imaginative incorporation of the *indígena* within the nation state. As an important element of cultural nationalism, *indigenista* discourses sought to recapture an Edenic notion of the many different Indian communities and to integrate them within the boundaries of the modern nation state (Noble, 2001: 86). Indeed, such was the success of Fernández' Edenic portrayal of the *indígena* that he is often considered solely as an indigenist director, when in reality films with an indigenist theme constitute only a small part of his oeuvre. Of these films, *María Candelaria* (1943) is continually cited as the film which best exemplifies both Fernández' depiction of the *indígena* and the project of cultural nationalism. This part of the chapter further explores the reasons why Fernández' portrayal of the *indígena* in *María Candelaria* came to embody the ideals of cultural nationalism and its sense of '*lo mexicano.*'

María Candelaria opens with a series of shots which frame in close-up ornamental heads of different pre-Colombian deities and nobility, dissolving from one shot to another and then eventually dissolving to the head of a real person with indigenous features. The shot then widens out to show the indigenous woman is posing as an artist's model and the ornamental heads are in fact masks on the wall behind her in his studio. The painter (Alberto Galán) is receiving reporters, one

Hybridity, *indigenismo* and whitening 81

of whom presses him to tell the story of a painting he has never wished to sell. Reluctantly the painter shows the persistent reporter the painting, saying the subject is 'of pure Mexican [sic] race... descendent of ancient Aztec princesses.' The film flashes back to Xochimilco, 1909, to the story of María Candelaria (Del Rio) and how the painter came to paint her.

The people of the village shun María Candelaria because her mother was a prostitute, but Lorenzo Rafael (Pedro Armendáriz) loves her. The two plan to marry just as soon as their little pig grows up and has a litter. However, their plans are jeopardized because of an outstanding debt to Don Damián (Miguel Inclán), the *mestizo* shopkeeper who wants cash for the pig and will not accept payment in vegetables or flowers. Lorenzo Rafael and María Candelaria therefore have to go to a market to sell their produce. At the market the painter spots María Candelaria and, seeing in her the model he has been searching for, asks Lorenzo Rafael if he can paint her. Suspicious of the white man's intervention, Lorenzo Rafael refuses and hurries María Candelaria home. Don Damián, embittered by María Candelaria's previous rejection of his advances, refuses Lorenzo Rafael government-supplied quinine and then kills their little pig, thwarting their marriage plans. When María Candelaria falls sick with malaria Lorenzo Rafael breaks into Don Damián's shop and steals quinine for her and a dress so that they can be married. She is cured by a visit from *la huesera* (the village healer) and a doctor sent by the painter. Two policemen and Don Damián wrongly accusing Lorenzo Rafael of having also stolen money from the shop interrupt their wedding. Lorenzo Rafael is put in jail. The painter intervenes to have Lorenzo Rafael released, but this cannot happen immediately as the judge is away. In the meantime María Candelaria poses for the painter, but refuses to disrobe so that he can complete his painting. Another model stands in. When the villagers see the painting of María Candelaria's face on a naked body they are enraged at such an insult to the integrity of their village and gather in an angry mob to kill her. They chase her and she flees to the prison. Lorenzo Rafael breaks out and runs to her side. But he is too late. They have already stoned her to death.

María Candelaria's narrative of Indian pride and dignity explicitly fits within the paradigms of *indigenismo* and indeed this is historically how the text has been interpreted. The opening shots of *María Candelaria* are read as further embodying the indigenist project by establishing continuity between the great Indians of pre-Colombian cultures and the nobility of contemporary indigenous people. The dissolves and graphic matches which suggest equality between these figures from the past and this figure from the present and a connection to the artistic tradition of the muralists Rivera, Orozco and Siqueiros. (The artist's model who appears in the film is played by Nieves, who often posed for Rivera.) However, on further examination, the text reveals itself to be a mass of contradictions and fissures in its depiction of Revolutionary racial ideology.

María Candelaria is set in Xochimilco close to the capital city (now part of the Federal District). Showing an indigenous community as close to, rather than remote to the nation's center (as opposed to locating it in Lake Pátzcuaro, Michoacán as in *Janitzio*) suggests *indígena* assimilation. However, by situating the film in the pre-revolutionary era, it remains remote to 1940s Mexico – hence problematizing the narrative's relationship to contemporary society. Furthermore, the specific location of Xochimilco is highlighted as a non-modern, peripheral space by the film's English subtitle 'A love story of Mexico's Floating Gardens.' Like the floating gardens on which it rests, Xochimilco is a 'backwater.'

A further contradiction stems from the film's anachronistic use of indigenous masks and the painter's self-characterization as an indigenist artist in the (1909) frame story, because *indigenismo* owes its existence (officially at least) to post Revolutionary (1920s onward) nationalism. The opening montage may refer to the Mexican indigenist tradition but it also references the Eisensteinian depiction of Mexico in *¡Que viva México!* in which ornamental heads/temples are juxtaposed with indigenous people within the same frame. This suggests that, rather than finding a truly autonomous and indigenous style as the project of *indigenismo* dictates, Fernández complicates this project not just by reproducing the Eisensteinian aesthetic but also by placing himself in the same position as Eisenstein – that of a colonial voyeur (Podalsky, 1993b: 27). He is partly redeemed by the film's awareness of how damaging the European tradition of representation is to the *indígena*. María Candelaria is stoned to death because the painter paints her as a nude, a form associated with the Western tradition (ibid.: 68). However, ironically, Fernández-influenced-by-Eisenstein and also Fernández-influenced-by-Hollywood is mirrored in the figure of the painter-influenced-by-a-European-style who causes the demise of the very subject he seeks to save. The following section explores the implications of this irony and asks whether Fernández' (mis)representation of the *indígena* is just as pernicious in ideological terms as that of the painter.

Although made in 1943 *María Candelaria* is considered to be more representative of the indigenist policies of the presidency of Cárdenas. The policies of his term (*cardenismo*), focused among other things (land reform, protectionism) on advocating assimilation of the indigenous population so that all could share equally in the life of the nation (Tuñón, 1995: 183; Miller, 1998: 19). However, the film's narrative explicitly contradicts this policy. Contact between *indígenas* and *criollos* in the film (María Candelaria and the painter), although well intentioned, brings about the death of the indigenous person. The narrative seems to suggest that rather than the incorporation of the *indígena* within the modernizing state, isolation is the only means to protect indigenous people. This interpretation challenges the dominant readings of the film such as that of French ethno-historian Serge Gruzinski, who reads it as a 'symbol of modern Mexico' because the contradictions of the story suggest that the film is really a parable against modernization/assimilation (2001: 266). Indeed, the film is clear on where the indigenous people stand in relation to the past, and questions their ability to live in the modern, increasingly urban Mexico. The central couple's moral exemplarity is based on a link to the past and a rural existence. First, María Candelaria and Lorenzo Rafael's moral purity is connected with the nobility of their ancestors through the initial montage sequence. Secondly, sequences where they touch and talk about the earth show that they are fiercely tied to it. Hence, by focusing on the past, the narrative elides the contradictions of the indigenist project, praising a dead *indígena* (María Candelaria as martyr) rather than dealing with the actual problems of the contemporary (live) *indígena* population (Dever, 1994: 40).

Furthermore, as Martín Barbero points out, the discourse of indigenism, situating national identity in a rapidly disappearing rural world as represented by 'lo *indígena*,' is contradicted by 1940s Mexico where, like the rest of Latin America, the populace's material conditions of living are increasingly shaped by the forces of modernization and urbanization (1998: 205).

This gulf between indigenist policies and Mexico's increasingly urbanized population is expressed though the negative representation of the other *indígenas*. They stone María Candelaria as punishment for her modernity (alleged liberated exhibition of her body and fraternization with the white man (*criollo*)). The film equates the following of indigenous traditions – killing María Candelaria for dishonoring the village – with backwardness (resistance to modernity), insularity and barbarism. Hence, the film presents a schizophrenic representation of the *indígena*: as both modern Mexico's central couple (María Candelaria and Lorenzo Rafael) and as the obstacle to its progress.

Representation of difference
Beyond the level of narrative, further contradictions in *María Candelaria*'s indigenist representation are evident at the level of mise-en-scène, particularly in terms of costume, makeup and performance. Because neither of the stars, Del Rio and Armendáriz, has indigenous features as has been widely noted, ethnicity has to be 'drawn on' through a number of specific cinematic techniques[6] (Huaco-Nuzum, 1992: 129). Unlike her glamorous Hollywood appearances in which she wears heavy makeup, Del Rio wears a 'barely there'/natural look. This minimal makeup was interpreted by some as the absence of makeup altogether. Sadoul, after watching *María Candelaria* in 1946 at the Cannes Film Festival, wrote: 'Without artifice, her *pure face* framed by long braids, and dressed with the *simple clothes* of a Mexican peasant . . . Del Rio appeared completely new and speaking her *native tongue*. Like her face, her acting lacked artifice. We did not face an actress, but rather, a woman' (López, 1998: 21, my emphasis). With the absence of artifice it was as if the 'real' Del Rio as opposed to the glamorous Hollywood starlet was appearing in the film; and hence, following this reasoning, *María Candelaria* showed the 'real' Mexico. However, rather than lack artifice, Del Rio's María Candelaria was a perfect illusion. The 'simple clothes' were actually designer-made (De los Reyes, 1996: 197–198). Rather than 'pure,' her face is made up with mascara, false eyelashes and rouge – creating a look no less stylized than her 1930s 'art deco look' (Monsiváis, 1997: 71). Far from speaking her 'native tongue' (like Armendáriz), she speaks a kind of pidgin Spanish which is neither the anti-bourgeois linguistic play of Cantinflas, a familiar character from 1940s Mexican comedies, nor indeed a respectful depiction of the way indigenous people speak (ibid.: 90).[7] When indigenous characters do speak an indigenous language it is only at moments of great anger – when Lorenzo Rafael's ex-girlfriend Lupe is pushed into the river by María Candelaria, she utters several expletives in Náhuatl – thus reducing it to incomprehensible

outbursts of primitive savagery. This creates not a sensitive depiction of the indigenous people's marginal relationship toward mainstream, 'white' society and modernity but, instead, characters whose speech further suggests backwardness.

Evident in Del Rio and Armendáriz' acting out of indigenous ethnicity is the influence of Hollywood otherness. Their performance consists of a number of stock 'Mexican peasant' traits as seen in the western: heavy-accented misuse of English/Spanish, stooping, cowering and exaggerated submissiveness around 'white' or *mestizo* characters (Woll, 1980: 88, 76). Indeed, it is this increased level of performativity that James Naremore suggests acts as an indication of 'otherness': 'As a general rule, Hollywood has required that supporting players, ethnic minorities, and women be more animated or broadly expressive' (1988: 43). One reason why ethnic minorities should be more animated is that as the dominant exists in a position of power it has no need to define itself as anything other than the norm against which everything else must be defined – hence actors playing the priest and the painter underplay and Armendáriz and Del Rio playing *indígena* overplay. What is ironic from this analysis is that it seems as if the pioneer of Mexican national cinema was reproducing the kinds of pejorative images of Mexicans (i.e., from Hollywood) that the national cinema was created to specifically challenge and destroy (Woll, 1980: 76; Paranaguá, 1995: 8).[8]

However, although in terms of performance Del Rio and Armendáriz are positioned as other to the dominant, the text is not totally coherent on this aspect of their representation. Other elements of their visual representation serve to align them with the dominant. This is effected through the lighting scheme within the film, particularly in terms of its representation of skin color. Lighting along with other aspects of mise-en-scène draws distinctions between Del Rio and Armendáriz and the community to which they belong in order to temper their status as others. What does such a tempering of otherness suggest at the level of post-Revolutionary racial ideology?

Mexican racial ideology and the value of 'whitening' in *María Candelaria*

From the colonial era onward, the underlying narrative of Mexican racial ideology has always been an aspiration toward, and an explicit valorization of, 'whitening.' Berg suggests that this valorization of white as a 'phenotypical ideal' emerges from the colonial era's complicated caste system which placed 'the European at the pinnacle and the Indian at the bottom' (Berg, 1992: 137). In the colonial system, as Claudio Lomitz Adler points out, 'Indian blood was entirely "redeemable"' [i.e., could become 'white'] through marriage (1992: 273). Despite Liberalism's egalitarian rhetoric after independence in the nineteenth century, the racial aspiration continued to be toward 'whiteness' now also attainable through the acquisition of wealth and status. (Lomitz Adler, 1992: 276). This valorization of whiteness as the nation's goal survived despite the Revolution's reappraisal of the *mestizo* (mix of Spanish and Indian) as 'the official protagonist of Mexican history' (Lomitz Adler, 1992: 277). It continues today as governments aspire to 'reaching the level of development of the United States or of Europe,' an idea often referred to as 'bettering one's race (*mejorar la raza*)' through 'whitening oneself (*blanquearse*)' (Lomitz Adler, 1992: 278).

Although not the majority in Mexico, where *mestizos* in fact do constitute the majority, white – as the political and economically dominant group – envisions itself as the 'universal' or the 'essential' as the 'nation's phenotypical ideal' (Berg, 1992, 137). Rather than depicting the *indígena* as a noble individual, *María Candelaria* textually universalizes Mexico's aspiration toward whitening.

As Richard Dyer argues, ethnicity is not actually skin deep. 'White' and 'black' people are not literally or symbolically 'white' or 'black.' However, ideas of ethnicity are figured through fallacious notions of skin color in which 'white' is the dominant and all 'non-whites' the marginalized others (1997: 42). Dyer argues that 'white' claims a position of neutrality and from this position posits itself as nothing and yet everything. He suggests that the strength of white representation is 'the sense that being white is co-terminous with the endless plenitude of human diversity' (1988: 46). In terms of Hollywood cinema, this power that white has manifests itself in the ability of whiteness to stand in for everything, to be universal. Hence a white actor can be 'raced' by the mise-en-scène to represent a 'non-white' character (for example Henry Brandon as Apache Scar in *The Searchers* (John Ford, 1956)), but a non-white actor can never play a role that is not racially marked – i.e., cannot be universal. With cinematic *indigenismo* we see the power of universality at work when 'white' actors Del Rio and Armendáriz play indigenous characters much in the same way that Debra Paget plays Sonserray, a Native American, in the otherwise progressive for its time *Broken Arrow* (Delmer Daves, 1950).[9]

The development of the photographic media and the cinema in particular has been influenced by this hierarchical organization of skin color. In keeping with the Western tradition of representation initiated by the Enlightenment and the process of Western imperialism, out of which it flourished, the cinematic apparatus as a photographic medium has developed to favor lighter skin. Dyer argues that 'photography and cinema, as media of light, at the very least lend themselves to privileging white people' (1997: 83). Lighting in *María Candelaria* takes on a function beyond just illumination. It is the key expressive element in the film and the one that most undermines the film's explicit racial ideology of indigenism.

Del Rio's and Armendáriz' biographies – and in the case of Del Rio her Hollywood career that preceded *María Candelaria* – can be understood to play a part in (and also contradict) their role in the project of Mexican cultural nationalism and specifically their representation as *indígenas*, the ideal Mexicans.

Del Rio (1905–83) was born Dolores Asúnsolo López Negrete into an aristocratic Mexican family. She married the equally aristocratic Jaime Martínez del Río shortly after her sixteenth birthday. Edwin Carewe, who talent-spotted her in Mexico, brought her and her husband to Hollywood in 1925. There she had a highly successful career playing first a series of sensual non-Americans in the silent period: a French girl (*What Price Glory*, 1926), several Russians (*Resurrection*, 1927, and *The Red Dance*, 1928), Spanish dancers (*The Loves of Carmen*, 1927) and 'half-breeds' (North American in *Ramona*, 1928). Then, as sound limited her to roles which could incorporate her heavily accented English she was constrained to 'Latin' parts as either a Mexican (*The Girl of the Rio*, 1932), a Brazilian (*Flying Down to Rio*, 1933) or other Latin others. As Hollywood's ethnographic imperatives shifted in the 1930s, influenced by the Good Neighbor policy which equated Latin America and its stars with music, Del Rio, as a non-musical star, found her career in severe decline. This and a failed romance with Orson Welles was part of her reason for returning to Mexico to become a part of its national film industry (López, 1998: 7–21).

Armendáriz (1912–63) was born in Mexico to an American mother and a Mexican father, but raised and educated in the United States. Completely bilingual in English and Spanish, he was not constrained by an accent when he spoke English, a fact which arguably allowed him to travel and be more successful at doing so than other Mexican stars with international appeal. In difference to that of Del Rio, his

Hollywood career took off notably *after* his success as an *indígena* with Fernández, potentially because he appealed to John Ford, who admired Fernández' work. In the US the majority of his 1940s and 1950s films were westerns such as *Three Godfathers* (John Ford, 1948) and *Fort Apache* (Ford, 1948) or quasi-westerns such as *The Fugitive* (Ford, 1947), in which he played mostly Mexican or Mexican American characters. In the 1950s and early 1960s he continued to travel, this time to Europe where among other roles he played an anglophile Turkish Agent Karim Bey (*From Russia With Love*, Terence Young, 1963).

While their Mexican and Hollywood star-texts emphasize them as 'white,' either in terms of Spanish ancestry (Creole) as with Del Rio (López, 1998: 13) or in terms of both North American and Creole parentage as with Armendáriz (Nason, 1984), in Hollywood they are almost always racially marked as non-white in terms of the roles they are able to play – a collection of different others. (Presound Del Rio did get to play Northern European parts in several films.) While in Mexico they function as white actors in a predominantly white cinema, in their postsound Hollywood careers Armendáriz and Del Rio were never allowed to be universally representative – i.e., play 'white' characters.

'Whiteness' in Mexican terms (being *criollo*) is carried through to Del Rio's portrayal of the *indígena* through a number of key concepts. It has been argued that the success of Del Rio's portrayal of an *indígena* is due in part to a certain 'cosmopolitanism' that she brings to the role. Although the role of María Candelaria calls for an onscreen image of a 'meek, ignorant barefoot Indian girl,' De los Reyes argues that the seemingly contradictory designer dress and star text effect a glamorization that is necessary to the overall project of the film. He goes on to argue that, although such glamorization is seemingly incompatible with indigenism, it and Del Rio's star performance are not totally incompatible with the nationalist project at the time. Both glamor and her star performance served the 'cosmopolitanism' of Mexican nationalism, which he defines as wishing to be as appealing to as many as possible, rather than only to the local (De los Reyes, 1988, 198–199).[10] This sense of 'cosmopolitanism' might potentially be increased for a Mexican audience by the fact that Del Rio had just returned from Hollywood when she played this role. But how can we read this sense of glamor/'cosmopolitanism' around Del Rio in *María Candelaria* in terms of racial imagery? If cosmopolitan means to have worldwide scope, it seems that we could also take cosmopolitanism as

Hybridity, *indigenismo* and whitening

being synonymous with universalism – i.e., with the ideology of 'whiteness' representing itself as the universal, everything and nothing at the same time.

The moral distinction drawn between the central couple (as exemplary) and the other *indígenas* (as barbaric) is echoed in the camerawork and lighting design. Del Rio and Armendáriz are constantly aestheticized with lingering close-ups and luminous lighting. When María Candelaria is sick there is substantial fill lighting making her forehead, temples and cheekbones more prominent (Figure 3.1). While the greater key lighting on them as stars is part of a classical lighting scheme that privileges important players, leaving unimportant players in shadow (Bordwell and Thompson, 2001: 167) it also has the effect of drawing a distinction in skin color between the principals and their supposed community. Lighting Del Rio and Armendáriz as luminous not only emphasizes their perceived ethnicity as actors but also (with backlighting that gives a halo effect) highlights the features associated with whiteness – i.e., moral superiority. Making them look visually lighter than the rest of the community is further

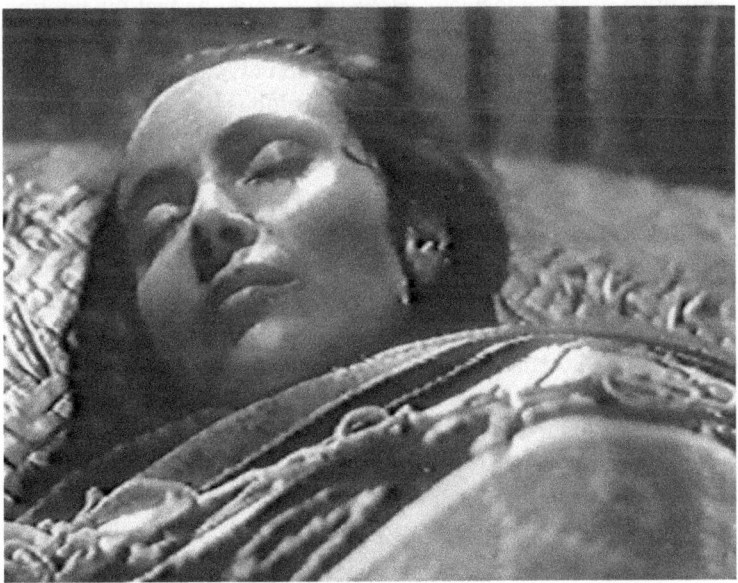

3.1 *María Candelaria*: María Candelaria is sick

morally inflected by variations in the lighting quality at key narrative points: for example, when indigenous characters behave badly their association with darkness is emphasized as they are lit to appear darker and, when Lupe rings the bell to call the town together to chase María Candelaria, her face is presented mostly in shadow cast by the bell. Then, when the other *indígenas* are chasing María Candelaria in order to stone her to death, their faces are mostly in shadow. Here, Western notions of white's moral superiority are mobilized (Dyer, 1997: 70). The central couple's moral exemplarity is expressed through lightness and the rest of the *indígenas*' immorality is figured through the absence of light. This lighting scheme undercuts *indigenismo*'s valorizing of the *indígena*, as it implies that not all *indígenas* are morally exemplary. However, it conforms with classical Mexican cinema's use of skin color as a mark 'of morality and social standing' where 'light skin confers righteousness and high social station; dark skin signifies a lower-class villain' (Berg, 1992: 27).

The schism between María Candelaria and Lorenzo Rafael and the rest of the *indígena* in terms of lighting and morality is incompatible with the nationalist project of assimilation and official post-Revolutionary racial ideology. However, it could be that the lighting design is not a textual contradiction, but that it merely highlights the binaries that regulate the representation of María Candelaria and Lorenzo Rafael as 'white' versus indigenous (darkness), and as modernity versus backwardness. Not only is the central couple not depicted like the other *indígenas* in terms of racially defined characteristics and qualities, but the text aligns them with a different group altogether – the white *criollos*. 'White' characters – doctors, the priest and the painter – are represented as the future. The film aligns María Candelaria and Lorenzo Rafael with these 'good' and 'reasonable' white characters. When María Candelaria is sick the painter gets a doctor. When Lorenzo Rafael is imprisoned he intervenes to get him released. That María Candelaria and Lorenzo Rafael are aligned with the *criollos* is often underscored by their positioning within the frame. At the blessing of the animals the shot places María Candelaria and Lorenzo Rafael on the side of the priest as he defends them from the other *indígenas*. Therefore, we could argue that it is not their *indígena* souls that are mythified through this expressionist lighting as has been suggested previously, but rather the (perceived/spiritual) whiteness of the actor and character.

Hybridity, *indigenismo* and whitening   91

A similar treatment of visible 'whiteness' in the face of otherness can be found in Orson Welles' *Touch of Evil* (1958), where Charlton Heston plays Miguel Vargas, a Mexican Police Chief. Heston is visually Mexicanized: he has curly hair, a moustache and darker skin. The narrative (Detective Quinlan in particular) reconciles this by constantly commenting on how he does not look Mexican. As the hero of the film, it is important that his whiteness is maintained, at least in terms of his star text: Heston is Moses (he went almost directly from Moses in *The Ten Commandments* [Cecil B. DeMille, 1956] to playing Vargas).

This cinematic highlighting of whiteness – against narrative – is also evident in *María Candelaria*'s articulation of race through gender. María Candelaria's positive virtues (virginity, humility) are coded as white – rather than indigenous – female virtues, inasmuch as they are inscribed within Western Christian morality. Christianity is not white but, as Dyer points out, as the religious export of Europe it is an important element in the 'white' project of imperialism. Similarly, Jesus and Mary were not white but their image has been gentilized and whitened from medieval times onward (Dyer, 1997: 17). Indeed, María Candelaria is continuously aligned with her namesake the Virgin Mary, '[t]he model for white women' (ibid.: 29). This is initially suggested through the camerawork when she is ill. Lorenzo lights a candle and places it in front of an image of Mexico's patron saint the Virgin of Guadalupe.[11] Then he looks between María Candelaria lying prostrate but luminous and the picture several times (see Figure 3.1). Del Rio is lit so that her forehead glows and there is a halo around her head. By cutting between the two, luminous María Candelaria is equated with the luminous Virgin of Guadalupe whose iconic representation includes an all-body glow. This equation also exists in the narrative in the confusion between the image of the Virgin and María Candelaria (Noble, 2001: 85). Early on, Lupe throws a stone at María Candelaria's Virgin – foreshadowing the stones she will later throw at María Candelaria. This analogy is further underlined and developed along racial lines when Lorenzo Rafael is arrested. She goes to the church and chastises the Virgin for her lack of sympathy. But rather than the visibly *mestiza* (mixed-race) Virgin of Guadalupe (also known as *La Virgen Morena*, the Dark Virgin), this representation is a more European 'white' statue.

At first, María and Mary are framed together; Mary in top left frame and María in middle right frame. The way María Candelaria holds her shawl mirrors Mary's hands clasped in prayer. When María Candelaria upbraids the Virgin, the priest tells her to stop, as she is making the Virgin cry (Figure 3.2). As they look to the statue the shot cuts to its contorted 'crying' face (Figure 3.3). Then it cuts to a close-up of María Candelaria who is also crying and lit to show tears in her eyes and on her cheeks (Figure 3.4). Again camerawork and dialogue make an analogy between María and Mary.

In this sequence, light plays a specific role in evoking 'religiosity' through 'luminosity' (Dyer, 1997: 112). Top lighting gives a sense of celestial lighting 'from above' connoting virtue and underlining the mise-en-scène's graphic match between the Virgin and María Candelaria (ibid.: 118).[12] This connection between spiritual devotion and light is further underlined by the dialogue when, after recanting her chastising of the Virgin, María Candelaria talks about how she was taught to 'see the light of heaven in Mary's eyes.'

This analogy between a European image of Mary – rather than the *mestiza* Virgin – and María continues on her funeral byre where her pose evokes a statuesque European Virgin: head surrounded by flowers, eyes closed and arms crossed.[13] María Candelaria represents

3.2 *María Candelaria*: 'Look the Virgin is crying'

Hybridity, *indigenismo* and whitening

3.3 *María Candelaria*: The Virgin is crying

3.4 *María Candelaria*: María is crying

the ideal of white womanhood 'bathed in . . . light. It streams on to [her] from above' (ibid.: 122).

At this point we return to the ethnic connotations of 'glamor' and 'beauty' that Del Rio brings to the project of the film. Dyer suggests that Western discourses of female beauty and glamor, as developed in European art and Christian imagery, are constructed around ideas of light and glow: the lighter the skin the more beautiful the woman (ibid.). Hence, glamor lighting in films, which has developed from these discourses, seeks to accentuate the glow of white women. That white women glow and that their beauty lies in luminosity is illustrated in the film when María Candelaria goes to rub mud on her face to 'hide her beauty' so she will not attract attention at the market. As well as emphasizing the 'lightness' of her skin this suggests her beauty can be taken away by darkening her skin.

As well as creating 'glamor', 'beauty', 'celestiality' and 'purity,' luminosity also constructs the ideal of white womanhood as a translucent, incorporeal image according to Western ideas of Mary, having no body and no carnal knowledge (ibid.: 131, 17). It is therefore significant that María Candelaria also has 'no body.' We never see the painting that causes her death. Classical convention leads us to expect a sighting of the painting (Noble, 2001: 85; Podalsky, 1993a: 68). We get several shots of characters looking at and reacting to the painting (including the other *indígenas* who are outraged at this 'dishonour' to their village), yet we never get the expected reverse shots of what the characters are looking at, which goes against continuity editing patterns.[14] The painting becomes codified as an absent image. The absence of her painted body further reflects how she is represented according to iconographic representation of white womanhood.

Mexican cultural nationalism is invested in the universality of mexicanness. As a technology developed to universalize whiteness, cinema becomes the privileged medium of Mexicanness in *María Candelaria*, offering a way of textually universalizing Mexico's Adam and Eve. Getting *indigenismo* right means confirming dominant ideas about the nation; providing a fantasy other which corresponds to stereotype and yet assures the Mexican nation that their Adam and Eve are white. Reflecting its glamorization (or 'whitening') of the *indígena* and postcard representation of Mexico, one critic jokingly retitled the film *María Calendaria* (Calendar María, García Riera, 1987: 48).

This analysis has shown that María Candelaria and Lorenzo Rafael are hybrids; they speak like the 'other' but are designer-dressed, they perform an exaggerated alterity but are lit to look morally and spiritually 'white.' However, rather than revindicating the actual other as alterity studies do, my analysis shows how their hybridity aligns them with the dominant position: white as the phenotypical ideal.

This analysis has reconciled *María Candelaria*'s positive and negative representations of the *indígena* as the source of the authentically Mexican, yet antithetical to the modern Mexican state. In the post-revolutionary period, progress for the community – reaching that on the level of the US or Europe – is thought of as 'bettering one's race' through 'whitening' (Lomitz Adler, 1992: 278). *María Candelaria* is organized around this racial binary; 'white' stands for modernity and order while 'non-white' stands for backwardness and chaos. Hence, Mexico's modern couple are portrayed as 'white.' The film reconciles *indigenismo* with the project of modernity in order to offer an idealized visualization of the *indígena*'s place within the modernizing Mexican nation.

Maclovia

Maclovia (1948) is often marginalized in analysis of Fernández films because it is viewed as a simple repetition of *María Candelaria* (García Riera, 1987: 129). However, while following some of its basic plot features, *Maclovia* rewrites and departs from many of the ideological principles of *María Candelaria*.

The story is located on the island of Janitzio with the Tarasco people (as in *Janitzio*). Maclovia (María Félix) and José María (Armendáriz) wish to be married. However, her father Macario (Inclán) objects to the union, forbidding José María to even look at his daughter. José María goes to school to learn how to write so that he can send letters to Maclovia. In the meantime, an army garrison is sent to the island, even though the presence of outsiders in their village is against the *indígenas*' customs. Sergeant La Garza (Carlos López Moctezuma), who has previously manhandled Maclovia in a nearby town, pursues her. Because an outsider is pursuing his daughter (and in the context that going with an outsider means death for the women of Janitzio) Macario agrees to the marriage between José María and Maclovia. However, their betrothal does not deter La Garza who tries to grab Maclovia, forcing José María to fight him. In a kangaroo court La Garza sentences him to prison for attacking an officer. Maclovia offers herself to the officer in order to save José María from a life sentence. José María escapes prison and kills La Garza before he can take Maclovia. The villagers, angry that she had agreed to give herself to a white man (which violates their customs), chase Maclovia to kill her. They stone her and José María as he tries to protect her. An older, private soldier steps in saving them from death. They paddle away from the island in a canoe.

Maclovia reflects the dominant discourse of the indigenist project in terms of explicit praise of the indigenous people and their traditions, and its criticism of the abuses of the white man against the indigenous people. However, it also embodies many of the contradictions of the indigenist project present in both *María Candelaria* and *Janitzio*. First, as with *María Candelaria* and *Janitzio*, by situating the story in 1914 during the revolution, and back on Janitzio, it remains remote to 1940s' Mexico thus problematizing the film's relationship to contemporary society and the modernizing intentions of *indigenismo* – i.e., to incorporate indigenous populations within the Mexican state. Also, as with *María Candelaria* and *Janitzio*, by being situated before or during the revolution, *Maclovia* suggests that the problems it deals with have been solved by the revolution and that subsequently none of these issues are relevant to contemporary Mexico. Furthermore, *Maclovia* like *María Candelaria* also contradicts the explicit national rhetoric around *indigenismo* (i.e., assimilation) by suggesting that without the presence of the white man (La Garza) all would be well on Janitzio. Thus the film appears, like *María Candelaria* and *Janitzio*, to be an isolationist fantasy rather than a parable of modernization.

But there are some significant differences in *Maclovia* which address the contradictions of earlier indigenist films and suggest a level of progressiveness in its ideology. These changes are either not commented upon in scholarship or not emphasized as significant. This seems to be a consequence of auteurist readings which seek to construct continuity across Fernández' oeuvre and suggest all his films are essentially the same.

One of the most significant changes in *Maclovia* is that, rather than ending in the death of one or both of the protagonists as in *Janitzio* and *María Candelaria* – thus praising a dead *indígena* (María Candelaria as martyr) rather than dealing with the actual problems of contemporary *indígena* – both Maclovia and José María escape the angry mob and get away from the island. Although the narrative has earlier stated that to leave the island is 'worse than death,' cinematographically Maclovia and José María's departure is not figured in tragic terms. They paddle away from Janitzio as the sun rises over the hills, suggesting that they

Hybridity, *indigenismo* and whitening 97

are moving into a more progressive (and hopeful) future. This escape from the island suggests assimilation, rather than isolation and also a move toward modernization. Further emphasizing the potential for assimilation is the fact that José María is one of the few adults on Janitzio who is learning to read and write.

A further significant difference in *Maclovia* lies in the film's less morally dichotomous representation of the *indígena* (and their practices). In *María Candelaria* a marked distinction is drawn between the central couple (as virtuous) and the rest of the *indígena* (as backward and barbaric) through lighting and narrative, thus problematizing the nationalist rhetoric of *indígena* incorporation. *Maclovia* on the other hand, particularly during long fishing sequences, aestheticizes both Maclovia and José María *as part of* rather than separate to the rest of the community. Further emphasizing their moral exemplarity, the rest of the villagers are not continually hostile toward Maclovia as they are toward María Candelaria, except for Sara (Columba Domínguez), the woman José María has thrown over in favor of Maclovia. And because Sara is a developed character (rather than a caricature like Lupe), we genuinely feel sorry for her. So although ultimately Maclovia and José María have to escape Janitzio, and the rest of the *indígena* figure at this point as a barbaric mob, the film as a whole offers us a much less schizophrenic representation of the *indígena* than *María Candelaria*. We have a much greater sense of the nobility and moral exemplarity of the entire community.

What is potentially most progressive about *Maclovia* is that it seems to question and explicitly criticize the racial hierarchy that privileges whiteness supported in *María Candelaria*. Although its central couple are played by white actors (Félix and Armendáriz) and most white characters (the teacher, the doctor, the lieutenant) are beneficent in the film, the villain (La Garza) is also a white character. In addition, the film very strongly counters the idea that La Garza's ethnicity affords him any special treatment. Early on in the film when he strikes Maclovia's father and is brought before a local judge, La Garza insists his '*ojos claros*' (light eyes) make his version of events more trustworthy than that of the '*malditos indios*' (damned Indians). But the judge (Manuel Dondé) who is visibly *mestizo* (mixed-race) refutes such a racial hierarchy, saying 'Todos somos indios aquí' (We are all Indians here) – i.e., all Mexicans are symbolically indigenous. Indeed, because *Maclovia* shows two Government institutions (the Courts and the Army) as respectful to the *indígena* (the army being fronted by the very reasonable Lieutenant (Roberto Cañedo) and the army saving Maclovia and José María at the end), the film suggests that the racist and belligerent Sergeant is an anomaly in what is otherwise a nonracist system. When the end to discrimination of the *indígena* owes its existence (officially at least) to post-Revolutionary (1920s onward) indigenist nationalism, this ideology of equality could seem anachronistic. However, what appears to be happening is an attempt to reconcile the narrative of indigenous oppression with a vision of contemporary (1940s) Government rhetoric – i.e., the idea that while prejudice against *indígena* remains it is only in isolated individuals, pointing to what is an idealized (if not unreal) nonprejudicial society.

However, the film's progressiveness in relation to the national project – i.e., suggesting that assimilation of the entire group of *indígena* is possible (and desirable) – is potentially undercut by the very same (fishing) sequences that idealize the *indígena*. These sequences, which narrate the practices of the Tarascos as 'sencillas costumbres y legendarias tradiciones' (simple customs and legendary traditions) have the effect of folklorizing the *indígena*, suggesting that like *Janitzio* the film is interested in exploiting them as picturesque subjects, rather than being an indigenist representation concerned with a socially meaningful depiction.

La perla

La perla (The Pearl, 1945), made as a coproduction by the Hollywood studio RKO and Águila Films and based on American author John Steinbeck's novella *The Pearl* (1975, originally published in 1945), was an industrially transnational film (García Riera, 1987: 85).[15] García Riera suggests that, as a result of this transnationality, the film subordinates the Fernandezian nationalist indigenist model to instead portray a Steinbeckian 'noble savage' (1987: 92). But while significant changes between novel (Steinbeck) and film (Fernández) are of interest, the following analysis suggests that contradictions in *La perla* are not necessarily traceable to clashes between its two 'authors' but to contradictions inherent in the ideology of *indigenismo*.

La perla is about Kino (Armendáriz), a pearl fisher who finds an enormous pearl. The pearl attracts the attention of a local pearl dealer and a doctor, who try to steal it from him. The pearl dealer will not give Kino a fair price for his pearl, and does everything to get it, even sending assassins to kill him. Having murdered the assassins he, his wife Juana

Hybridity, *indigenismo* and whitening

(María Elena Marqués) and their child Juanito flee to the city to sell the pearl there. The pearl dealer follows, eventually cornering Kino and his family on a rocky mountain. The film climaxes when the pearl dealer shoots Juanito and Kino stabs him. Juana and Kino return to their village and toss the pearl into the sea.

La perla is an explicitly indigenist text praising the indigenous people and their traditions (particularly pearl fishing) and criticizing the abuses of the white man against them (Figure 3.5). It is also a text

3.5 Pedro Armendáriz as Kino in *La perla*

that reflects contemporary government discourse. For example, in Steinbeck's novella Kino and Juana are descendants of an ancient people tied to an ancient past. The pearl dealers, the doctor and a priest are all Spanish or of Spanish descent, a 'race which for four hundred years had beaten and starved and robbed and despised Kino's race' (Steinbeck, 1975 [1945]: 12). In the film Kino and Juana are still marginalized indigenous people, but the doctor and the pearl dealer are not white of Spanish descent but German (the characters are played by Austrian and German actors Fernando Wagner and Charles Rooner respectively who both speak Spanish with German accents). This change in the provenance of the 'villains' reflects contemporary codes of Mexican cinema – i.e., wartime antifascism.[16] In addition, Steinbeck's money-grubbing priest (who is anxious to also share in the riches of the pearl) is elided altogether. Both of these changes are consistent with contemporary Mexican ideological imperatives, first the institutionalized Revolution's post-1940 rejection of anticlericalism and secondly the promotion of national unity (hence Europeanization/de-Mexicanization of bad white characters).

The contradictions in *La perla* are seemingly the familiar contradictions noted in *María Candelaria* and *Maclovia*. Supposedly, indigenist policy is to incorporate the *indígena* into the Mexican state (while contradictorily holding them up as the essential Mexican which in turn belies their marginalization). However, because in *La perla* it is the wicked ways of white men – i.e., a capitalist economy in which one can sell one's product or labor to the highest bidder – that corrupt *indígena* purity and ultimately lead to tragedy (Juanito's death), the text suggests that separation or even protectionist isolation of the *indígena* would be preferable. As with *María Candelaria*, in *La perla* it is suggested that the death of Juanito could have been avoided had the indigenous characters remained 'in their place.' And yet other elements within *La perla* suggest that it is not an isolationist fantasy in the way *María Candelaria* and *Maclovia* are interpreted as isolationist fantasies, but a film that deals with the issue of assimilation in all its complexity and difficulty.

First, the involvement with white capital and the system of exploitation it produces is already a part of the *indígena*'s lives. The film makes clear that they already sell their pearls to the pearl dealers at fixed low prices. Hence they are not unassimilated but marginalized within an unjust economic system. It is Kino's finding of the pearl – and the fact that the disparity between its value and the money he is offered for it is so great – that reveals the reality of this system, to both Kino and the rest of the *indígenas*. That the pearl itself will create changes in Kino's life – i.e., potential further assimilation and demarginalization – but that the system will ultimately not allow such upward mobility, is suggested the moment the pearl is found, and then in a subsequent moment in the film. When he finds the pearl Kino lifts it skyward and is shown in long shot laughing maniacally while Juana cowers in the boat. The low angle of the shot and dark clouds overhead are ominous, suggesting the pearl will bring tragedy. Then, when vendors come to sell the newly rich Kino all kinds of things, one significantly hands his son a candy skull and a toy gallows.

The film deals with the complexity of the assimilation process by tracing Kino's journey to consciousness of his position within an exploitative system. He goes from the infantilized *indígena* (frightened by such symbols of Western scientific knowledge as a doctor's stethoscope or the pearl dealer's magnifying glass) to a moment of politicized clarity. When the pearl dealer suggests the pearl is defective or a mere oddity, in order to drive the price down, Kino responds 'Our pearls are never good enough for you' and takes the pearl away from him. Kino, with the help of his *compadres* (friends) in the village, realizes he has to leave the village and go to the city to try to sell his pearl at a fair price. (His departure is precipitated by the attack of the pearl dealer's henchmen.)

Readings of *La perla* often stress the film's opening shots which figure groups of immobile *indígenas* in which 'the women are so still that only the fluttering of their clothes in the wind reminds us that this is a moving image' (Tuñón, 1995: 185). Emphasis on such moments underlines auteurist interpretations of Fernández' representation of the *indígena* as the unchanging, essential Mexican. In turn, few readings focus on elements within the film that would contradict the Fernándezian vision or the tenets of *indigenismo*. At the end of the film, for instance, Kino and Juana return to the village. Their son has been killed and Kino has killed the pearl dealer. At this point he no longer resembles the stereotypical submissive, infantilized cinematic *indígena* who cowers in the presence of white men. In the final shot of the film, after Kino and Juana throw the pearl into the sea, he grasps her wrist and we see both their fists clenched. The action of throwing the pearl into the sea could potentially be read as abdication or acceptance of a system in which Kino and Juana are to occupy the bottom rungs and not aspire to 'wealth.' But their clenched fists suggest an alternative reading; not the submissiveness of Fernández' stereotypical *indígena* but the potential of radicalism and resistance.

Notes

1 *Malinchista* is used to refer to Mexicans who have been corrupted by foreign, particularly North American, influences.
2 Tin Tan was a popular comedian who specialized in musical comedies. He was criticized by some critics for incorporating English phrases in his speech, and for symbolizing transculturation (Mraz, 2001: 132).
3 In *La perla* for example, Fernández mixes customs from two different coasts (the West and the East) and landscapes. The Taharumara guides who help the pearl dealer track Kino and Juana are from Chihuahua (a landlocked state on the border with the US). The music played during the celebrations are *sones* from Veracruz (on the gulf of Mexico) (García Riera, 1987: 92).
4 See Introduction, note 2 on the omission of the accent on Del Rio's name.
5 The problems with Vasconcelos are widely acknowledged. See Dever (2003: 16–23) for a discussion of some of these problems.
6 Although Del Rio is always portrayed as 'white' (creole), a photograph of her and her grandmother shows her grandmother to have distinctly indigenous features. Significantly, this photograph is not in De los Reyes (ed.) (1996), *Dolores Del Río*. This suggests that her official biography elides this aspect of her genealogy.
7 However, on another level 'pos' is acceptable as a *campesino* variation of 'pues' going back to the nineteenth century, and can be found in literature. The screenwriter Mauricio Magdaleno may have been using the vernacular language popularized by the novel of the revolution, such as Mariano Azuela's *Los de abajo* (1916) or his own *El resplandor* (1929).
8 'The rejection of Hollywood's images of Mexicans was one of the principal factors that led to the establishment of a local industry' (Paranaguá, 1995: 8)
9 *Broken Arrow* is considered to be one of the first progressive westerns of the postwar era. Its progressiveness is usually traced to its attempt to depict Native Americans with their own culture, practices, way of life and systems of belief. *Broken Arrow* was also the first western to use the culturally accurate term Wicki-up to denote Native American dwellings, instead of the more frequently used (and inaccurate) Wig Wam.
10 It is useful to note here how Mexican nationalism actually presented itself as anticosmopolitan, opposing itself to the cosmopolitanism of elite intellectuals such as the *Contemporáneos*. However, as De los Reyes points out in his description of *María Candelaria* and also Jorge Cuesta in a 1935 essay 'La nacionalidad mexicana' (Cuesta, 1991 [1935]), Mexican cultural

nationalism was actually more cosmopolitan that it would admit, imitating the European values against which it was supposedly meant to define itself.
11 The Virgin of Guadalupe is said to have appeared in 1531 to Juan Diego, an indigenous man, on Tepayac hill outside Mexico City. When he picked roses growing miraculously at the site where she appeared, as proof for the Church authorities, the Virgin's image was indelibly marked on his cloak.
12 Dyer talks about the way this kind of top lighting is often referred to in Hollywood as 'North' or 'Northern light.' This light is literally and symbolically superior in terms of being seen as coming from the North, which in Eurocentric geography (standardized during the process of European expansion) is placed above the South (1997: 118).
13 Though it is also of note that her plaits – a sign of her indigenous identity – are also visible, making her a hybrid figure.
14 One reason Fernández omits a shot of the painting is to avoid the self-reflexive question 'is this film a more reliable representation of the indigenous community than the painting of the artist?' (Podalsky, 1993a: 69).
15 There are in fact two versions of *La perla*, a Spanish version and an English version which was shot simultaneously with the same cast and crew, and is more or less the same text (with some telling Production Code-mandated omissions). For the purposes of this study I only analyze the Spanish-language version.
16 In 1940 the Allies feared that Germany had already targeted Latin America for fascist infiltration via diplomatic, commercial and cultural routes. It was thought that Mexico in particular was susceptible to such infiltration given the bad relations between it and the allies following Cárdenas' expropriation of US and UK oil interests in 1938, a policy which had forced Mexico to look to Germany and Italy as markets for its oil (Peredo Castro, 2004: 84). To counteract this and encourage plenty of antifascist, pro-Allies propaganda, the United States set out to build close economic, diplomatic and cultural ties with Mexico, particularly with its film industry (as an industry with commercial distribution throughout Latin America) (ibid.: 78). At the same time the US industry proposed to isolate Argentina, which had declared itself 'neutral' during the Second World War (but had in reality already been penetrated by the Reich's commercial and diplomatic forces – a situation fictionalized in Alfred Hitchcock's *Notorious* 1946) to circumscribe any Spanish-language, pro-German propaganda that could emanate from the Southern cone by limiting the supply of virgin film stock (a product it controlled) to Argentina (ibid.: 78–79, 88).

4

Gender, sexuality and the Revolution in *Enamorada*

As part of Mexico's ongoing Revolution, 'the ideological vision of society and culture... offered/accepted by the State' (Monsiváis, 1976: 305), the cultural reelaboration of Mexicanness also involved a cultural redefinition of gender. Fernández, both the individual and his oeuvre and their intersection in the figure of the auteur, become a part of that redefinition. For example, Tuñón said that the first time she spoke with Fernández, she was surprised that a man with such a 'macho' persona should have such a thin and watery voice (1988: 11). Similarly, García Riera observes that in *La cucaracha* (Ismael Rodríguez, 1958), Fernández' *altiplada* (high) voice was dubbed with the deeper voice of another actor (Narciso Busquets) for his portrayal of the revolutionary Colonel Zeta (1987: 251). What both these observations suggest is that for a director so closely allied to the Revolution, Fernández' own, high voice was in some way incommensurate not just with his public persona but also with the redefinition of masculinity in the post-Revolution era. However, apart from these two observations, the question of Fernández' voice is something which does not arise in traditional auteurist accounts of his work (although everything else about his life and being does). This question of incompatibility between voice and man, and the fact that it is a matter largely suppressed, presents us with interesting issues in relation to gender and the Revolution and also to the question of authorship which can be more fully explored by looking at how these issues intersect in his oeuvre.

This chapter looks at how Fernández' *Enamorada* deals with the Revolution's renegotiation of gender identity. It argues that Fernández' and the Revolution's explicit gender discourses of 'lo macho' and female submission are often undermined by the melodramatic mise-en-scène and borrowings from the Hollywood screwball comedy.

Gender and the Revolution

In the 1920s the Porfirian 'effeminate,' 'refined,' 'bourgeois' model of masculinity was symbolically defeated by a – supposedly more Mexican – 'virile,' 'savage,' proletarian hypermasculinity, resulting from the Revolution's identification with working-class peons. This is evident in the so called 'virility debates' around the topic of national literature, in which, as Robert Irwin points out, the *Estridentistas* valorized a nebulous 'virility' in literature (exemplified in the novel of the revolution *Los de abajo* (1916)) over a similarly nebulous 'effeminacy' in the writing of the *Contemporáneos* (1997: 71–74). However, as Irwin argues, the 'virility debates' often involved a blurring between the notion of 'virile' writing and 'virile' writers, in which the *Estridentistas* attacked the *Contemporáneos* for being 'effeminate' and therefore – within the *Estridentista* logic – associatively foreign, upper-class, antinationalist and antirevolutionary. This chapter attempts to read against a similar blurring between work and artist, between the accepted model of Revolutionary masculinity and a hypermasculine filmmaker – if either actually exists. It asks how the eliding of Fernández' high voice in biographical auteurist accounts suggests a repression of 'other,' less 'virile' readings of his work.

At this point, however, so as not to oversimplify the question of gender, it might be pertinent to contextualize the somewhat heterosexist language used within the rhetoric of the Mexican Revolution to construct gender. First, the use of the potentially offensive oppositions 'effeminate' vs 'virile' and 'savage' is not my choice of words but a reflection of the specific terminology used in the so-called 'virility debates:' 'Individuals of doubtful morals who are holding official posts with their effeminate acts, besides constituting an example worthy of being condemned, create an atmosphere of corruption that reaches the extreme of preventing the maturing of virile qualities in our youth ...' (Monsiváis, 1977: 277). As Daniel Balderston points out in reference to the above quotation, these are the 'fighting words' used by one group of Mexican intellectuals against another (1998: 57). Furthermore, within the context of post-Revolutionary Mexico, these terms and their synonyms are also circulated within the texts of the 'the philosophy of Mexicanness.' In one of the most famous of these texts, 'Los hijos de la Malinche' (The children of La Malinche) from *El laberinto de la soledad* (1951), notions of gender revolve around the verb *chingar* and its specific translation. In the Manichean scheme that Paz outlines, there is the active, violent '*chingón*' (he who fucks) who is denoted as masculine and as the 'macho' and the passive, open *'chingado'* (1997 [1951]: 83) ([s]he who is fucked) who is denoted as feminine and as the *'hembra.'* Paz regards machismo as an attempt to compensate, through greater masculinity, for the inferiority complex suffered by most Mexicans as a result of their racial and economic status as well as their heritage as a conquered, colonized people (O'Malley, 1986: 8). As Ilene O'Malley points out, this figuration of Mexican masculinity is actualized and institutionalized in the heroes of the Revolution, Emiliano Zapata and Pancho Villa, who are constructed as the prototypes of the macho (ibid.: 3). 'Lo macho' is also a recurrent theme within auteurist accounts of Fernández' work and also part of his myth. He is even rumored to be an ex-villista General himself (Monsiváis, 1992: 29). He and the characters he creates are *perceived* as being like the *'chingón'*. For example, his daughter Adela writes about her father in terms associated with 'lo macho' as a possessive, gun-loving womanizer. It is also suggested by Adela Fernández and by Tuñón that he behaved like many of the male characters in his films (Adela Fernández, 1986, 161–201; Tuñón, 2000: 49).

The idea of gendered national identity, as it is constructed in this and other auteurist accounts of Fernández' work, correlates closely with the texts of 'the philosophy of Mexicanness.' After outlining the *chingón/chingado* scheme, Paz argues that since Mexican independence, the problem of national identity in Mexico has been presented as a problem of male identity. The Mexican male subject has been constituted as a violent rejection of 'la chingada' ('La Malinche'), Doña Marina, the indigenous woman given to and subsequently *chingada por* (fucked by) the Conquistador Cortés. She is perceived as inferior, first as a traitor to the nation for having facilitated the taking of the Aztec city Tenochtitlán and secondly because she was open, passive and allowed herself to be *chingada* (fucked) (Paz, 1997 [1951]: 94–95). The legacy of this psychological scar, Paz argues, is a concept of women as passive, transmitting and conserving but not creating the values and energies which nature and society pass on: 'In a world made in the image of man, the woman is only a reflection of male will and desire' (Franco, 1989: 133).

However, as Roger Bartra points out, in *La jaula de la melancolía* (The Cage of Melancholy), his deconstruction of *El laberinto de la soledad* and the philosophy of Mexicanness *'La chingada'* along with the other 'foundational' myths of Mexican national identity do not necessarily reflect a particular Mexican self but are merely constructions serving the dominant ideology. Concepts of 'La chingada' along with the Virgin of Guadalupe, simply construct and reify a *machista* perspective on Mexican national identity, discounting the agency of women by treating them as merely vessels or instruments of male desire (1996: 171–185). It is also important to point out that Bartra shows how the philosophy of Mexicanness constructed by Paz, Leopoldo Zea and 'Agusto Salazar Bondy is really nothing but Western philosophy redressed in indigenous form; hence La Malinche the treacherous woman is not necessarily an indigenous figure but really a reconfiguration of the Western myth of Eve (1996: 181).

In line with this dominant current, the hypermachismo of Fernández is read as symptomatic of a Mexican national identity locked into a permanent rejection of the female ('la chingada'). A typical Fernández film is taken to be one in which 'there is a required unconditional submission of the woman' (Tuñón, 1993: 169). In the narratives of Fernández, women are thus read not only as a means of masculine self-determination but also as a means to the definition of the nation itself as male (the fatherland) against the female. Evidence of this gendered national identity shows in the fact that many of the titles of these nationalist films are female proper names or refer to women: *Flor Silvestre María Candelaria* (1943), *Las abandonadas* (1944), *Enamorada* (1947), *Víctimas del pecado* (1950).

Fernández' films could be read in other, more subversive ways that are obscured by traditional criticism's focus on 'lo macho' as authentically Mexican. Hence, although in this chapter Fernández and the myth of his hypermachismo provide a link between the aesthetic strategies of nationalism and the concurrent gender issues of postrevolutionary Mexico, these do not figure as a hegemonic force weighing on the reading of the films.

The advantage of *Enamorada*, in a reading which attempts to go against the grain of cultural nationalism, is that it does not repeat the images of aesthetic nationalism as mythified by nationalist discourse: Eisenstein-inspired Mexican landscape, Posada's maguey cacti and Rivera's *indígenas*. Furthermore, the explicit discourse on gender of the Hollywood screwball comedy tradition from which the film borrows further facilitates attempts to locate this film outside Fernández' vision of gender relations and also outside a purely national paradigm. It is, moreover, interesting to note Monsiváis' suggestion that, although Mexico borrowed a lot from Hollywood in its construction of a national film industry, the screwball comedy was one genre that Mexico was unable to translate due to a lack of reliable scriptwriters and of a culture of humor, a point which the heavily screwball-influenced *Enamorada* contradicts (1993: 141).

Enamorada: woman or man in love?

Enamorada is a loose adaptation of William Shakespeare's *Taming of the Shrew*, and revolves around a 'Fernándezian' central couple. Set during the historical revolution, the narrative deals with the 'taming' of Beatriz Peñafiel (María Félix), an antirevolutionary and conservative (yet fiery) middle-class girl, by a lower-class, *zapatista* revolutionary general, José Juan Reyes (Pedro Armendáriz). Jean Franco has read this narrative as one which seeks to refeminize the 'masculinized' woman, returning her to her proper place within patriarchy after the disruption of the revolution: 'The broken family, the cult of violence, and the independent "masculinized" woman have to be transformed into a new holy family in which women accede voluntarily to their own subordination not to a biological father but to a paternal state' (1989: 147). Franco interprets the film's project to be a restoration of the balance in gender relations by affirming masculinity and subduing the 'virile' female. Franco echoes the language of the postrevolution redefinition of masculinity by using this precise word, seemingly not just applicable to men. (ibid.: 149) This perception of coherence between the Revolutionary rhetoric of 'lo macho' and the text itself is typical of Fernández criticism. However, the film's supposed trajectory toward the triumph of machismo is contradicted by certain cinematic elements within the film which, rather than subduing the 'virile' Beatriz, actually serve to 'feminize' General José Juan. Furthermore, although entitled *Enamorada/Woman in Love*, the film's narration is predominantly concerned with a man in love: the General. This would seem to question the film's place within a monolithic Fernández oeuvre, and its connection to Fernández as a director figure and male-oriented Mexican cultural nationalism. If the film can be seen to embody contradictory drives – i.e., a cleavage between the text and the ideological project of the film – how then can we interpret its discourse on gender in relation to the Revolution?

Genre, gender and the Revolution

How do melodrama and action work in relation to the idea of gender in the film? The use of the terms femininity and masculinity does not in this case signal biological sexual categories – i.e., male or female – but points to gender attributes established by the text in terms of genre-based cultural associations.

In the shots immediately following the credits, the film begins by establishing masculinity in the action adventure style, a genre which, Yvonne Tasker argues, itself embodies a masculinist aesthetic (1993: 1). When General José Juan first appears we see him shot from a low angle on horseback, an image which implies power and, within the rhetoric of action cinema, masculinity. A subsequent long scene, which lasts for a substantial part of the film, also seems to serve as a means of establishing the General with respect to masculinity. In particular, the scene serves to establish him as a man of power and leadership: able to call upon the richest men in the town and leave them to cower as he decides their fates. This dominating sense of puissance can be seen from the way in which the initial encounter with the town crier is framed: when the crier is forced down to the General's boot level to write down the names of the *ricos* (rich), he is shot from behind and between the General's legs, a position which suggests both his submission and the General's power. Similarly, when the General orders Bocanegra to bring the rich men to him, the camera quickly tracks into an extreme close-up of his face – again implying forcefulness and authority.

Later, when the *ricos* arrive, there is a key shot in which the General is filmed with the back of the men's heads in the foreground as the camera tracks left and right, following him as he shouts his beliefs at them (as Bernal the shopkeeper cowers on the floor). The shot makes the men anonymous (placing them in a 'weak' dramatic pose), they are silent and lined up, suggesting they are condemned men at the General's mercy.

General José Juan is forceful and severe in his decisions, although he presents himself as being righteous too, a quality that is also portrayed as masculine. He despises the shopkeeper, who exploits both the revolution and the town, whereas he is generous to the schoolteacher, not only doubling his salary but also paying him from his own purse, an action which is linked with his idea of honorable machismo.

However, the film also starts to hint at cracks in the General's macho image, and this suggests that some of the attributes that have been set up in relation to masculinity will be reversed later in the film. The first hint at a 'gentler' (synonymous with feminine in Paz' outlining of gender binaries) General is that he had once been in the seminary along with the priest, and they are thus old friends.¹ We also detect cracks in his macho image when we hear he has an adopted daughter, and in his performance when he grants Roberts (the American) passage to Mexico City to get things for his wedding to Beatriz. The General agrees to let him go because of his nationality, but his silence and the tiny head shake he gives after saying, 'Only a guy like that could think of marriage in these times,' suggests other reasons.

Indeed, it is when Roberts returns that we get some idea of what these other reasons could be, when he asks the General whether he has ever been in love. We cut to a close-up of the General, who suddenly registers the question and goes into distracted and slightly troubled thought by arching his eyebrow and looking down and away from Roberts/the camera into thin air, then looking back and offering a hesitant 'No,' as melodramatic music begins on the soundtrack.

If we can presume as Christine Gledhill does (1987: 10) – though not unproblematically so – that melodrama, as a 'women's' genre, is in some way a more 'feminine' genre than the 'masculine' action film, then the increasing shift to melodrama in the mise-en-scène, – which includes music, soft-focus close-ups, pensive and anguished facial expressions – can be seen to point toward a certain feminization in the text. The fact that this should happen from the moment 'love' is first mentioned suggests that the film sets up a tension between being macho/masculine and being in love. Overtly, within the rhetoric of the Revolution the two are presented within the text as compatible: Mexico's future (the coming together of the conservative upper-class Beatriz, and the lower-class revolutionary José Juan) depends on a proper organization of gender roles. However, the workings of the text show the two are not so easily compatible, as José Juan goes through a definite 'feminization' in terms of filmic representation when he falls in love. Further evidence of the fact that being in love is in some way incompatible with Revolutionary masculinity is the fact that the film would have been more accurately titled *Enamorado/Man in Love* as it is more about José Juan's love pangs than those of Beatriz. However, to call the film *Man in Love* in Mexico in the 1940s would have been culturally inappropriate and politically insensitive.²

A reversal of 'traditional' gender attributes is seen in the serenade sequence. Franco reads the scene in terms of Laura Mulvey's visual-pleasure paradigm, as a reproduction of the male as holder of the gaze and the female connoting only 'to-be-looked-at-ness' suggesting that the scene works on a conventional axis of male desiring the female (1989: 150–151). Monsiváis, however, suggests a more ambiguous reading of the scene: 'During the serenade of *Enamorada*, the eyes of María Félix perform the most elaborate version of courting and surrender, siege and surrender' (1988b: 94). Monsiváis hints at the active (courting) and aggressive (siege) role of María Félix in this scene, implying she plays the active part. Gabriel Figueroa's camerawork suggests María Félix plays the active part by undoing the male as looker/female as to-be-looked-at-ness dynamic of classical cinema (Mulvey, 1990: 38). With the concentration on Beatriz' eyes, the emphasis is upon not José Juan's but Beatriz's act of looking at the male body – José Juan's. He, does not have access to see her but she does spy on him. Furthermore, although this scene is very much about the beauty of Félix's eyes – 'Qué bonitos ojos tienes' (What beautiful eyes you have) is a literal translation of the first line of the serenade – these are eyes that look knowingly straight at the camera, connoting defiance rather than submission (Figure 4.1).

4.1 Eyes that look knowingly . . . connoting defiance rather than submission

Genre/Gender-bending: the screwball comedy

A main structural theme running through *Enamorada* seems to be a contrasting of what is considered feminine or masculine – in particular, the relationship between love/charity/humility and power/wealth/oppression. As we would expect from a revolutionary (action) film, the opening few shots of the film of the attack on the village all seek to establish action and movement: rapidly cut cannons, a swift tracking shot of cavalry, grand explosions. But then this appears to be contradicted (although it turns out to be more complicated than simple contradiction) by María Félix's appearance from a house and the title caption *Enamorada*.

This immediately gives rise to certain tensions. One is that the opening shots establish action/adventure, but then we are presented with the film's title and the promise of 'María Félix en . . .' (María Felix in . . .) which seems to jar with that action. For instance, the title 'Woman in Love' suggests the tragic melodrama of a lonely woman, since it is not 'Women in Love' or 'Man and Woman in Love.' This tension is perhaps most interestingly captured in the manner in which the title suggests melodrama and matters of the heart – *Enamorada* – but it is superimposed over a shot of battle and explosions, and is rendered in a kind of adventure movie style font (uneven, 'chipped' lettering). Similarly, one could read a process of gender-bending in the manner in which María Félix is given top billing ('María Félix en'), such that when Armendáriz first appears (low angle, on horseback) the machismo of the image is undercut somewhat by the titles 'con Pedro Armendáriz' (With Pedro Armendáriz) implying he is playing second fiddle to a woman.

Indeed, with such a credit sequence the film seems to suggest that femininity and machismo (or 'love' and 'violence' as established by textual convention) go in tandem with each other, and that these contradictory drives are always in a state of flux. For example, much of Armendáriz and Félix's 'falling in love' is expressed and developed through comic verbal and physical conflict. This expression of love through conflict suggests a strong influence of Hollywood screwball comedy on the film, thereby introducing a third genre, and given that it is a genre that is self-conscious about gender roles, it seems further evidence of the way the film seems to be investigating masculinity.

One important feature in screwball relevant to *Enamorada* is the way in which it organizes the couple. The female protagonist of the screwball is usually a free and assertive (working) woman (Lent, 1995: 318). And although screwballs are usually admired for the progressiveness of their representations of women, this is somewhat hampered by the fact that they are still presented and defined largely in relation to marriage and men. To a certain extent the Hollywood screwball can also be seen to 'tame' the women, in the same way that *Enamorada* does. The casting of María Félix, whose star persona in Mexico very much revolved around a notion of assertive, even masculinized, femininity seems therefore made with the screwball aesthetic in mind: 'María Félix is the *hembra* [woman] who becomes a macho in order to survive and to ensure the humiliation of those other women who lack beauty and personality, who are incapable of imposing their will and or wielding the lash' (Monsiváis, 1985: 42).

The male lead of the screwball is on the other hand often a weaker character, his weakness often being suggested through a certain feminization: see Cary Grant in a woman's dressing gown in *Bringing Up Baby* (1938) or his passing as a woman at the end of *I Was a Male War Bride* (1949). Another manner in which the film is comparable to the Hollywood screwball tradition is the use of an 'unsuitable suitor' to make the lead seem the heroine's 'natural mate' (Lent, 1995: 326). Indeed most screwballs depict one of the leads as having an ill-suited fiancé, who is usually a wet fish, arrogant or just too straitlaced for the wacky leads: for example King Wesley in *It Happened One Night* (1934). In *Enamorada* the 'unsuitable suitor' is Roberts. Not only is he a foreigner, which is a good way to paint a character as ill-suited, he is also presented to be very stiff – Beatriz even says to him at one point, 'You are all tight and wrapped up, I don't understand you.' Roberts is also quite camp with a pencil moustache, cravat, smug grin, slicked-back hair, dapper suit and, most sickeningly, a very soppy view of love.

Therefore, the screwball aesthetic, which comes into play almost directly after the initial establishing-of-masculinity scene, can be seen to question masculinity as constructed within the rhetoric of the Revolution and the action adventure style. When José Juan first sees Beatriz, he makes a few macho catcalls at her expense, praising her legs but saying she must have a '*cara de espantapájaros*' (scarecrow face). First we get a shot of Beatriz from behind (echoing the earlier shots of the *ricos*) in a 'weak' dramatic pose – not facing the camera, hunched with head low and shoulders high, bows in her hair (suggesting a childishness which is stereotypically associated with femininity). But then she turns round and empowers herself against

José Juan's sexist teasing. First she shows off her legs, using them as weapons of a sort, recalling Claudette Colbert's hitchhiking technique in *It Happened One Night* and prefiguring Sharon Stone's flashing in *Basic Instinct* (1992). As she approaches José Juan and stands close to him, he leans back away from her and she slaps him. As he falls we hear screwball, Laurel and Hardy-style music. Then he stands up and, as he rubs his sore cheek fetishistically and talks of how he is going to marry her, he is significantly filmed from the same low-angled shot used to establish his masculinity in the credit sequence, an angle which suggests a certain ironizing of this masculinity – i.e., that it is being made fun of (Figure 4.2).

Indeed, screwball itself is a contradictory genre, using violence between couples as coding for romantic interest: see for instance, the physical and verbal abuse usually, but not exclusively, inflicted by the woman on the man in films such as *Bringing Up Baby* or *The Lady Eve* (1941). Later in *Enamorada*, for instance, there is a scene in which Beatriz and José Juan exchange blows through and across the door of

4.2 *Enamorada*: José Juan rubs his cheek fetishistically

Gender, sexuality and the Revolution, 1

her father's house (Figure 4.3).³ The door is potent screwball metaphor for a certain sexual barrier. José Juan's ramming of it is furthermore suggestive of attempted penetration (which ultimately he achieves). In the Hollywood films, this kind of physical interaction (violent, comic, playful, childish) was used as a code/metaphor for the more sexual kind of interaction the Production Code forbade from 1934 onward. This scene also portrays the screwball feature of the exchange of comic banter where both Beatriz and José Juan call each other names or trick each other with language. The scene is shot with José Juan and Beatriz taking up parallel positions on either side of the door, a framing which suggests that as parallels of each other they are also in physical harmony – i.e., compatible. *It Happened One Night* uses similar parallel construction to suggest the compatibility of Ellie Andrews and Peter Warne (Clarke Gable) when they sleep on either side of the blanket in identical single beds. This textual evidence contradicts Franco's notion that gender relations are only in balance (harmony) at the end when Beatriz is placed in a subordinate position (1989: 152).

4.3 *Enamorada*: Beatriz and José Juan, violence as romantic interest

Furthermore, equality as a particular generic feature of screwball, which *Enamorada* embodies, is somewhat at odds with Mexican national (gender) identity and also with the Fernández mythology of the 'unconditional submission of the woman' (Tuñón, 1993: 169; 2000: 100).

In particular, this kind of screwball interaction (female dominant, male subordinate and both in a constant state of antagonism) is very appropriate to the Revolutionary conflict with which the film deals. Franco argues that this conflict is played out in the contemporary setting of the film's production, 1946 – i.e., subduing the militant conservative women who had increased in numbers during the Lázaro Cárdenas regime. Hence the winning over of Beatriz is emblematic of how militant conservative women scared of a revolution which for them signals violence can be won over (Franco, 1989: 149).

I would argue, however, that the way in which the film figures the problem of the revolution is much more as a male problem than a female one, and hence more across the character of José Juan than that of Beatriz. The trajectory of José Juan's development is played out through a theme of love versus oppression and this is figured through his differing interpretations of a painting which hangs in the sacristy at the church. Painted by a Juaréz, José Juan initially thinks of it as another commodity, displaying his initial insensitivity toward art. But then, when he sees the painting for the first time – which is, significantly, after he has fallen in love – his reaction to it is far more spiritual. As the shadow of a cross falls on José Juan he reads the painting of the Magi at Jesus' birth as representing rich, powerful and oppressive men bowing humbly before a baby (Jesus – who would go on to represent purity, charity and goodness). The earlier scene with the rich businessmen appears to be a version of this same narrative. In particular, the earlier scene represents José Juan's attempt to place himself as a God/Jesus figure. The problem is that José Juan only achieved this power through force and terror, which paints him symbolically as more of an Old Testament God rather than a New Testament God of Love.

The trajectory of the film, therefore, is for José Juan's character to find his own humility, marking a move from where he too is actually a symbol of power and oppression to where he is humble and asking for forgiveness. In his case, the transformation is brought about through Beatriz (and the appreciation of beauty/art) rather than through a small baby. Such an interpretation makes the film seem ultimately more concerned with *his* taming rather than with the taming of Beatriz – a taming which is achieved through love. At the end of the film, it is important that José Juan decides to retreat (without fighting the Federal Forces), and finally earns the true respect of his friend the priest. Thus the assurance from a post-Revolutionary regime that the violence of the past has been left behind is derived, not from a relocation of woman within patriarchy as Franco has read the film, but textually from a demasculinization, or a humbling that is figured through use of screwball and melodrama in generic feminine terms.

How, then, does *Enamorada* adopt the screwball form and adapt it to local (Mexican) concerns? At the beginning of the film we could interpret General José Juan as representing the revolutionary (Fernandezian) model of masculinity: lower-class, powerful and somewhat savage. Roberts (as an American) represents the (rejected) Porfirian model of masculinity: foreign and effeminate. The film then takes this further by challenging and undermining the revolutionary masculinity of General José Juan, sending him in the direction of Roberts toward qualities which have been repressed in him, love and romance, which are perceived as feminine. It could be that the film poses that the problem of Mexican post-Revolutionary male identity is one of excessiveness. José Juan is excessively macho while Roberts is excessively effeminate. The trajectory of the film, therefore, is about finding a more tamed version of both.

Furthermore, the presence of Roberts within the film, as the American suitor defeated by the Mexican revolutionary hero, could also be a playful reference to postwar Mexican-US relations; a kind of reversal of Hollywood's depiction of US-Mexican gender relations where the Anglo suitor always gets the girl (Fein, 2001: 160).

Screwball plots usually revolve around a wacky couple who can find no place in society as individuals or as a couple. Hence such plots often finish with the couple having to leave the world to find their own space, as in *Holiday* (1938) where Johnny and Linda go off on a cruise or *It Happened One Night* where Pete and Ellie go off to their own 'private island.' Indeed, *Enamorada* does end with a similar departure of the couple. José Juan leaves the town of Cholula and Beatriz goes behind him with her hand on his horse's rump. We presume he is going to continue fighting the revolution and she follows him as his humble *soldadera*. However – in the light of the screwball – this departure, rather than being interpreted as her submission to the 'virile' male and the requirements of the Revolution, can now be seen as a mutual escape from a world in which they do not belong (Figure 4.4).[4]

Thus, from this genre-based reading of *Enamorada*, we find that it turns out to be a very different kind of film than most Fernández scholarship suggests. The film sets up the issue of defining a national identity in Mexico in 1940s in relation to gender issues through the use of the screwball genre. The lack of coherence in the text between ideology and image becomes a deliberate strategy of representation, a means of suggesting an even non-*machista* approach to post-Revolutionary politics. Indeed, the film seems to offer a critique of machismo when Don Joaquím tells José Juan that men who 'por lo macho' (out of machismo) do not express their emotions lose out.

We could of course attribute the critique of machismo in the film to Figueroa's photography – i.e., the melodramatized moment which often cuts in to action scenes using techniques of soft-focus close-ups,

4.4 *Enamorada*: Beatriz and José Juan leaving a world where they do not belong

Gender, sexuality and the Revolution, 1

showing pensive and anguished facial expressions, or the transcendental 'Ave María' scene in the splendid baroque church. Indeed it has been suggested that the masculinist discourse of nationalism is subverted and feminized by the melodramatic sensibility of the many melodramas of the 1940s onward which often elide the complex issues of the Revolution itself, e.g. land reform, class conflict, social injustice and violence (Kraniauskus, 1997: xviii).

However, rather than ascribing feminine or masculine traits to Fernández and/or Figueroa, which is arguably problematic, it might be more useful to suggest that this chapter shows there is room for other readings of *Enamorada* than Mexican cultural nationalism and the basic Fernández mythology allow for – i.e., in this case a feminist reading. This would be a position consistent with Hall's 'Encoding/Decoding' essay. Such a cultural-studies polysemy questions the success of the totalizing ideology of cultural nationalism, and gives rise to the 'others' and 'other' readings it would repress. This does not mean that *Enamorada*'s questioning of masculinity means it must be read as a feminist text nor Fernández as a feminist, but the acknowledgement that the tensions in the text between traditional perceptions of masculinity and femininity do create multiple readings.

Notes

1. This not only hints at his capacity for goodness, but also is also reminiscent of *Angels With Dirty Faces* (1938), in which James Cagney and Pat O'Brien play lifelong friends. Cagney is a gangster and O'Brien a priest. O'Brien ultimately brings about Cagney's redemption, persuading Cagney to pretend he is 'yellow' when he is executed, so that the Dead End Kids who worship him will learn a lesson and choose a better path.
2. On the other hand, in 1951 Pedro Infante starred in a comedy entitled *El Enamorado (Man in Love)* directed by Miguel Zacarías. That Infante could appear in a film of such a title is arguably, following the thesis of De la Mora's *Cinemachismo* (2006), because of the very different type of masculinity that Infante embodies. Unlike Fernández and his surrogate Armendáriz, Infante frequently cried and showed emotion in the parts he played, e.g. as Pepe El Toro in *Ustedes los ricos* when his son El Torito is killed in a fire. Hence this sentimental title is okay for him, but not for Armendáriz in a Fernández film.
3. The idea of a barrier as an added incentive to innocent sexual play is also used in *It Happened One Night*, where a blanket hung between the beds

of the lovers-to-be is called 'The walls of Jericho' – a name which itself suggests that the blanket like the Old Testament walls will come tumbling down.

4 The very similar ending of Josef von Sternberg's *Morocco* (1930), when Marlene Dietrich leaves with Gary Cooper as he departs with the Foreign Legion, supports this interpretation. Indeed, García Riera has suggested that Fernández' film is purely derivative in its copy of the ending of *Morocco* (1993d: 60).

5

Gender, sexuality and the Revolution in *Salón México*, *Las abandonadas* and *Víctimas del pecado*

If *Enamorada* narrates an[o]ther model of Mexican masculinity, *Salón México* (1949) narrates an[o]ther model of Mexican femininity. One of few urban films to be considered part of Fernández' canonical (culturally nationalist) work, along with *Las abandonadas* (The Abandoned Women, 1944) and *Víctimas del pecado* (Victims of Sin, 1950), *Salón México* belongs to the *cabaretera* (cabaret/brothel melodrama) genre. In films like *Salón México* and *Distinto amanecer* (A different dawn, Julio Bracho 1944) which proliferated during the late 1940s, women are the breadwinners forced by growing economic hardship to work as prostitutes. These films deal with this apparent crisis in patriarchy (and in the ideals of the Revolution) by forwarding an ideology of family orthodoxy and national unity, recuperating the other – the prostitute – within a narrative of conventional morality (Hershfield, 1996: 77).

Elsewhere I have argued that *Salón México* embodies the patriarchal conservative values of the institutionalized Revolution which map female virtue onto to a sense of nationhood (Tierney, 1997). Here I argue that Fernández' revolutionary moral and ideological discourse of female sacrifice and patriarchal orthodoxy is in fact undermined by an emotional and visual investment in the interests of the other. While *Salón México* is read as a depiction of the dominant ('el México que debe ser'/Mexico as it should be), the camerawork displays greater pleasure in depicting the forbidden other ('el México que no debe ser'/Mexico as it should not be) (García Riera, 1993d: 264).

The *cabaretera*, like Fernández' *Enamorada*, is also read as depicting a sense of proper gender roles in post-Revolutionary Mexico. Fernández' *Salón México*, *Las abandonadas* (actually a fallen-woman film), and *Víctimas del pecado*, like other *cabareteras*, such as *Aventurera* (Alberto Gout 1949), and proto-*cabareteras*, such as *La mujer del puerto* (Arcady Boytler, 1934) and *Santa* (Antonio Moreno, 1931 and Norman Foster, 1943), ostensibly offered symbolic narratives around the new role of Mexican women in the public sphere. The archetypal figures of the *cabareteras* were defined through the sacrifice of their bodies as sexual objects for men and for their families. In *Salón México*, *Las abandonadas*, and *Víctimas del pecado* Mercedes, Margarita and Violeta give their lives (in one case literally) for their 'children.' Although, as 'fallen women' Mercedes, Margarita and Violeta are others, excluded from society, they are largely pardoned for their prostitution and in some cases stealing by narratives which cast them as heroines, albeit tragic heroines. Thus, rather than questioning the status quo, the narrative positions these characters as both victims and abnegated women, reifying them within a dominant perspective of Mexican cultural nationalism in terms of its representation of the female.

Salón México

In *Salón México*, the protagonist Mercedes (Marga López) works as a *fichera* (dancer, code for prostitute), to support her younger sister Beatriz (Silvia Derbez) at an exclusive boarding school. In many ways Mercedes is a codified representation of a single mother: nurturing and providing for her younger sister. Mercedes and Paco (Rodolfo Acosta) her *padrote* (pimp) win a *danzón* competition, but because he will not share the prize money which she needs to pay her sister's school fees, she steals it from his room. Lupe (Inclán), the neighborhood policeman, witnesses the crime, but protects Mercedes because he knows why she took the money. Later he saves her from Paco's beating because he is in love with her. Mercedes regularly visits her sister at the school and learns she is to be married to Roberto (Roberto Cañedo), the Second World War hero son of the headmistress (Mimi Derba). But Mercedes is unable to meet her sister's fiancé when, after Paco hides from the police in her room, she is subsequently imprisoned as his accomplice. Lupe asks Mercedes to marry him and, knowing Roberto will look after her sister, she accepts. However, Paco escapes from prison, comes to Mercedes' room and threatens to tell her sister what she really does for a living. To protect her sister from the truth Mercedes stabs Paco. As he dies he shoots and kills her.

In the previous chapter we examined (and sought to problematize) how the conquest as the 'originary moment' in the development of an 'essential Mexican psyche' produces the 'macho,' a form of hypermasculinity that compensates for feelings of inferiority, and how this is worked through in the texts of cultural nationalism. In this chapter we question the reproduction of similar motifs of cultural nationalism in relation to the production of the *hembra* (female), an exaggeratedly submissive and abnegated female identity, and femininity in conventional readings of *Salón México, Las abandonadas* and *Víctimas del pecado*.

In conventional readings of *Salón México* and the *cabaretera*, it is understood that the Mexican female subject, like the male subject, is also derived from the violent rupture of colonial encounter (Hershfield, 1996: 79, 83; López, 1993a: 150–1). Mexican woman is reduced to a duality of Malinche/traitor/*chingada* (fucked) vs the Virgin of Guadalupe – the mother of Mexico, as both an object of ridicule *and* of praise. Thus the Mexican female subject is caught in a duality of whore/virgin. It is largely understood that the tragic heroines of the *cabatereras* represent this divided female subject. Hence, although the *fichera* is effectively a prostitute, she retains a spiritual virginity. This is represented visually in *Salón México* by the braids and bows Mercedes curls on her head, connecting her both to the countryside (the locus of purity and authenticity) and also to a childlike innocence which Tuñón points out is a feature of all Fernández' women, even the urban ones (2000: 42). In Mercedes' case the braids and bows stand in for the pre-seduction sequence which is commonly part of *cabareteras* or fallen women films, but not part of *Salón México*. This spiritual virginity (i.e., absence of blame) is achieved narratively by blaming the *fichera*'s downfall on economic necessity – as in *Distinto amanecer*, *Salón México* and *Víctimas del pecado* – or on the seducer who subsequently abandoned her – as in *Las abandonadas, La mujer del puerto* and *Santa*. In the sense that they do not blame women, *cabareteras* differ to Mexico's founding fiction, the novel *Santa* (Federico Gamboa, 1903), which they otherwise take as their model. In the novel Gamboa blames Santa's downfall on her fatal flaw, a 'natural' propensity for vice (Castillo, 1998: 42). So, although like the *fichera* she is also seduced and abandoned, her fall into prostitution is always positioned as a result of her own lustful desires.

Hershfield suggests that in *Salón México* the duality of Mexican female identity is expressed through and reflected in the oppositions which structure the film:

> The film mirrors ['the double life of women in this period of economic instability'] visually and conceptually through the alternation between darkness and light, good and evil, and mother and whore. The world of the cabaret with its smoky dance halls, its dark and shabby hotels with unlit staircases and broken windows, is transformed with a mere cinematic dissolve to the brightly lit rooms of the College for Young Women, where cigarette smoke, alcohol, and prostitution cannot intrude. (1996: 91)

The dualistic argument common in Hershfield's and others' readings of *Salón México* and other *cabareteras* follows the Manichean scheme that Paz outlines, locking the female into a dichotomy of *mujer buena/mujer mala* (good woman/bad woman) (Ayala Blanco, 1993: 108–109), effectively imprisoning her as the other or as the object to be read without any alternative space for autonomous female desire (Paz, 1997 [1951]: 195). *Salón México* is, however, altogether less dichotomous and more ambiguous in its representation of Mexican women in the 1940s, and makes space for marginalized groups or ideologies through melodramatic excess, (dis)organization of the narrative and specific use of song and dance.

Melodrama

> 'In so far as [melodrama] is a genre that mobilizes emotion, melodrama is always potentially subversive, refusing containment.' (Kraniauskas 1997: xviii)

In chapter four it was suggested that, once love is mentioned in *Enamorada*, there is a shift from action toward melodrama and that this suggests a certain feminization in the text, challenging the overt gender ideology of the Revolution. This chapter looks at how melodrama offers a space for subversive pleasure within an otherwise restrictive moral context that challenges gender ideology as it relates to racial identity.

Melodrama has occupied an ambivalent position in film studies. In the early days of film theory it was dismissed as less appealing critically by film theorists for its (female) excessiveness and its highly emotional context in favor of the (more manly) gangster movies and westerns – or art cinema. In Latin America the theorists of the New Cinema of the

1960s and 1970s dismissed the 'colonizing tendencies' of melodramatic films like *Salón México* for 'reducing' complex social problems and injustices to an emotional level and for being ideologically conservative and complicit with the interests of the ruling classes (Colina and Díaz Torres, 1972: 14–16). However, in Europe and the US during the 1970s, feminism, psychoanalysis and a changed attitude toward the products of mass culture, such as melodrama, redeemed these texts from the accusation of superficiality and brought about a revalorization of the subversive potential of the genre – especially in the films of Douglas Sirk – to question (rather than uphold) the norms of patriarchal bourgeois society (Landy, 1991: 14, 20). In Latin America, changed perspectives toward mass culture in general, as well as restricted access to an official literary or institutional culture, have led theorists to proclaim melodrama in its different manifestations in radio, cinema, television and novels as *the* privileged genre of Latin American identity that 'personalises the political' and 'unifies' Latin America (Martín Barbero, 1998: 181; Monsiváis, 1994a: 8).

As well as this continental specificity, melodrama has also been linked to the development of (Mexican) national identity. Peter Brooks traces the emergence of melodrama as a dramatic and novelistic form in eighteenth-century Europe, arguing that melodrama 'fill[s] the vacuum of a post-Revolutionary world where traditional imperatives of truth and ethics had been violently questioned' (1991: 60). Monsiváis offers a similar explanation for the popularizing of melodrama within the national cinema, arguing that in Mexico's post-Revolutionary society, classical Mexican melodrama takes on the role of religion offering a marker of transcendental values and a means of making sense in an increasingly secularized society (1994a: 116).

These perspectives have provided the impetus in US studies for revaluations of the melodramatic form, the classical Mexican melodrama and the *cabaretera* genre in particular. López points out how melodrama in the more contemporary form of *telenovelas* (soap operas) has revealed the genre's radical potential (1991: 596–606). Podalsky rereads the disjointed story-frame in *María Candelaria* as a melodramatic element that contradicts national orthodoxy in terms of land reform and the indigenous population (1993a: 66–73).

In Mexican scholarship on the melodramatic genre, however, there has been little reevaluation of the genre and its subversive potential. Mexican melodrama is characterized as a series of oppositions, a struggle between good and evil, obligation and desire, sanctity and prostitution, fidelity and adultery (Monsiváis 1994b: 9). Monsiváis characterizes melodrama of the nineteenth and early part of the twentieth centuries as a vehicle of traditional bourgeois morality promoting the acceptance of social, racial and sexual inequality (ibid.). However, Monsiváis is also one of few Mexican cultural theorists to reevaluate melodrama and acknowledge a shift toward subversion. He suggests that from *La mujer del puerto* (1934) onward melodrama, impacted by industrialization and urbanization, begins to loosen its hold on moral absolutes giving 'oportunidad visual al pecado, a la concupiscencia y el deseo' (visual opportunity to sin, concupiscence and desire) (ibid.: 10). The simultaneous urbanization, industrialization and emergence of the 'fallen-woman' film in *Santa* and then *La mujer del puerto* is no accident. Prostitutes become the focus of this morally ambiguous melodrama. From the 1940s to 1960, Monsiváis suggests melodrama subverts traditional values via 'la presentación incitante del pecado' (the inciting presentation of sin) (ibid.). Ayala Blanco, on the other hand, positions the melodrama of the fallen woman (which develops into the *cabaretera* in the late 1940s and early 1950s) within more conventional melodramatic bourgeois morality, suggesting that it ultimately reinforces the status quo:

> Matrona burguesa o prostituta: no hay otra alternativa en el horizonte femenino. Polo opuesto a la madre y a las mujeres maternales, la prostituta restablece el equilibrio familiar, fundamenta la búsqueda mexicana de un arquetipo amoroso, compensa las insatisfacciones del macho, sublima el heroísmo civil y desencadena las pasiones melodramáticas; tras haber amenazado el *status*, terminará sirviéndolo.
>
> (Bourgeois matron or prostitute: there is no other alternative on the female horizon. As the opposite pole to the mother and the maternal woman, the prostitute reestablishes family equilibrium, lays the foundation in the search for an amorous archetype, compensates for the dissatisfactions of the macho, sublimates civic heroism and unleashes melodramatic passions; having already threatened the status quo she will end up serving it.) (Ayala Blanco, 1993: 108)

Ayala Blanco's and Monsiváis' evaluations of the melodrama diverge radically. Ayala Blanco's more conservative examination of *cabareteras* is strictly narrative-based, while Monsiváis' more subversive analysis is mise-en-scène-oriented. As such Monsiváis' work resembles that of Thomas Elsaesser and Geoffrey Nowell Smith. Elsaesser argues that, because melodrama is all about sublimation, dealing with everything that happens 'inside,' critical importance should be given more to the mise-en-scène rather than to the intellectual content of the story (1991: 76). Similarly, Nowell Smith's intervention suggests that as a bourgeois form, melodrama siphons off unrepresentable material into an excessive mise-en-scène (1987: 74). According to López, *cabareteras* similarly escape narrative constrictions through the excesses of mise-en-scène: 'And even when their narrative work suggests utter complicity with the work of the law, the emotional excesses set loose and the multiple desires detonated are not easily recuperated' (1993a: 153). Hence, rather than following the dichotomous approach to sexuality, female identity and femininity of the philosophy of Mexicanness that is repeated by film critics, my approach to *Salón México* and later *Víctimas del pecado* will be via those extranarrative elements of 'multiple desires' which act as a potential location of subversion as suggested by Elsaesser, Nowell Smith and López.

It is also important to take into account *Salón México*'s similarities to the Hollywood women's film of the 1940s. According to Christine Gledhill the Hollywood 'women's film,' a melodramatic subgenre, has been read as representing the needs of the male psyche to both disavow castration anxiety through fetishism and also affirm patriarchal domination through voyeuristic punishment (1987: 10). In Mexico, the women's film therefore seems eminently suitable to the expression of local concerns; the gender imperatives of dominant post-Revolutionary society; seeking to sooth a patriarchy in crisis through images of voyeurism, female castigation and dominant machismo.[1] However, in *Salón México* the greater emphasis on melodramatic elements, particularly the use of music, work against the containing patriarchy of the 'women's film.'

Music and dance, race and sexuality

The *cabaretera*, like most Mexican genres, is not a simple 'copy' but instead a transnational negotiation between national and Hollywood models. The *cabaretera* emerged in its initial form at a time when sound opened a window of opportunity for the Mexican film industry. Post the advent of sound (1927), Hollywood's temporary inability to satisfy the linguistic needs of the Latin American market allowed Mexico's nascent film industry to capitalize on the local audience and exploit national musical talent. *Santa* (1931), one of the first sound and 'fallen-woman' films, included several numbers, most importantly the title song 'Santa' written by Agustín Lara. From *Santa* onward the proto-*cabaretera*'s narrative structure grew out of a symbiotic relationship between narrative and music. The *cabaretera* is therefore a hybrid of the melodrama and the musical, in which music and dance become highly important as a 'central register for [melodramatic] excess' (López, 1997: 335). In the *cabaretera*, music is diegetically motivated through the locale (the cabaret) and the protagonists who are either performers/prostitutes or dancers. As with the Hollywood musical, in which the shape, movement and feeling as films are dictated by music, diegetic music plays an important part in shaping and developing narrative concerns. Unlike the Hollywood musical, however, these films 'do not weave music and dance in to a dual-focus narrative focused on heterosexual romance and the joy of coupling' (ibid.: 322). Instead, they arrest the narrative and invest it with emotion:

> In these and other films the narrative stoppage usually generated by performances was reinvested with emotion, so that melodramatic pathos emerged in the moment of performance itself (through gesture, sentiment, interactions with the audience within the film, or simply musical choice) . . . music and song rather than dramatic action propel the narrative. (López, 1993a: 149)

To date, other than the work of López, little detailed study of music and dance in these melodramas exists. However, the work of Dyer on the ways in which song-and-dance numbers in Hollywood musicals can function ideologically provides a useful basis for study of the *cabaretera*'s subversive potential. He argues that the emotional qualities offered by musicals – abundance, energy, intensity, transparency and community – work politically in relation to 'everyday life' by filling a compensatory role: for example, 'abundance' compensates for 'actual poverty in society', or 'intensity' makes up for dreariness (Dyer, 1992: 20–1, 24). Taking these conclusions a step further, Dyer then argues that the only political issues which entertainment addresses (or compensates for) are those which it is capable of solving *itself* – ultimately leading to the exclusion of marginal concerns such as 'class, race and sexual caste' that the musical as a bourgeois form cannot incorporate within its dominant ideology. In the *cabaretera*, however, those marginalized concerns which Dyer suggests are excluded from bourgeois forms are actually often incorporated through popular strategies, particularly song-and-dance numbers. In *Salón México* the conservative Revolutionary moral and ideological discourse of female sacrifice and patriarchal orthodoxy is in fact undermined by an emotional and visual investment in the interests of the other which is largely expressed through music and dance.

How can music and dance as emotive factors within melodrama function politically, not just in a 'compensatory role' but in a radical one? Dyer argues that the taken-for-granted description of entertainment as 'escape' points to its central thrust: 'utopianism.' Dyer's ideas are not unlike those of Monsiváis, who himself has suggested that the realm of sentiment is not to be undervalued or dismissed politically (Monsiváis, 1997). In a history of the *bolero*, one of the most popular song-forms in Mexico and highly important to the shape and form of the *cabaretera*, Monsiváis charts its development from a rural love song to an urban form of expression with political resonances intimately linked to melodrama. For example, the *boleros* written and recorded by the singer-composer Lara, which frequently provided 'the central dramatic impulse propelling the action of many *cabaretera* films' (López, 1993a: 159), expressed sympathy with marginalized groups, usually prostitutes. Lara's *boleros* have also been read as signifying Mexico's passage into modernity, through their focus on the nocturnal, perfidious existence of urban living. Indeed, with respect to this transitional moment in Mexican culture, Monsiváis writes about *bolero's* metamorphosis. He suggests that '[s]ong adds psychological credibility to cabaret, and through the medium of jukeboxes, collectivities gathered in bars and cafés hear songs that make intimate history a public concern – the autobiography of everyone and no one' (1997: 192).

Monsiváis is suggesting that music functions ideologically as a vehicle of subaltern or marginalized subjectivity. A *bolero* sequence from the *cabaretera Aventurera* demonstrates his point when the lyrics are linked to the subjectivity of the female protagonist. In one scene, Pedro Vargas sings the title song 'Adventuress' written by Lara while Elena (Ninón Sevilla), a *rumbera* (dancer, but also it is suggested prostitute) in a smart nightclub, wanders around in front of the stage. Rather than focusing on the singer, the very popular Vargas, the camera follows Elena around the room and eye-line matches suggest he is really singing to her. The lyrics implore: 'Vende caro tu amor Aventurera/ Da el precio del dolor a tu pasado/Y aquél que de tus labios la miel quiera/que pague con brilliantes tu pecado' (Sell your love expensively Adventuress/Give a price to the pain of your past/And he who wants honey from your lips/Let him pay for your sins with diamonds). Interestingly enough, this proto-feminist moment of self-awareness is considered by conventional criticism to be an anomaly in the otherwise patriarchally organized *cabaretera* genre. The music in *Salón México*, for example, is considered more representative of how music works in the genre, seemingly never commenting on Mercedes' predicament or state of mind, nor motivated from her point of view as with *Aventurera*. And *Aventurera*'s ending, in which the *rumbera* emerges alive and happy (i.e., unpunished for her 'sin'), is not common in the *cabaretera* where most (like Mercedes) end up dead (or at the very least punished and excluded from society).

Dance and the way in which it functions in *Salón México* provides an interesting perspective on how the film fits within both the generic features of the *cabaretera* and auteurist understandings of what constitutes a Fernández film. Although initially the music and dance in *Salón México* seem to confirm its status as a women's film in terms of female suffering and castigation by not offering Mercedes subjective perspective as in *Aventurera*, music and dance actually work to undermine the moral dichotomies of the women's film and Mexican cultural nationalism.

In an influential essay (1993) Dyer examines the formal qualities of couple dances in cinema in relation to the construction of the heterosexual ideal: the 'heavenly feeling' in the Astaire-Rodgers films of the 1930s (*Top Hat*, 1935), a number of MGM musicals of the 1940s and 1950s (*On the Town*, 1949) and several 1980s musicals (*Dirty Dancing*, 1987). Dyer's interpretation of dance as it is used in Hollywood musicals helps us to examine sites of subversion in the *cabaretera* cinema. He argues that the steps of the dance in these different films represent in each case different developing gender dynamics between the couple (1993: 49–51).

Near the beginning of *Salón México* we see Mercedes dancing in a *danzón* competition with her pimp. There is an initial establishing shot where we see the dance taking place. Then we cut to an exchange between Paco and someone offstage, telling the person to make sure that he wins the competition. This sets up the dance as important to Paco's sense of manhood, suggesting that winning it (by coercion) is important to his sense of masculinity. Dance here functions more as part of the women's film narrative (in terms of asserting an insecure masculinity) rather than in terms of the musical (coupledom). We then cut back to the long shot of the couples dancing onstage. The shot dissolves (though there is no musical break) to give a sense of time-lapse and reveals a reduced number of couples dancing. Then the shot cuts to a medium shot of Paco and Mercedes dancing together. When she tells him she needs the prize money he tells her: 'Muévete bien y ya veremos' (Dance well, and we'll see what happens). Here, dancing is explicitly tied to economic survival (and hence Mexican cultural nationalism). The shot cuts to their feet as the music swells on the soundtrack. The camera is almost at floor level as it shows us Mercedes and Paco dancing: a position which prioritizes footwork and, of course, her extremely high shoes.

On a narrative level, the camera position is used to express the sacrifice of the female body for the greater good of society. In this sense *Salón México* is a typical 'women's film', one which, as feminist film theorists have argued, inscribes patriarchy's attempt to access (then symbolically control and repress) that female desire which remains one of its threatening others. And indeed we do get the impression that Mercedes is suffering through the dance rather than experiencing the 'heavenly feeling' of heterosexual coupledom. This sacrifice of body (because within the terms of Mexican cultural nationalism there can be no pleasure) is expressed through the camerawork and the rhythms of the editing around Mercedes, who gives up her body as a *fichera* in order to educate her younger sister. When the film cuts to two other couples dancing, the camera pans upward from feet to heads and shoulders so that we get more of a sense of their complete bodies, whereas with Mercedes and Paco the film cuts between their heads and shoulders and feet, thus fragmenting their bodies. Mercedes is represented not as a whole, but as a fetishized object for the male gaze. Furthermore, the camera's concentration on shoes (which appear even sexier in close-up, and are her 'tools of the trade') signal the fact that Mercedes is a prostitute. All the women at the respectable College for girls significantly wear flats. As a classic fetish object the high heel shoe is inscribed within patriarchal codes, immobilizing woman in order to better display her as an object for spectacle.

The use of the high-heeled shoe is a common iconographical feature of *cabaretera* films. Another *cabaretera*, *Trotacalles* (Street Walker, Matilde Landeta, 1951) makes a similar use of high heels as graphic shorthand for prostitution in a sequence which depicts a 'pick-up' entirely through shots from the knee downward. In the credit sequence of *Trotacalles* we see a dingy, noirish pavement lined with women's feet wearing high heels. A pair of men's shoes approaches a pair of these women's shoes. After a brief pause where the two pairs of shoes linger together (as if their wearers were coming to an agreement) the man's shoes and woman's shoes walk together down the street and into a doorway. After a dissolve suggesting a time lapse, the woman's shoes reemerge from the doorway and come back out onto the street. As in the opening of *Trotacalles*, in the *danzón* sequence in *Salón México*, the close camerawork – also from the knee downward – and editing, coupled with the smoky room and chiaroscuro lighting, creates an erotically charged atmosphere: dance between a man and a woman becomes a sublimation of the sexual act itself, of what goes on from the knee upward. Through the way it is shot, the environment in which it is placed (a smoky dance hall) and the morally repressive context of which it is a part, the dance in *Salón México* is explicitly sexualized and patriarchal, in the sense of physical male domination and female subordination. Mercedes dances when Paco orders her to. Proper gender roles, male domination and female submission, are emphasized and guaranteed.

However, we could offer a reading of dance in *Salón México* in less morally descriptive terms that takes account of the other perspectives the film offers. It is not the presentation of dance as an erotically charged metaphor for sex that problematizes its easy identification with a patriarchal conservative moral orthodoxy. Dance as sex is a commonplace in classical Mexican cinema (Tuñón, 1997: 239). However, the camera's greater pleasure in depicting this 'Mexico que no debe ser' (Mexico as it shouldn't be) as opposed to moral orthodoxy and the resultant blurring of Fernándezian moral and social polarities (Hershfield, 1996: 83) does present certain problems to placing it within an industrial and authorial context. On the level of pleasure, the very close attention to the movements of the dance, matched by the increased volume of the music on the sound-track as we cut to the footwork, signals the camera's investment in following Mercedes and Paco as they flawlessly execute the very intricate and controlled steps of the *danzón*. García Riera writes about the closeness of the camera and what this might signify: 'La misma camera que guarda una respetuosa distancia en el colegio se siente autorizada en el Salón a participar gozosamente . . . del relajo general. Inquieta y curiosa seguía los sabrosos movimientos de los bailarines' (The same camera that remains at a respectful distance at the school feels authorized in the Salon [dance hall] to lustfully participate in the general debauchery. Restless and curious it follows the racy movements of the dancers.) (1993d: 264–6). Also at this point we hear exclamations from the diegetic audience '¡Mueva!' (Move it), their pleasure emphasizing the camera's pleasure at the scene it is depicting. This intense focus on and pleasure derived from sublimated sex challenges an auteurist reading of the film because Fernández is famous for his puritan tendencies as a director. So great was his disapproval of any sexual display in his films that he would not even show a romantic couple kiss on the lips (Tuñón, 2000: 166).

The intensely pleasurable *danzón* sequence is matched by a number of equally pleasurable dance sequences throughout the film. These dance sequences, which are offered directly to the audience unmediated by characters' point of view and seemingly not integrated into the narrative, further disrupt the morally conservative narrative of *Salón México* by investing in the depiction of a different order. These interstitial dance sequences allow the other to interrupt into the rigid racial and sexual dualities that shape dominant Mexican identity, the *mujer buena/mujer mala* (the good woman/bad woman), the Creole/Indian. With respect to these spaces López argues that 'beyond the national paradigm, music and dance operate in "other" spaces – domestic and semi public spheres – where they serve as vehicles for different forms of transgressions and crossings linked to desire and other processes of identity formation and contestation' (1997: 312).

Looking at these interstitial moments of excess in the text as sites of subversion is an approach commensurate with the many cultural studies, queer theory and postcolonial theory advocates who all suggest the 'in-between' or 'moment of slippage' is a useful way of theorizing how subaltern culture may counter the dominant (national or metro-politan) culture outside a scheme that reifies center/periphery relations (Bhabha, 1994: 25).[2] Furthermore, the cabaret itself represents according to Monsiváis a kind of interstitial space: 'a moral hell and sensorial heaven, where the "forbidden" was normalised' (1995c: 118).

The first interstitial dance significantly comes almost immediately after Mercedes and Paco's *danzón*. Mercedes has followed Paco to the door of the Salón México to 'beg' him for a share of the prize money. He pushes her back and we hear drums on the soundtrack. As she goes to follow him the camera (which is lingering at the door), rather than following her (the principle character as classical convention dictates), cuts back inside (as if called by the drums) to a shot of a lady frantically dancing an accelerated rumba.

Although it is within the bounds of classical continuity editing for the camera to follow aural as well as visual cues, that the camera leaves

Mercedes – the main character – suggests an alienating departure from the norms of narrative convention. However, this is merely one example of what is in fact the organizing sensibility of the film – i.e., the camera's focus on 'forbidden' spectacle. As the credits end a *danzón* begins and, as the first few notes ring out, the camera pans upward to a lighted sign 'Salón México' and then down to observe women entering the dance hall. It comes to rest on Mercedes as Lupe lights her cigarette. Then it cuts inside to a close-up of a smiling percussion player then pulls back to show the rest of the band and then couples dancing on a stage. This opening gives the sense that the camera is drawn in to the dance hall by an attraction to its music, and also to 'el México que no debe ser' (Mexico as it should not be) that it represents.

When the camera cuts away from Mercedes to the energetic rumba dancer we note that, whereas Mercedes dances with Paco because he tells her to, this lady dances alone and of her own free will. The fact that she dances in a ring of people and not on the stage behind her, gives her dance an air of spontaneity rather than performance. She wears a *rumbera* outfit exposing her thighs, midriff and chest (in contrast to Mercedes' quite demur outfit). She is filmed in long shot – not in the fetishistic sequence of close-ups as with Mercedes. Her movements are fluid and liberated, in contrast to the rigid restraint and elegance of the *danzón* (Aspden, 1992: 41). She leans backward, constantly wiggling her breasts and hips. The audience, gathered round her in a circle, shouts and exclaims. With the woman's semi-nudity, enjoyment and physical display, this sequence is as suggestive a sexual display as the *danzón* sequence – the musicians, who accompany her, enthusiastically tap and bang on a variety of phallic-shaped percussion instruments.[3] However, dance is not displayed voyeuristically but in long shot which allows us to see the woman's face and more importantly her own enjoyment. Sexuality is not sublimated but out in the open. After a few moments a man joins the woman. They dance apart for a while and then he takes her and swings her around. But he does not hold her with any sense of permanence or control as with the *danzón*, still allowing her to pull away from him and do her own steps.

Reading the film according to sexual mores of cultural nationalism, Hershfield has interpreted this and the other showcased dance sequences as offering an image of exotic sexuality, of an other which underscores Mexico's own more conservative sexual code (1996: 103). The display of this and other women who dance in later sequences, free from the bounds of patriarchal and restrictive coupledom as in the terms of the dance, suggests, according to Hershfield, a liberated sexuality not permissible within the bounds of Mexican morality. The fact that she dances solely to drums and other percussion instruments, as well as the semi-nakedness of the performer/dancer, also problematically suggest ideas of primitivism. Hershfield argues that the liberated sexual display is only permissible because this woman is clearly signalled through the Afro-Cuban music, dance and costume as other, as non-Mexican and hence outside the bounds of Mexican national identity. Indeed, it is a generic convention of the *cabaretera* genre to locate its sexual excesses outside of Mexico – this is perhaps why the Cuban *rumberas* Ninón Sevilla and María Antonieta Pons were so successful in films of this genre. Although they play Mexicans in the films, it is sufficient that they speak (and dance) like Cubans to suggest that they are really from elsewhere.

However, rather than reading these interstitial dance sequences as necessarily a projection of 'unacceptable' sexualities onto other nations, it could also be read as a highlighting of Mexico's own African heritage. Part of the difficulty with Hershfield's reading of the showcased dance sequences in *Salón México* is the way she positions them within Mexico's racial history. In relation to the *cabaretera*, Hershfield does not take into consideration Mexico's Afro-Mexican population, presuming that these sequences are necessarily about an external (i.e., Cuban) rather than an internal other.[4] Hershfield repeats the processes of Mexican nationalism as described by Lomitz Adler, which forge the *mestizo* (mixed-race) son of an Indian mother and a European father as its protagonist and elide the third racial component in its history, the African (Lomitz Adler, 1992: 262).[5] Lomitz Adler points out how, from the complicated colonial caste system onward, in which Indian blood was entirely redeemable through marriage (i.e., could become 'white'), whereas African blood was not, the Afro-Mexican element has always been denigrated/disavowed by Mexican cultural nationalism (ibid.: 273). Analyses of *cabareteras* which read its *rumberas* and Afro rhythms as necessarily other continue this nationalist disavowal.

Admittedly, even if the provenance of the dancers in these sequences is potentially more local than allowed for by most readings, the music played in these free-style sequences, which have been read as depicting an alternative to the rigid, structured *danzón*, is Afro-Cuban and the musicians who play are often famous Cuban or at least non-Mexican performers.[6] However, juxtaposing these two rhythms to contrast with each other, like a set of polar opposites (like those of the melodramatic form) in which one (the rumba) acts as a counterpoint to the other, in this case dominant sexuality and gender behavior (the *danzón*), does not work either. The *danzón* is *also* a Cuban form and therefore problematic in the way it is meant to stand in for a certain kind of gendered Mexican national identity. And, like the rumba, it is also a syncretic music form as a mixture of French Creole *contradanza* and Afro-Cuban and Spanish rhythms which problematizes its representation as a national essence of either Afro-Cuban or Afro-Mexican identity (López, 1997: 311, 336). After all, although to a lesser extent, French Creole, African and Spanish elements have *also* combined in the formation of a hybrid Mexican cultural and racial identity. As López points out, 'the idea of these specific rhythms as emblems of the nation already involves the process of appropriation and assimilation of differences . . . when we talk about the circulation of such rhythms outside the nation-state in question' (ibid.: 312).

In a later interstitial sequence, the shot cuts from the brightly lit girls' school where at a very proper tea party Beatriz first meets Roberto, to a trumpet player writhing around in seeming ecstasy on the stage of the Salón México. It is a very pleasurable sequence both formally and in terms of the way music is the leading element in the organization of the shot. The trumpeter times his writhing so that he comes to a stop with the trumpet playing directly into camera, the trumpet horn appearing huge within the frame. Hershfield suggests the film is structured so that 'cigarette smoke, alcohol, and prostitution' cannot intrude into the Mexico of moral orthodoxy (1996: 91). This sequence, however, implies the interconnectedness of the two Mexicos; that of moral orthodoxy in which Beatriz will marry the Pilot and gain ascendance into 'Mexico's Revolutionary family' and that of the underworld of the cabaret where pimping, prostitution and robbery happen daily, and on which, ironically this union depends. (If Beatriz' education had not been funded by this underworld, she would not have met and become engaged to Roberto, the headmistress' son). The textual organization of the film suggests that these two Mexicos are not polar opposites, as traditional Fernandezian scholarship contests, but symbiotically related. This interdependence is further underlined when Roberto turns up at the Salón México, with some American soldier buddies, and Mercedes is called on to 'entertain' them.

Las abandonadas

There is a similar 'continuity' between the Mexico of moral orthodoxy and underworld Mexico in the earlier Fernández 'fallen-woman' film *Las abandonadas*. *Las abandonadas* is often interpreted as reinforcing conservative discourses about the Revolution: patriarchal dominance and female sacrifice. However, the film can also be read as a questioning of the rigid hierarchies of conservative post-Revolutionary cultural nationalism. Like *Salón México* and *Aventurera*, *Las abandonadas* shows a 'respectable,' professional middle class subsidized by and dependent on the processes of crime and the labor of the poor. As Tuñón suggests, '[in *Las abandonadas*] the traditional fields of good and evil share the same foundations' (2000: 159). To a certain extent this continuity between Mexico as it should be (conservative) and Mexico as it should not be is already signified in the prostitute paradigm where the protagonists in these fallen-woman films are often both decent women and 'bad women' – i.e., they retain a spiritual morality.

The film begins in 'turbulent Mexico of 1914' in a coastal town. Margarita (Del Rio) abandoned by her new husband (Victor Junco) discovers he is already married. Pregnant, she is thrown out by her father and travels to the capital in search of work. She works in a laundry until her child is born, and then becomes a high-class prostitute to support the child, Margarito. One night a group of soldiers appear at the brothel where she works. General Juan Gómez (Armendáriz) is stupefied by her beauty and takes her to live with him in a huge house. Their idyllic life together is marred only by his jealousy and possessiveness which lead her to hide the fact that she has a son. Everything comes to an abrupt end when it emerges that he is a false general, leading the infamous Grey Car Gang, using army uniforms to rob wealthy Mexico City residents. He is killed resisting arrest while she is sentenced to prison. On release from prison eight years later she visits Margarito at the orphanage and seeing in him someone who could become a 'great man like those who appear in newspapers' chooses not to tell him she is his mother. To pay for his education she returns to prostitution, first on the streets and then in dingy bars. Her son becomes a lawyer (also played by Junco) and, now old and ragged, she listens to him defend his first client, a woman accused of murder. He wins the case and is carried by the public out of the courtroom. Bumping into Margarita, he takes her for a beggar, giving her a coin which she clasps to her bosom.

To a certain extent *Las abandonadas* can be read as supporting a conservative post-Revolutionary system. The film suggests that in the meritocracy made possible by the revolution there are no social classes or boundaries. An 'orphan' (like Margarito), thanks to a beneficent state (that runs the orphanage he grows up in), can become a great lawyer. Further emphasizing the film's conservative ideology is the way it recounts Margarita's downfall which ends up with her in a brothel. Unable to get a job elsewhere due to the lack of a union card she works before the baby is born at a laundry. (The film hence performs a subtle criticism of union practices.) As part of this conservative ideology the film also displays the 'proper' segregation of underworld Mexico from morally orthodox Mexico. Margarita (like Mercedes in *Salón México* and Violeta in *Víctimas del pecado*) hides her profession from her child. One scene in particular illustrates the segregation of these two worlds. At his birthday Margarito is to have his photograph taken dressed as a *charro*. Margarita's 'colleagues' withdraw one by one from the picture as if not wanting to 'taint' the pure little boy with their 'shame.' (They all wear very lavish but also very gaudy clothes, which signal they are prostitutes.) Eventually, Margarita also withdraws, leaving her little boy alone in his photograph. His mother and her career are symbolically expunged from the boy's life, thus ensuring the proper division between respectable and 'disrespectful' worlds. However, the fact that Margarita and her colleagues linger at the edges of the frame, just out of the photograph but close to the boy within the diegetic frame, hints at the interdependency of these two worlds. This is further underlined and developed by the fact that Margarito's education as a lawyer has been funded (unbeknownst to him) by his mother's prostitution and stealing.

That the film plays with the discrepancy between appearance (moral orthodoxy) and reality (underhand dealings), and that the former is often dependent on the latter, is further suggested by the film's false-general plot: Juan and Margo lead an upper-class, cultured life on the proceeds of his robberies, until the subterfuge is discovered and their magical world instantly falls apart. That this points toward a similar discrepancy in contemporary Mexico is suggested by the fact that *Las abandonadas* had problems with the censors. It appears that the scenes of military misbehavior unsettled military powers who feared it would threaten the prestige of the armed forces – especially because the leader of the historical Grey Car Gang was rumored to indeed have been a real general (García Riera, 1987: 63, 67). To calm such concerns and conform to the censors' demands, Fernández had to add a scene in which Juan Gómez takes the uniform from the body of a dead general on the battlefield, and to add a subtitle situating the film in a 'turbulent' 1914 (ibid.: 63).

Víctimas del pecado

When *Víctimas del pecado* premiered in France in 1952 it was a huge success, and many French critics preferred it to *Aventurera*. Although considered part of Fernández' canonical 1940s work, it is generally given less attention in criticism, potentially because it does not conform to auteurist paradigms.

Violeta (Niñon Sevilla) is a *rumbera* but also *fichera* at the Changoo cabaret. Rosa (Margarita Ceballos), another *fichera*, has had a baby by Rodolfo (Rodolfo Acosta) her pimp. Rosa, desperate to get back with Rodolfo leaves her baby in a bin. Violeta arrives just in time to save the baby from the garbage truck. Fired from her job, in order to survive and look after the baby Violeta must become a street prostitute. One night Rodolfo finds her and tries to harm the child. When the fight brings them before a judge she denounces him as perpetrator of a recent robbery. Feeling sorry for her, one client – Santiago (Tito Junco) – offers her a job in his cabaret, the Maquina Loca (the Crazy Machine). Santiago and Violeta fall in love and baptize the baby Juanito. Six years later Juanito is at boarding school and calls Violeta and Santiago mum and dad. Rodolfo gets out of prison and kills Santiago. The cabaret is closed. Rodolfo takes Juanito out of school with a plan to use him in his next robbery. Violeta arrives just as Rodolfo is beating Juanito. She shoots him dead. She is imprisoned and Juanito becomes a newspaper boy and shoe-shine. One day he arrives at the prison too late to give Violeta the shoes he has bought her for mother's day. The prison Warden (Arturo Soto Rangel) finds Juanito outside the prison and, after a phone call to the President, Violeta is pardoned. She and Juanito walk out of the prison hand in hand.

On a narrative level the film supports conservative cultural nationalism through the ideology of family orthodoxy and national unity emphasizing maternity (Violeta's strong maternal instinct: her release from prison is largely on the grounds that her imprisonment means a child is left without a mother) and patriarchy (Santiago offers Violeta a job when he sees the child and they subsequently form a family). As with *Salón México*, in *Víctimas* aspects of the women's film are key, in forwarding this conservative ideology. Showcased dance sequences where Violeta performs Afro-Cuban numbers in revealing costumes for a largely diegetic male audience (at times because she is forced to by her abusive boss), seemingly disavow castration anxiety through voyeurism. (Gledhill, 1987: 10) Similarly, sequences where Rodolfo either beats Violeta, or where she struggles on hands and knees to wash the floor in the prison, seemingly affirm patriarchal domination through voyeuristic punishment (ibid.). Indeed *danzón* itself becomes a much more literal female punishment in *Víctimas* than in *Salón México*. After Rosa is forced to abandon her baby Rodolfo puts her straight back to work dancing. She dances with a client and with tears in her eyes but a smile on her face, suffering the loss of her child so she can be with Rodolfo. As the title of the film suggests, women are passive, suffering victims reinforcing the conservative discourse of post-Revolutionary gender imperatives and the women's film.

But there are elements in *Víctimas* which allow for readings in less morally descriptive terms. As with *Salón Mexico*, ideological discourses of female sacrifice and patriarchal orthodoxy are potentially undermined by the film's emotional and visual investment in the interests of the other, particularly during dance sequences.

First, although Violeta is victimized by men – specifically Rodolfo (who beats her up, kills her husband and tries to take Juanito from her), and also by the law (sent to prison for shooting Rodolfo when she was only defending her son), she and other women are not always presented as victims. Violeta is by no means an abnegated woman in the way Mercedes and Margarita are, but an active agent (and her dancing is an important part of this). When Violeta is put upon, she fights back (first at her boss Don Gonzalo and then at Rodolfo when he tries to harm Juanito). At the Changoo, although she is a *fichera*, she significantly appears not to have or need a pimp. Instead she has Rita Montaner as her godmother, giving her the chance to be a *rumbera*. Furthermore, Violeta does not display the passivity associated with victimhood. She is resourceful. So are the other women who burst in when Rodolfo is beating her and start beating him. Women are not necessarily depicted as victims of *sin* (as auteurist readings of the film suggest), but as victims of patriarchy and an economic crisis, which gives them few options other than prostitution.

Secondly, although it is made clear that dancing is her job (and sometimes she is forced into it), it is also communicated (particularly when she tells Montaner how happy she is at being allowed to perform numbers at the Changoo) that Violeta thoroughly enjoys dancing. Even when she is just dancing as a *fichera* and not performing as a *rumbera*, Violeta steps away from her client to do her own steps in a way that appears completely for her own pleasure. This relationship toward dance problematizes the notion that as a *cabaretera* the film necessarily offers scenes of female punishment in order to soothe an insecure patriarchy. The camerawork in the dance sequences is also not voyeuristic in terms of fragmenting her body for male consumption (unlike the *danzón* sequence in *Salón Mexico*). Violeta's dance sequences are shot mainly in high angle, long shots or plan américain that show her whole or almost her whole body.

With the chiaroscuro lighting and smoky atmosphere in the Maquina Loca, dance sequences are as erotically charged as dance sequences in *Salón Mexico*. However, this eroticism is not necessarily figured as one of patriarchal domination. This is largely because Violeta's pleasure at dancing is continually highlighted. One dance sequence in particular emphasizes Violeta as agent of her own dancing pleasure and thus questions the mores of Mexican bourgeois morality. One night, Violeta offers to stand in for the *rumbera* who has walked out. The spontaneity of her performance is emphasized by the fact that she is not wearing the *rumbera* outfit (which exposes thighs, stomach and breasts), but a more demure evening dress (which has the effect of making her less of an object of male voyeurism). Violeta dances freestyle initially in front of the band, half facing toward them, taking her cue from their rhythms. She then drags one of the black musicians up to dance with her. Although they dance together, they do not hold each other, but mirror each other's steps in a kind of duel format – she does a step and then he answers with a different step. The smiles on their faces make it clear that they are taking mutual pleasure from each other's dance. At one point she lies on her back and at another she wiggles her behind in his face. This is an immensely erotic sequence and highly unusual in classical Mexican cinema because of its interracial nature – a white woman dancing with a black man. This dance sequence works against the containing patriarchy and racial ideology of Mexican cultural nationalism (which excludes the Afro Mexican in favor of the *criollo, mestizo* or *indígena*). The protagonist's dance in *Salón México* is explicitly patriarchal, in the sense of physical male domination and female subordination (Mercedes dances because Paco tells her to) – but not in *Víctimas* (Violeta dances of her own volition and furthermore picks someone to dance with her). Whereas in *Salón Mexico* the challenge to bourgeois morality happens in interstitial dance moments, in *Victimas* this challenge is presented through the major character.

What is most progressive about *Víctimas* is that, unlike in *Salón México* and *Las abandonadas*, the protagonist is not ultimately punished through either death or debasement. Violeta is released from prison so she can be with her son. However, other aspects of the ending recuperate the narrative and its subversive elements within a discourse of patriarchy. Violeta is pardoned by the president (the ultimate patriarch). The agent of her release is the paternal prison Warden (whose voice-over sends Violeta and Juanito off into the world of moral orthodoxy, a world in which 'goodness and love still reign despite evil and ambition').

This analysis has sought to destabilize the rigid melodramatic, social, racial and gender paradigms upon which readings of *Salón México, Las abandonadas* and *Víctimas del pecado* are based. It has attempted to show how the unacceptable 'other' (the liberated sexuality of the lone female dancer) is not necessarily the opposite but in fact an integral part of the image of the nation. In the case of *Salón Mexico*, through a focus on camera work, this analysis has shown the slippages between the college and the dance hall, the respectable world and the world of vice and corruption, and how these exist in a continuum rather than in a dichotomy. To a certain extent, rather than an anomaly this is another critically disavowed generic feature of the *cabaretera*. Like *Salón Mexico* and *Las abandonadas, Aventurera* also posits a link between Mexican propriety (the world of Guadalajara's upper classes) and the brothel and between the decent woman and the *mujer mala* (Tuñón, 2000: 159). In Guadalajara, Rosaura (Andrea Palma) maintains her sons in the upper-class life to which they are accustomed by, unbeknownst to them, running a brothel in Ciudad Juárez.

Salón México, Las abandonadas and *Víctimas* are less morally dichotomous in their representation of Mexican women and the struggle for modernity in the 1940s than much of conventional scholarship allows for. In the case of *Salón México* and *Víctimas*, some dance sequences open a space for marginalized groups (Mexico's disavowed Afro-Mexican population). Music and dance work to undermine the dichotomies of the film. The distinction between 'el Mexico que no debe ser' (Mexico as it should not be) and 'el Mexico que debe ser' (Mexico as it should be) is further blurred by the fact that the contemporary proliferation of cabarets and brothels, violence and

Gender, sexuality and the Revolution, 2

indeed the *cabaretera* film itself is often interpreted as a reflection of the corrupt economic policies of President Miguel Alemán (1946–1952) which were in turn considered to be 'prostituting' the country (Ayala Blanco, 1993: 133, De la Vega Alfaro, 1999: 167).

Notes

1   However, the women's film has also been valued by feminists inasmuch as it reveals the contradictions of patriarchy, for 'the large space it opened to female protagonists, the domestic sphere and socially mandated "feminine" concerns' (Gledhill, 1987: 10).
2   In Bhabha's 'The Commitment to Theory' he discusses the ability of theory to open up the dichotomies of master/slave or oppositions in culture to an in-between space that is *'neither one nor the other'* but something else besides (1994: 25).
3   There is a similarly suggestive sexual display that functions both for the enjoyment of a diegetic audience and that of the female performer, and also happens in semispontaneous mode in the 1949 remake of *La mujer del puerto* (Emilio Gómez Muriel). Noticing an attractive stranger, Rosario (María Antonieta Pons) does an impromptu jazz routine in a bar. Her pleasure at dancing and that of the bar's occupants in watching her make this one of the most sexually charged sequences in classical Mexican cinema.
4   Elsewhere, Hershfield (1999: 92–96) does a very useful analysis of two classical Mexican films which feature Afro-Mexican characters and the problematic issue of the marginalized Afro-Mexican population: *La negra Angustias* (Matilde Landeta, 1949) and *Angelitos negros* (Joselito Rodríguez, 1948).
5   Like most of the Americas, Mexico began importing Africans as slaves in the sixteenth century. Over a period of three centuries until its abolition in 1829, slavery brought around 200,000 Africans to Mexico.
6   In *Salón México*, the featured band El Son Clave de Oro are a Cuban band. *Víctimas del Pecado* features the famous Afro-Cuban singer Rita Montaner both performing and acting.

6

Progress, modernity and Fernández' 'antimodernist utopia': *Río Escondido*

In earlier chapters we have explored and sought to problematize the role that Fernández' films play in the project of cultural nationalism. In this chapter, through Fernández' *Río Escondido* (Hidden River, 1947) we question another key element within the post-Revolution redefinition of Mexico – necessary consonance of Fernández' films with conservative, Government ideology. Specifically, we explore the tensions between Government discourses of progress and modernity and *Río Escondido*'s representation of Mexico. At the same time, this chapter takes issue with the idea that this film (along with all Fernández' films) represents an 'antimodernist utopia' antithetical to progress and modernity, and suggests instead that it is firmly rooted in the contemporary moment (and problems) of its production (Acevedo-Muñoz, 2003: 66).

In *Río Escondido*, Rosaura Salazar (María Félix) is sent by the President to Río Escondido, a village located in an arid and desert-like environment north of Mexico City. Her efforts to set up a school and educate the village's indigenous population are opposed by Don Regino Sandoval (Carlos López Moctezuma). He is the *Presidente Municipal* (Mayor) who exercises a *cacique* (boss)-like control over the village and its inhabitants.[1] With the help of Felipe (Fernando Fernández), a student doctor doing his rural service in a nearby village and also sent 'personally' by the President, Rosaura establishes a school, successfully rids the village of smallpox, and rehabilitates the drunken local priest (Domingo Soler). When Don Regino kills her adopted son, Rosaura defies him by holding an all-night *velatorio* (wake). Don Regino attempts to 'subdue' Rosaura and save his 'loss of face' by raping her. Instead, she shoots him dead. The newly emboldened villagers rise up and kill his complicit henchmen. She suffers a heart attack, surviving only to write to tell the President of her success in educating Río Escondido and to receive his grateful reply. She dies and is buried in Río Escondido.

Although, *Río Escondido* seemingly furthers the State's claim to be Revolutionary by figuring a revolutionary struggle and victory – a dispute over *land* and *resources* (evil cacique bars villagers access to water and education) solved by a heroic schoolteacher via a popular uprising of armed and angry peasants returning land and power to '*los de abajo*' (the underclass) – as a direct result of centrally organized state reforms (i.e., the Government literacy program), we find that the very revolutionary actions the film celebrates are simultaneously disavowed as part of Mexico's contemporary reality.

The Government and the (myth of the) revolution

> This story is not about the Mexico of today, nor has it been our intention to situate it there. [This story] attempts to symbolize the drama of a nation that, like other great nations of the world, has emerged *out of a bloody past* and is on its way toward great and wonderful achievements. (*Río Escondido*)

Most readings of *Río Escondido* figure it as emblematic both of the Fernández-Figueroa 'nationalist aesthetic' and the cultural institutionalization of the Revolution (Berg, 1994: 14). Indeed, inasmuch as it presents itself as a revolutionary-inspired yet at the same time conservative narrative of State-orchestrated defense and enablement of the underclass (Rosaura is sent by the President) *and* as a self-reflexive commentary on the project of Mexican cultural nationalism – i.e., educating the masses in Mexican national identity – *Río Escondido* is considered Fernández' most canonical and 'nationalist' film. But one of the most curious facts about the supposedly 'ultra'-nationalist *Río Escondido* is that it opens with the above disclaimer, disavowing its connection to the contemporary moment of Miguel Alemán's presidency (1946–52). This disavowal sets up an opposition between *alemanista* discourses and those of the text. The disclaimer also sets up a suggested time frame of before and after: before as the events and ideologies of the revolution (the '*bloody past*') and after as the period post-revolution up to and including the contemporary moment (the 'Mexico of today'). The following reading of *Río Escondido* analyzes the ways in which the film sets up the notion of the historical revolution (the before as a struggle of ideas, land reform, social justice) and goes on to analyze how the content and style of the film represents a threat to the notion of an after (a Mexico 'on its way to great and wonderful achievements'). This reading suggests that by placing the 'before' moment of insurrectionary violence in 1940s Mexico, the film threatens the ideological legitimacy and stability of the Alemán Government.

Río Escondido (like the rest of classical Mexican cinema and the state-sponsored arts – e.g. Rivera's murals) is read as part of the propagandizing of a 'myth of the revolution' (Peredo Castro, 2004: 410). In the 'myth of the revolution' the historical revolution (the events of 1910–20) and its complex political reality (that it was fought by opposing factions – urban middle classes and peasants groups – with different goals) disappears behind a fiction of Government propaganda (O'Malley, 1986: 113). This fiction supports a version of Mexican politics in which the Government (synonymous with an institutionalized Revolution) becomes the champion of the underclasses when in reality it only pays lip service (in films like *Río Escondido* and in Rivera's murals) to the actual revolution's values and beliefs (economic help for the indigenous and *campesinos*) (Peredo Castro, 2004: 410).

Disclaimer aside, with it being a part of 'myth of the revolution' and a film that received funding *directly* from Alemán's Government (rather than State support from the Banco Cinematográfico), we would expect the rest of *Río Escondido* to unproblematically unite its discourse with that of the Government (ibid.: 409). Indeed the text initially does this through an opening sequence heavy with the iconography of Government-centered nationalism. Its opening shots of the Plaza de la Constitución, the Mexican flag, the Palacio Nacional (the Government Seat), the Campana de Dolores,[2] Rivera's murals, the figures of Hidalgo and Juárez[3] and finally the President (an actor double) evoke nationalism as a struggle for independence from colonial forces and the revolution as a continuation of that struggle, centralized and institutionalized within the State, its buildings and the President himself.[4] However, the contrast between voice-over and image that emerges in *Río Escondido*'s opening sequence also reveals the myth of the revolution as historical falsification. When Rosaura stops on the stairwell to look at the (recently finished) Rivera murals (of the preconquest, through the revolution to the contemporary moment) the voice-over effectively neutralizes Rivera's Marxist interpretation of the revolution as class struggle. While one panel shows the rural teacher (significantly in the likeness of Rivera's wife Frida Kahlo)

Progress, modernity, 'antimodernist utopia'

6.1 *Río Escondido*: National Palace Mural *maestras rurales*

6.2 *Río Escondido*: National Palace Mural *campesinos* held at gunpoint

wearing a pendant bearing a Soviet star and other peasants being held at gunpoint, the voice-over elides issues of ideology by referring to the revolution as 'a fight for human dignity' (Figures 6.1 and 6.2).[5] So although Rivera's Government-patronized murals were effectively part of the 'myth of the revolution' convincing the masses of the Government's own Revolutionary nature, at moments like this one where class (poor peasants held at gunpoint) and ideology (the Marxist star) are represented, the disjunction between Government discourse and Rivera's discourse becomes evident.[6] Significantly, the voice that narrates (and neutralizes) the murals for Rosaura (and the spectator) belongs to the same actor (Manuel Bernal) who plays the President in the following scene. This cleavage between voice-over and image evidences the contradictions that exist in the Government's cultural nationalism, and is emblematic of further cleavages in the rest of the text.

Río Escondido contradicting the myth of an ongoing Revolution

In March of 1947, the year *Río Escondido* was filmed, Daniel Cosío Villegas published his famous essay 'La crisis de México' (The Crisis of Mexico) in which he suggested the State had failed to achieve the goals of the revolution. This crisis had actually begun in 1940 when the Revolution (Government) had officially taken 'a turn to the right,' away from the agrarian reformist policies and radical fervor of Cárdenas (1934–40) (Joseph et al., 2001: 8; Podalsky, 1993b: 65). By 1947 the 'pro-business, pro-industry, economic policies' and ties with the US that Alemán was setting in place (those that were effectively 'prostituting' the country according to Ayala Blanco) made it increasingly difficult to invoke ideals of the revolution or suggest that the Government was working toward 'improv[ing] the conditions of the masses' (Ayala Blanco, 1993: 133; Acevedo-Muñoz, 2003: 58–59). This crisis gave rise to increasing social unrest to which the Government responded with the repression of any form of dissent. It seems extraordinary, therefore, given the need to maintain an appearance (rather than an actuality) of ideological coherence between contemporary government policy and the revolution, that a film like *Río Escondido* whose narrative explicitly espouses 'old' revolutionary ideals should begin with a disclaimer. However, that Fernández was forced to put in a disclaimer, at the request of Alemán who was anxious to

Progress, modernity, 'antimodernist utopia' 149

situate the film elsewhere than in his own presidency, creates even greater contradictions in the text (García Riera, 1987: 108).

The disclaimer acts as a prologue to the film, appearing in the credits over the first of a series of *grabados* (engravings) by Leopoldo Méndez, the famous Mexican engraver. The engravings (including one of a man sitting back on his chair giving orders to a group of men loaded down with heavy sacks in the background) suggest a downtrodden people oppressed by an evil *cacique* (Figure 6.3). The engravings effectively preview the film's internal revolutionary narrative while significantly omitting the framing narrative of the President and Mexico City. The engravings' subject matter, together with the opening words of the disclaimer 'This story is not about the Mexico of today' and the alternately jaunty and lyrical (western-style) music that play over them, construct several expectations. First, we expect that the film will play out in a pre-revolutionary rural setting, in the manner of some other Fernández films – *Flor Silvestre* and *María Candelaria*. Secondly, we also expect that the problems which the credit sequence previews have subsequently been eradicated by the revolution in the same way *Flor Silvestre* and *María Candelaria*'s pre-revolution time frame is read as

6.3 *Río Escondido*: Engraving of *cacique* issuing orders

suggesting these films' respective problems – unequal land distribution and prejudice toward and isolation of the indígena – have been eradicated. However, once the credits finish, the film proper opens not in the pre-revolution countryside, but in a contemporary, visually modernizing city.[7] Furthermore, the policies the President outlines in his speech to Rosaura are those of the Alemanista regime – i.e., concerns of infrastructure and road building, etc. (Acevedo-Muñoz, 2003: 60).[8] This jarring between the disclaimer's temporal abstraction (that the film is not set in contemporary Mexico) and the opening scenes (which suggest that it is) is heightened by the fact that the President is represented by an actor (Bernal) who physically resembles Alemán.[9] Because of the resemblance between Alemán and Bernal and the 1940s Zócalo, the disclaimer does not effectively disassociate the film from the contemporary Government and its policies.

Río Escondido as a threat to the myth of the revolution

Río Escondido threatens the myth of the revolution (and more significantly Alemán's discourse of progress and modernity) in its depiction of the underdevelopment of Río Escondido. Río Escondido is a dry, arid village far from the rural utopia of Xochimilco depicted in *María Candelaria* where María Candelaria and Lorenzo Rafael could harvest lots of flowers and vegetables and raise a little pig (before Don Damián kills it). Furthermore, the long sequences which depict Rosaura and Felipe trekking to the village emphasize rural isolation and a disconnect between city and *provincia* (countryside). *Río Escondido* accentuates just how dry the village is by concentrating on the arduous task of gathering water which comes from one well and eventually runs out. The film also insists on disease in the village and the absence of health care. There is a smallpox epidemic in the village when Rosaura arrives. Rosaura tends to a woman with three children and a face filled with sores in the moments before she dies. A doctor (like the one sent to a neighboring village) was not sent there. The film also emphasizes how the children in the village (Rosaura's students) are initially dirty and unkempt.

By detailing different aspects of the village's underdevelopment and insisting visually on its contemporary setting, *Río Escondido* becomes an indictment of the failings of the institutionalized Revolution. The film becomes a testimony to the fact that almost thirty years after the historical revolution's 'victory' the problems it sought to solve – widespread poverty, illiteracy and disease – still exist in Mexico. Despite the frame narrative's emphasis on desired progress (the President's speech), the work Rosaura is able to do and her frequent mentioning of the President's desire to 'regenerar México' (regenerate Mexico), *Río Escondido* like *Los olvidados* (Luis Buñuel, 1950), a film that is more often read as an indictment of underdevelopment, 'dramatizes' the Government's failure 'to improve the conditions of Indians and Indian rural communities' (Acevedo-Muñoz, 2003: 69). Following Cosío Villegas, Acevedo-Muñoz suggests that this was one of the Revolution's (the Government as the institutionalized revolution) great failures (ibid.).

Another way in which the film challenges the myth of the revolution is in its depiction of Don Regino's control over the village. Some critics, in line with conservative cultural nationalism and the dominant hegemonic reading position, read his ownership of the village (and its inhabitants) as the remnants of eighteenth- and nineteenth-century neofeudal (i.e., Spanish) power arrangements (Hershfield, 1996: 63). Hence, the film is about completing the revolution's unfinished business, by destroying pre-revolution power structures. This is already antithetical to the myth of the revolution, as it suggests the Government has failed so far to do away with unjust political practices. However, the text actually suggests an even greater contradiction/threat when it implies that Don Regino is actually a *product* of the historical revolution and the institutionalized Revolution (i.e. the Government). First, Don Regino is identified as *Presidente Muncipal* (a government-appointed post) and referred to as a 'funcionario' (government employee). Secondly, while having his photograph taken he says he wants to appear like 'mi General Villa cuando entró a Torreón' (my General [Pancho] Villa when he entered Torreón). Indeed, rather than supporting the myth of the revolution, in which the Government was and remains the just guardian of its ideas, the text seemingly supports a version of history in which 'bossism' – the manipulation of local politics for personal gain by abusive politicians – is actually produced by the revolution and supported by the institutionalized Revolution (Fein, 1999: 3). Furthermore, this 'bossism' becomes an allegorical way of referring to corrupt power structures facilitated by Alemán.

A yet further way in which *Río Escondido* presents contradictions to the institutionalized Revolution is in its fomentation of rebellion. Dever, reading the film in line with nationalist discourses (that figure Fernández as supporting Government interests), has suggested that the credit sequence engraving of a man with a raised torch refers to the prologue's 'bloody past' a torch Rosaura is supposed to extinguish (2003: 58) (Figure 6.4). Dever's reading runs contrary to the narrative and visual strategies of the film which suggest that education, rather than extinguishing the torch of rebellion, actually seeks to light it. Significantly, the raised torch is not only the first image in the film but also the last, acting as an echo to the film's denouement when the villagers with raised torches bear down on Don Regino's henchmen. It is Rosaura's defiance of Don Regino and more importantly her education of their children that emboldens the villagers to take action. It is her selective account of Mexican history (taught to their children) that leads them to think they can (and should) face up to 'malos mexicanos' (bad Mexicans) like Don Regino. As a film that seems to actively promote rebellion and peasant and worker activism as a means of solving problems of *caciquismo*, violence, ignorance and poverty, *Río Escondido* runs counter to the mass-media project of Alemán's Government which aimed to 'pacify proletarian and agrarian demands' (Fein 1999: 126).

Furthermore, the project of education carried out in *Río Escondido* is not the education in *lo mexicano* of conservative cultural nationalism

6.4 *Río Escondido*: Engraving of Raised Torch

– i.e., the nationalist, lay education brought in by the Alemán Government thirty days after its instalment in 1946 (Peredo Castro, 2004: 361). With her exhortations to the rights of the poor and indigenous (using Juárez to symbolize these), her teaching resembles both the socialist education of radical *cardenismo* (1934–40) *and* a proto-New Cinema-like *conscientización* (consciousness raising).[10] At one point, when she has successfully got Don Regino and his armed henchmen to stand down (intimidated both by her and by the mass of torch-wielding villagers behind them), Rosaura says to the villagers: 'Now you have learned that there is no injustice that can be imposed on a united people.'

Stylistic contradictions in *Río Escondido*

Although criticism generally insists upon a stylistic continuity between all of Fernández' canonical films, with *Río Escondido* featuring as the apotheosis of this nationalist style (Berg, 1994: 14), the film is stylistically very different to the rest of Fernández' oeuvre and more experimental than the classically shot *María Candelaria*, *Flor Silvestre* or *Enamorada*. Both in its stark, black-and-white decentered compositions and its focus on adobe ruined houses, the film resists the classical romanticization of the rural landscape and the 'coherency' between land and people in Fernández' other canonical rural dramas (Rozado, 1991:71). In fact, in terms of consistency, although all Fernández' canonical films are generally read as Eisensteinian (Berg 1994:13–14) – inasmuch as they are taken to have Eisensteinian/Posada/muralist-inspired maguey cacti, or immobilized geometrically organized indigenous people and expansive Mexican skies – close examination reveals that *Río Escondido* is the only canonical Fernández film that closely resembles throughout the (adopted as Mexicanist) Eisensteinian techniques of *¡Que viva México!* (Long Live México, 1932). *María Candelaría's* opening montage uses similar strategies to those of *¡Que viva México!* but the remainder of the film establishes a very different aesthetic based on creating a picturesque, utopian environment – and there are no maguey cacti in the film. Taking the maguey as a kind of test case with which to examine the kinds of analyses Tuñón and others perform of Fernández' style (because many critics assert the maguey is a ubiquitous element in his 1940s canonical films), we note that there are no magueyes in *Flor Silvestre* (Tuñón, 1993: 167). Magueyes are similarly not present in *Maclovia*. In *Enamorada* magueyes appear only very briefly in the opening sequence and do not form a significant compositional element. Even in *Río Escondido* where the maguey does form a significant compositional element, it does so in only three different shots: an *indígena* is yanked out from behind one by one of Don Regino's henchmen; a maguey appears at the right side of the frame as two of the henchmen escort Don Regino's ex-girlfriend Merceditas (Columba Domínguez) 'to the train' (to kill her); and then one appears on the left side of the frame after she kills herself.

The problem with the kinds of analyses which identify a feature (the maguey) as nationalist and go on to count (or as is the case here take for granted) its appearance in different films, is that they merely assert similarities between works by Fernández and Eisenstein, and a continuity between Fernández and the popular Mexican art forms Eisenstein mined. While this kind of analysis supports nationalist auteur readings – i.e., positing stylistic continuity between director, film and a nationalist cultural canon – what it also suggests is that Fernández' films support a politically conservative agenda.

According to Tuñón and others, Fernández' supposed stylistic continuity speaks to an essential, eternal Mexico (an 'antimodernist utopia' or a 'mythic [cosmic] order') (Tuñón, 1993: 165; Acevedo-Muñoz, 2003: 66; Rozado, 1991: 10–61). Tuñón and Rozado use this stylistic continuity and the cosmic order or eternal Mexico which they suggest it creates to propose that Fernández' films are either 'fatalist in relation to issues of poverty and injustice' or simply just 'not critical' – i.e., that Fernández' films negate any change or desire or need for change (Tuñón, 1993: 165; Rozado, 1991: 85, 23). Within these readings, the immobilized indigenous people (which appear at the beginning of *La perla* and the beginning of *Río Escondido*) support the notion that there exists an 'unconquerable force and inertia of an essential nature' (Tuñón, 1993: 165). This kind of analysis of recurring elements also obscures the presence of other significant compositional elements that might counter the interpretation of these films as essentially conservative. Furthermore, auteurist structuralist analysis does not (as argued in chapter 2) suggest how a particular feature may produce meaning in relation to the narrative of the film. For example, although in *Río Escondido* there are some initial sequences in which villagers are passive, immobile figures, they do not remain so but are mobilized to fight against the man who oppresses them. The villagers become angry, pick up torches and lynch Don Regino's henchmen,

Progress, modernity, 'antimodernist utopia'

beating them to death. (Similar mobilizations of 'immobilized *indígena*' take place in *Maclovia*, *La perla* and *María Candelária*.) This suggests that *Río Escondido* carries a very definite desire for and figuration of possible change. And yet these elements (that *indígenas* do not remain passive in Fernández' films) are ignored because they remain unreadable through a matrix of conservative cultural nationalism.

Other elements in *Río Escondido* unreadable through auteurist structuralist paradigms that support conservative cultural nationalism are the 'dead trees' (which Mora makes note of, but only as they effect an Eisensteinian framing) (Mora, 1989: 79–80) and semi-deserted, half destroyed houses that appear throughout *Río Escondido*. These, much more ubiquitous (than the maguey) compositional elements, continually emphasize the reality of the village's barrenness and underdevelopment, and point to the issue of contemporary rural depopulation. Simply identifying the formalized signifiers of an Eisensteinian Mexicanness in *Río Escondido* means ignoring elements that contest the hegemonic representation of Mexicanness and Government discourses of modernity and progress.

Acevedo-Muñoz uses *Río Escondido* as an intertext to Buñuel's depiction of urban poverty and underdevelopment in *Los olvidados*. He suggests that *Río Escondido* offers an idealistic representation of Mexico which ignores the impact of economic changes, and that *Los olvidados* deals head-on with the impact of these changes (Acevedo-Muñoz, 2003: 57). However, reading *Río Escondido* through its text and not through auteurist or nationalist discourses contests the commonly held idea that Fernández' films represent a utopian and romanticized Mexico that is countered by Buñuel's critical, harsher Mexico (King, 2000: 130; Acevedo-Muñoz, 2003: 72; Rozado, 1991: 23). My reading of *Río Escondido* reveals how it cannot be unproblematically incorporated into a supposed stylistically nationalist and conservative mainstream against which *Los olvidados* and Buñuel measure their otherness. Both films share similar strategies, opening with disclaimers that work *too hard* either to position the films in another time (*Río Escondido*) or to suggest that the problems (urban poverty and juvenile delinquency) are endemic to all major cities (*Los olvidados*), and as a result fail to position the films elsewhere than in contemporary Mexico. My reading of *Río Escondido* also problematizes the version of Mexican film history in which Buñuel figures as the reverse of Fernández.[11]

Unlike *María Candelaria* or *Flor Silvestre Río Escondido* like *Los olvidados* refuses to idealize the poor or make them contented in their poverty. Instead the film reveals a reality of underdevelopment, poverty and hunger. This suggests we cannot read Fernández' relationship toward contemporary Mexico uniformly across his films. The discourse of nation building (which all Fernández' films supposedly embody) emphasized Mexico's development, the stable process of 'nation building [of which indigenous assimilation is a part] and material progress sometimes doing this by framing the past with contemporary frames' (Schmidt, 2001: 25). This discourse is contested in *María Candelaria* in its contradictory representation of the *indígena* (as physically white or barbarously dark and incapable of assimilating into modern Mexico), and is also contested in *Río Escondido* where the 'before and after' of institutionalized discourse come together to reveal the before and after as falsification and to reveal the stalling of the Revolutionary process. The poverty of the village is not the lyrical beauty or utopian idealized poverty of Xochimilco where, as María Candelaria says, there is always *frijol* (beans) and *maizita* (corn), and bountiful flowers and vegetables spill over from baskets and canoes. The material reality of scarcity is a pressing issue in *Río Escondido*. It is not that *Río Escondido* is arguing against progress, just that it is arguing for social justice in the midst of progress.

The ending

As David Bordwell points out, the 'ending' of the classical system of narration performs an important ideological function. It gives the semblance of (rather than actual) resolution of the film's ideological conflicts and closure to the story (1985: 159). But *Río Escondido*'s ending – a letter from the President thanking Rosaura for her work, Rosaura's death while listening to it, her subsequent burial and canonization as martyr for 'progress' – does not adequately perform its ideological function of resolution and closure. In part, the rapidity with which she dies, is buried and eulogized (all of two minutes) in comparison to her lengthy agonizing and other speeches has the effect of questioning the ideological closure the ending supposedly affects. In the case of *Río Escondido* the ending does not redeem the classical system, or recoup the story into the ideological system of Government discourse. The President's words in a letter: that he 'can now begin the process of rehabilitation of *Río Escondido*' (now that Rosaura and the villagers have killed the corrupt politician and his henchmen) leave more questions than they provide answers. For example, why would a system of social reform send a civilian woman (feminist considerations aside) to do a job that is quite clearly the responsibility of the Government and Government institutions (the police, the army, the courts)?

Podalsky has noted a similar failure of classical closure in two other Fernández films (*María Candelaria* and *Flor Silvestre*). In these two films the narrative frames that open and close the films are, in Podalsky's opinion, 'disjointed.' Podalsky suggests that this is partly because the frames take up such a short space of the screen time that they make the endings seem 'forced and unconvincing' and '[t]he conflicts created within the frame hang over or exceed its attempt at closure' (1993a: 62–63). In *María Candelaria* the painter introduces the story of María Candelaria and the painting he has never exhibited, and closes it with one sentence in voice-over as she appears on a funeral byre 'This is the story of María Candelaria.' Podalsky suggests that the film breaks with the framed structure by not returning visually to the master narrative of the painter who is telling the story (1993a: 69). In *Flor Silvestre* Esperanza tells her son the story of his father's death during the revolution before a flashback to that story. The film ends with a speech back with Esperanza and her son. Podalsky argues that 'despite Esperanza's words [which are supposed to convince us that José Luis died so that the revolution could triumph and bring about a fairer Mexico] her husband's death seems futile' (1993a: 63). Effectively in both cases, the story 'outweighs the ending.' A comparable hangover occurs in *Río Escondido* where the President's letter acts as a similarly disjointed frame, not sufficiently responding to the profound conflicts elaborated within the body of the narrative, and thus problematizing classical and ideological closure within the film.

Both Fein and Podalsky have argued that Golden Age Mexican Cinema 'sought to resolve or distract from the contradictions between the official rhetoric and actual practices of the post-Revolutionary state as it made its rightward turn in the 1940s' (Fein 1999: 105). For Podalsky the disjointed melodramatic frames in *Flor Silvestre* and *María Candelaria* are simultaneously part of an acknowledgement of these contradictions within the Revolution and an affirmation of it as a 'meaningful system' (1993a: 63). *Rio Escondido* with its nationalist trajectory toward the Revolutionary (i.e., Government) triumph of progress and modernity through education has been interpreted as simply affirming the institutionalized Revolution. However, this analysis has shown how various formal and narrative elements (the disjunction between voice and image during the mural sequence, the opening and closing with an engraving of a raised torch, the nature of education, the disjointed frame) contradict the official rhetoric of the State. There is a cleavage in *Río Escondido* between the 'myth of the revolution' and the underdeveloped 'reality' of rural Mexico, a reality tinged by poverty, exploitation and ignorance. This cleavage is underpinned by what the text makes clear to be the contradictory (and increasingly divergent) drives of ideological revolution (social justice, socioeconomic emancipation, national sovereignty, education, etc.) and the political and economic projects of the institutionalized Revolution (private interests, increasing alliance with the US, institutionalization of authoritarian controls in Alemán's Government). Hence, although *Río Escondido* seemingly endorses the State as the *just guardian* of the revolution, at the same time the film suggests that the State has practically and ideologically abandoned revolutionary ideals.

Notes

1 *Caciquismo* or 'bossism' is the manipulation of local politics for personal gain by abusive politicians. Local *caciques* or bosses would use their power against the federal government's social reforms (Fein, 1999: 3).
2 On 16 September 1810, the Bell was rung in the town of Dolores in the state of Hidalgo by Padre Miguel Hidalgo, an event that was later perceived to signal the start of Mexico's war of independence. The bell was later moved to hang above the central entrance to the Palacio Nacional where it continues to be rung every year on 16 September by successive Mexican presidents.
3 The depiction of nineteenth-century President Benito Juárez throughout *Río Escondido* (his portrait hangs in the school Rosaura establishes and she uses him as an example for the pupils) is commensurate with his depiction in mainstream Mexican culture as a friend of the humble classes. However, in reality the picture is not quite so clear. Nineteenth-century liberalism which Juárez came to symbolize 'viewed the lower social elements as collective obstacles to development'. Rather than wanting to help the lower classes, liberals wanted 'to transform them for their own good and the well-being of the country.' (Machlachlan and Beezley, 1999: 77)
4 The soundtrack further underlines the action in nationalist terms. We hear voices singing 'Mexico' and the chiming of a bell suggesting that Rosaura

Progress, modernity, 'antimodernist utopia'   159

is being called by the cumulative weight of Mexico's history (i.e., condensed in the Campana de Dolores) to the services of the Republic (García Riera, 1987: 125).

5 We also see other Marxist-inspired imagery: a fat priest and images of masses of workers rising up. These are all not commented upon by the voice-over.

6 Although Rivera's murals presented a communist interpretation of Mexico's history and future, they also acted as a part of the institutionalization of the Revolution, making excellent revolutionary propaganda for a Government which wished to convince the masses of its own revolutionary nature. 'As part of the metalanguage of the myth of the revolution, [Rivera's murals] buoyed up the image of a new government as nonracist, and tolerant of communist views when in practice it was not' (O'Malley, 1986: 122).

7 Further underlining the film's 1940s setting are the many 1940s-style cars parked in the National Palace courtyard and the fashions worn by the female teachers: pencil skirts and waisted suits. Rosaura on the other hand wears a *rebozo* (shawl) and bows in her hair.

8 'We have to bring health to our coasts and our high land villages. Mexico lacks water, high ways, locals roads, literacy and official morality . . .'

9 In fact, so close is the resemblance between actor Bernal and Alemán that Fein (and other scholars Hershfield, Mora and Acevedo-Muñoz) have mistakenly understood that Alemán himself appears in a cameo role in this scene (Fein, 1999: 124; Hershfield, 1996: 61; Mora, 1989: 78; Acevedo-Muñoz, 2003: 24).

10 Films of the New Latin American cinema in the period 1960–73 were revolutionary and explicitly political, calling for an end to hunger, exploitation, illiteracy and ignorance. Central to one of the movements of New Latin American Cinema, that of 'Third Cinema' was the idea that film itself could act as a tool of consciousness-raising about the problems of neoimperialism and underdevelopment plaguing the continent. See Fernando Solanas and Octavio Getino's 'Towards a Third Cinema: Notes and Experiences for the Development of a Cinema of Liberation in the Third World,' in Martin, 1997: 33–58).

11 A flip side that is reflected in the oft recounted anecdote: 'While *Nazarín* was being filmed on location near Cuatla . . . Gabriel Figueroa carefully prepared an outdoor scene for the director Luis Buñuel. Figueroa set up the camera with the snow-capped volcano Popocatépetl in the background, a cactus at the right-angle of the composition, circle of clouds crowning its peak and the open furrows of the valley in the foreground. [This is the Eisensteinian aesthetics that are considered central to the Fernández-Figueroa style] Looking at the composition, Buñuel said: "Fine, now let's turn the camera so that we can get those four goats and two crags on that barren hill"' (King, 2000: 130).

Epilogue: Mexican cinema and Emilio Fernández post the Golden Age – from golden boy to 'the man in black'

Río Escondido (1947) is Fernández' last 'great' epic while the much cheaper genre film *Víctimas del pecado* (1950) is his last 'critically' acclaimed, canonical film. After *Víctimas* no other Fernández film registers universally in criticism. In the following decades Fernández goes from being *the* Mexican and Latin American director of the 1940s, to nobody.[1] He makes films with less success and less acclaim and suffers periods of industry-imposed directorial inactivity (García Riera, 1987: 251–279). Accounts of his career post the Golden Age paint him as a 'tragic' figure, making poorly received films and acting (in black *charro* costume) in others' films (an activity he purportedly did not like) in order to survive when he could not find work as a director (De la Vega Alfaro, 1999: 186).

Fernández and the Mexican film industry in the 1950s

The decade of the 1950s was a period of breakdown in Mexican cinema, when both the ideological – i.e., the political institution of the Revolution as it passed from Alemán to Adolfo Ruíz Cortines (1952–58) – *and* institutional 'systems' of Mexican classical filmmaking began to fall apart (Berg, 1992: 37).[2] This institutional failure in Mexican cinema had been looming since the end of the Second World War, when Hollywood; withdrew technological and financial support, returned to full production and competitive practices but also attempted to gain a greater share of the Mexican market and take control of its industry (Fein, 1999: 134, 138–40). Hollywood encroachment and other factors precipitated a deep problem in the Mexican film industry. First, the Jenkins' monopoly (after American mogul William Jenkins) that controlled not just exhibition but what kind of films were exhibited, pushed producers to exploit certain profitable genres (urban themes, musical comedies) to the point of exhaustion (Mora, 1989: 75; King, 2000: 129; García Riera, 1998: 152). The low-budget, rapidly made films that resulted from this overly commercialized production strategy (*churros*) divided the film audience into two groups; the growing urban mostly illiterate audience who watched them and the middle-class audiences who were driven away by them to European and Hollywood cinema (Paranaguá, 1998: 33; De la Vega Alfaro, 1995: 89). The quality of production was further worsened by the closed-shop union policy that excluded new directors, competition from television and 'a lack of risk-taking on the part of producers' (De la Mora, 1999b: 5). Therefore, although the total number of films produced remained high – up to 124 in 1950 and 114 in 1959 – overproduction of certain genres by a limited number of directors occasioned a kind of 'qualitative' and 'metaphysical' crisis (García Riera, 1987: 167).

Fernández, still considered in the early 1950s a director of 'quality' films, was negatively impacted by these factors and the production strategies they encouraged. In 1950 for example, he made four films, the most he had ever made in one year and with much smaller budgets than his 1940s epics, including *Un día de vida* (One Day Left To Live), *Las Islas Marías* and *Víctimas del pecado*. Only *Víctimas* was a critical and public success but, like Fernández' other 1950 films, it was ignored at the *Arieles* in 1951 (García Riera, 1987 171–9). When these and subsequent Fernández films including *Cuando levanta la niebla* (When the fog lifts, 1951) failed to make money, he was marginalized by producers now interested only in *churros* for whom his costly films (in the context of declining audiences and the 1954 peso devaluation which increased costs) were too much of a financial risk (García Riera, 1987: 127).

Although in 1953 Fernández won international (Cannes) and domestic acclaim (though not box-office success or awards) for *La red* (The Net), after two more films (*Reportaje*, Reportage, 1953, and *El rapto* (The Snatching, 1953), limited Mexican directorial projects forced him abroad. He made three films in quick succession in Cuba (*La rosa blanca*, The White Rose, 1953), Spain (*Nosotros dos*, We Two, 1954) and Argentina (*La Tierra del Fuego se apaga*, Tierra del Fuego's flame is put out, 1955), countries where his reputation was still intact or, as in the case of *Nosotros dos*, capital could be made from the European success of *La red* (Taibo, 1986: 145–50; García Riera, 1987:

233). In between travelling projects in 1954 he was sacked from *La rebelión de los colgados* (The Rebellion of the Hanged), thus deepening his reputation as a 'difficult director' and further isolating him. Reportedly, Fernández quarrelled with the producer José Kohn when the latter asked him to speed up the shoot. He was tellingly replaced by the *churro* director Alfredo B. Crevana (García Riera, 1987: 229).

Post *La Tierra del Fuego*, Fernández made two films in 1956, *Una cita de amor* (An appointment with love, his last with Figueroa) and *El impostor* (The Impostor). His first period of directorial inactivity followed. During this period he made anti-Semitic tirades blaming Jewish producers Gregorio Wallerstein and Arturo Ripstein Snr. for an overly commercialized film industry that had abandoned 'quality filmmaking' (García Riera, 1987: 239–45). In 1958 the *Arieles* (the industry's own marker of esteem) were suspended for lack of suitable nominees (García Riera, 1998: 213). It was in the context of his own inactivity and the suspension of the *Arieles* that he uttered the words 'El cine mexicano soy yo' (I am Mexican cinema) – a phrase which, from this perspective, is less the nationalist self-affirmation that auteur criticism suggests it is and more the insecure protestation of someone who feels isolated and boycotted. In this same period the famed shooting of a journalist took place. What provoked Fernández' murderous rage was a journalist who contradicted his assertion that Mexico was best known for his films (García Riera 1987: 253–5, Taibo, 1986: 155–60).

Fernández' first recession coincided with various events which further intensified the national cinema crisis: the closure of several film studios and the loss of the Cuban market (because of the Cuban Revolution) (Garcia Riera, 1998: 231). In order to survive financially, Fernández returned to acting (his most recent previous performance having been as the bandit Rogelio in his own film *Flor Silvestre*, 1943). Fernández was a success in his starring role as Coronel Zeta in *La cucaracha* (Ismael Rodríguez, 1958) and went on to act in his first Hollywood film since working as an extra in the 1920s and 1930s, playing a small part in John Huston's *The Unforgiven* (1960).

In the late 1940s Fernández had achieved world fame both for himself and Mexican cinema by 'dominat[ing] the festival circuit in Europe' and winning a number of international prizes (García Riera, 1998: 150). But from the beginning of the 1950s, he was displaced as Mexico's most prestigious director by Luis Buñuel. With *Los olvidados* (1950) Buñuel won best director at Cannes and swept the *Arieles* in

Epilogue: Fernández post the Golden Age

1951, continuing his critical success in Mexico through the 1950s and early 1960s. In the meantime, French critics, who had been the first foreign critics to praise Fernández' work, began to find his films repetitive (García Riera, 1987: 121).

Fernández and the Mexican film industry in the 1960s

The 'crisis' in Mexican cinema worsened in the early 1960s. For the first time feature production decreased, kept up only by the production of series films (García Riera, 1998: 234). At the same time a group of young critics, aspiring cineastes and writers (Salvador Elizondo, Carlos Monsiváis, García Riera, Paul Leduc, Alberto Isaac and others) formed the Nuevo Cine group. This group launched a magazine, *Nuevo Cine*, which ran to seven numbers between 1961 and 1962. Their articles called for a director-led cinema (García Riera, 1998: 235). Fernández' films fared well in the pages of *Nuevo Cine*, while 'nude' films and 'puerile' Cantinflas comedies did not (García Riera, 1987: 245). Seemingly gripped by the vogue of auteurism, Nuevo Cine praised Fernández' work but at the same time recognized the public was tired of '[his] loving focus on magueyes' (García Riera, 1998: 245).

In the early 1960s members of the Nuevo Cine group made low-budget independent films which added to the growing climate of cinematic innovation, already blossoming out of the cine club movement at the National Autonomous University and the newly opened film school the CUEC (Centro Universitario de Estudios Cinematográficos). Jomí García Ascot's *En el balcón vácio* (On The Empty Balcony, 1964), shot at weekends and on 16mm, won prizes at 'European festivals' and paved the way for the Government-sponsored Experimental Cinema competition in 1965. The festival launched future successful new cinema directors including Isaac, whose *En este pueblo no hay ladrones* (There Are No Thieves In This town), based on Colombian writer Gabriel García Márquez' short story, won second prize (García Riera, 1998: 236).

However, despite admiration from the Nuevo Cine group and the artistic (but not industrial) renovation of the early 1960s, Fernández remained out of favor with producers. In the 1960s he suffered two lengthy periods of directorial inactivity (García Riera 1998, 240). But first, in 1961 he made *Pueblito* (Little Town) which had a similar plot to that of *Río Escondido*. Although the Nuevo Cine group praised its auteurist vision, *Pueblito* did not revive his domestic or international career. In 1962 Fernández made *Paloma herida*, about indigenous exploitation. The film was badly received by the critics, who suggested that Fernández work was now not only static but going 'backward' (García Riera, 1987: 256, 262).

Fernández' made one film as an actor in 1961, a chili-western *Los hermanos del hierro* (The Steel Brothers Ismael Rodríguez) and another in 1962 *La Bandida* (Roberto Rodríguez) a color superproduction in which he starred as a revolutionary General (García Riera, 1987: 260–267). In 1963, during the second hiatus in his directorial career, he found his niche in a series of westerns currently enjoying a resurgence in Mexico (as well as the US and Europe). He played mostly starring roles in Mexican films *El revólver sangriento* (The Bloody Revolver, Miguel Delgado) and character parts in Hollywood films *The Night of the Iguana* (Huston, 1964). In 1964 he made four Mexican films including *Los hermanos muerte* (The Brothers Death, Rafael Baledón). In 1965 he acted in five Mexican westerns as a character actor or star, including *Duelo de pistoleros* (Duel of the Gunfighters, Miguel Delgado). His characters in these films were gunfighters, killers or bandits and were often dressed '*de charro negro*' (in black 'cowboy' gear) (García Riera, 1987: 267).

After a three-year absence from directing, in 1966 Fernández directed only one film *Un Dorado de Pancho Villa* (One of Pancho Villa's Men). This was his first color film and the only time he directed himself in a starring role. (García Riera, 1987: 271) In the same year, although the Moscow Film Festival paid him homage it awarded no prizes to *Un Dorado de Pancho Villa*. The film was likewise poorly received in Mexico.

In 1968, Fernández made only one film, *El crepúsculo de un dios* (The Twilight of a God), to which the public and the critics were indifferent. In the same year he acted in three Mexican films, including a parodic western coproduction with the US (*El pistolero fantasma* [The Ghost Gunfighter, Albert Zugsmith]). In 1968 Fernández began his third and longest period of directorial inactivity (lasting five years). In 1968 he also made one of his most notable Hollywood performances as the cruel womanizing General Mapache in Peckinpah's *The Wild Bunch*. He also acted in three Mexican films including *Duelo en el Dorado* (Duel in El Dorado, René Cardona). Although in 1968 Fernández' acting had protected him through the recession, as parts dried up in later years he went through financial difficulties (like other film-industry veterans Julio Bracho and Fernando Soler) (García Riera, 1987: 279–80; 1999: 275).

Fernández and the Mexican film industry in the 1970s

By the beginning of Luis Echeverría Álvarez' presidency (1970–76), the classical filmmaking apparatus had collapsed and the state itself was in crisis, hastened by the Tlatelolco massacre in 1968 (Berg, 1992: 29).[3] Echeverría set in place 'unprecedented financial and infrastructural' state backing for the film industry in order to 'promote Mexican cinema throughout the world' (Berg, 1992: 29). Much of the initial backing was for projects by the Nuevo Cine directors who had emerged in the 1960s, including *El rincón de las vírgenes* (The Corner of Virgins (Alberto Isaac, 1972) in which Fernández appeared.

Later in the 1970s, state funding helped struggling veteran directors like Fernández, and also Bracho, Gavaldón and Galindo. With state help Fernández made *La Choca* (1973) and *Zona roja* (Red Zone, 1975). As a sign that fortunes were changing, the *Ariel* was reintroduced in 1972. Fernández' *La Choca*, set in the jungle amid a backdrop of drug trafficking, won six *Arieles* in 1975 including prizes for best film and best director (García Riera, 1987: 283). *La Choca* was also a box-office success in 1974, earning as much as Arturo Ripstein's new cinema classic *El castillo de la pureza* (The Castle of Purity, 1973). The new and old cinema critics liked *La Choca* despite the considerable female nudity, 'a by product of Echeverría-era liberalization' (Berg, 1992: 125).

Fernández' other Echeverría-era film *Zona roja*, a prostitute, cabaret and prison drama (popular genres in the 1970s and early 1980s), did less well with critics and at the box office. Like other films from this period such as the remake of the 1941 *Cuando los hijos se van* (Juan Bustillo Oro) by Julian Soler (1969) *Zona roja* demonstrated poor production values and a lack of basic filmmaking craftsmanship (ibid.: 31). *Zona roja* was criticized both for these imperfections and for its excessive nudity. The film won no *Arieles* and made no impact abroad (García Riera, 1987: 289).

In the meantime, Fernández' acting during the early 1970s included another of his most significant roles in 'Hollywood' (actually filmed in Mexico) – as the vicious patriarch who initiates a series of bloody murders – in Peckinpah's *Bring Me the Head of Alfredo García* (1974). He also acted during these lean years in various *churros* and another Peckinpah film, *Pat Garret and Billy the Kid* (1973) (García Riera, 1987: 281–283).

At the end of Echeverría's *sexenio*, the new president José López Portillo (1976–1982) withdrew initiatives to encourage quality Mexican cinema. López Portillo also named his sister Margarita director of a new organization Radio, Televisión y Cinematografía (Radio, Television Cinema). She made various disastrous decisions, undoing much of what had been achieved (including dismantling state production companies) with Nuevo Cine in the preceding six years. Directors now faced 'lower budgets, stricter censorship and tighter distribution policies' (García Riera, 1998: 305; Berg, 1992: 51).

Fernández' final films – *México norte* (1977) and *Erótica* (1978) – were made under Portillo and were funded by the remaining state producer Conacine. The production of *México norte* was delayed when Fernández shot and killed a man. According to Fernández, the man had been bothering him and a group of gypsies and he had had to defend himself/them. He was convicted of murder, sentenced to four a half years in prison, and released on bail (García Riera, 1987: 292–9, 303).

México norte is considered a retelling of *Pueblerina* (1948) one of Fernández' semicanonical 1940s films. Despite his desire that the film would go to Cannes as did *Pueblerina* in 1949, *México norte* remained in Mexico receiving a very low-key reception (García Riera, 1987: 300). *Erótica* (1978), Fernández' final film, was also a remake of another of his films, *La red*. Fernández was actually arrested (for having not completed his sentence) before he could complete the film, but was eventually pardoned and the film finished. *Erótica* did badly at the box office and received only narrow distribution (García Riera, 1987: 306). Post *Erótica*, Fernández made no more films, but maintained the hope that producers would allow him to direct one of many planned projects. To this end he established an 'office' at a table in the cafeteria of Churubusco Studios, to which he would determinedly go every day in the final years of his life.

Fernández – an auteur in decline

For the biographical auteurist critics, the narrative of Fernández' post-Golden Age career is one of increasing marginalization, which in turn is part of the ongoing institutionalization of Mexico's racial ideology. In the same way that it is fitting for Mexico's first internationally renowned auteur to be of mixed racial heritage, for auteurist critics it is equally fitting that he should go into decline along with the cinema and ideological absolutes (Mexican cultural nationalism) which he represented, *and* that this directorial exclusion should reflect discrimination against him as '*Indio*' (Tuñón, 1993: 165) rather than reflecting the industrial crisis which ruled out the kind of expensive quality filmmaking at which Fernández had excelled.

The blurring between director and film which is part of his construction as an auteur happens increasingly in interpretations of his post-Golden Age acting career between director and character. For example, in *La Bandida* he plays a General who despite having just fought a duel for the woman he loves (María Félix) is rejected by her. For critics the plot mirrors Fernández' rejection by the industry and heightens his already tragic status (García Riera, 1987: 260). In auteurist accounts, certain events and speculation about his post-Golden Age life dominate (while the films themselves are rarely analyzed) – for example, that he was responsible for the extreme torture scenes in *La rebelión de los colgados* (Fernández, 1986: 46), that he shot at journalists and that he killed a man in a shoot-out. These events and speculations are focused on to suggest that he has reverted to the 'dark side' of the noble savage or become the violent *chingón*. Fernández' construction as the *chingón* represents in part what Andrea Noble calls 'Mexico's reflection and refraction of Hollywood' (2005: 37). Despite Mexico's rejection of Hollywood's image of Mexicans as greasers and *bandidos* in the early sound days, Mexican cinema embraces those very images in the late 1950s, 1960s and early 1970s in the chili-westerns in which Fernández acts. Mexican criticism does the same when it suggests that the characters he plays in these films are thinly veiled versions of himself. Similarly, Fernández' violent encounters (with the journalist and man he killed) become, following Ramos' ideas about the Mexican macho, the manifestation of a Mexican inferiority complex.

Fernández' decline and stagnation are blamed on the repetition and anachronism of the same images of nationalism that brought him great success during his most prestigious years (García Riera, 1987: 274). This reading is in part symptomatic of auteurist approaches which decide a paradigm of nationalist images (the themes of Fernández' cinematic nationalism, isolationism, indigenism, tragic love) and then examine films as they fit into that paradigm, discarding those films which do not fit the predetermined paradigm as anomalies – notably *Pepita Jiménez* (1945) and *Bugambilia* (1944).

The basis for authorship during the 1940s – difference from the run-of-the-mill commercial fare and the fact that his films incorporated a nationally specific message – became the basis for Fernández' 'falling out of fashion' post the Golden Age, in a film industry governed by commercial concerns and a country in which there was increasing divergence between Government rhetoric and popular politics.

However, there is potentially space to reevaluate the films Fernández made in the post-Golden Age (as reevaluations have been made of the 1950s *churros*, particularly the nascent exploitation genre), to retain them both for a Fernández canon and for Mexican national cinema (Syder and Tierney, 2005).

In conventional readings of classical Mexican cinema, the country's proximity to Hollywood has been suffered as a constant reminder of Mexico's comparative underdevelopment and its marginal position within the global economic system. The study of Mexico's classical cinema has reproduced this relationship of subalternity by emphasizing its cinema as an imperfect/poor copy of Hollywood (Paranaguá, 1995: 8). The grounds for valuing this cinema in traditional scholarship is as the location of the 'national' or '*lo mexicano*,' a loose collection of images, voices and faces that define the nation and defiantly resist the colonizing culture (Hollywood). This has resulted in scholarship's emphasis on sociohistorical approaches to its cinema, which stress how intensely 'local' this cinema is, and in turn produce readings of Fernández' 1940s films in particular as a coherent representation of post-Revolutionary Mexican cultural nationalism. This emphasis is supported by the cultural-studies approaches of Monsiváis, Martín Barbero and García Canclini which, rather than giving voice to discourses silenced by state hegemony, instead highlight audience 'agency' in the reception of what is still perceived as a monolithic text of cultural nationalism.

What this book has attempted in its reading of Fernández' canonical films is a retheorization of Mexico's proximity to Hollywood and the way in which Mexican classical cinema is studied. By rethinking the cultural dimensions of nationalism (the project of the institutionalized Revolution), imperialism (Hollywood domination) and modernization (incorporation/assimilation of the *indígena* and urban masses into the nation state, education), rather than as a relationship of suffering or marginalization, this proximity is re-viewed through the concept of the transnational as a source both of invention and of qualified national expression.

Hence Mexico's cinematic history emerges not as one of simple domination and resistance but as a more complex process of adaptation, contestation and innovation of transnational forms. Through

Epilogue: Fernández post the Golden Age

approaches that prioritize the transnational (Hollywood and Europe) within the national, this book has developed reading strategies which treat Fernández' films as polysemic texts – rather than sociohistoric documents – and reveal the fissures and gaps in the supposedly monolithic text of cultural nationalism. From this analysis it emerges that, rather than narrating and solving the internal conflicts of post-Revolutionary Mexican society – modernity and progress, indigenous assimilation, national unity, 'proper' gender roles – as conventional Fernández scholarship posits, *Enamorada, Salón Mexico, Víctimas del pecado, Las abandonadas, Maria Candelaria, La perla, Maclovia* and *Río Escondido* reveal internal conflicts and inassimilable others in a (seemingly less) monolithic text of *lo mexicano*. This challenges the myth or the institutionalized readings of the role of cinema in cultural nationalism in which film narrated the formation of the nation, linked diverse regional groups, and 'taught migrants how to adapt to city life' (García Canclini, 1997: 246–7).

García Canclini asks whether the transnational conditions of the 1990s – the North American Free Trade Agreement (NAFTA) and border crossings which increasingly characterize the production, circulation and reception of films – have made coherent scenarios of national identity like those of Golden Age Mexican cinema impossible (ibid.: 247). This study of Fernández has highlighted how Mexican cinema has *always* been a transnational phenomena, and has questioned whether, even at the apex of its 'nationalist' period, Mexico's film industry – and Fernández in particular – ever produced this unproblematic national self-image.

And rather than positing transnationality as a threat to the 'imagined commonality' maintained by the circulation of films, this book highlights how the many transnational forces that shaped and determined Fernández' films – transnational stars like Del Rio and Armendáriz; Hollywood's screwball comedy; the women's film; use of Afro-Cuban rhythms – actually allow for an understanding of the nation in terms of plurality, hybridity and heterogeneity. At the same time, Fernández' transnational texts are inserted within a trajectory of national self-determination in the film industry, a process that began as early as 1897 with Mexican entrepreneurs using foreign technology to exhibit moving images in major cities (De los Reyes, 1995: 63).

What also emerges from the textual focus on Fernández' canonical films is how, contrary to the opinion of Monsiváis, not only do these texts withstand textual analysis but also they reveal an incredible richness and technical complexity which challenge the notion of aesthetic 'poverty' often circulated in Mexican cinema scholarship. For example, reading the ethnically motivated lighting scheme in *María Candelaria* illustrates the Eurocentric bias within *indigenismo*, but also celebrates the technical mastery of Figueroa. Furthermore, the mise-en-scène analysis also shows how these different films, far from representing a coherent authorial or nationalist vision, actually represent a great textual diversity ranging between the orthodox and the heterodox.

In this study the motivation has not been to center upon marginalization as part of a national psyche (as is done with the *auteur* figure of Fernández himself), nor indeed to rescue these films as necessarily progressive texts, but instead to suggest that classical Mexican cinema and specifically the films made by Fernández have been misunderstood as solely readable via a myth of post-Revolutionary Mexican culture. As for the implications of this study for future approximations of Fernández' post-Golden Age cinema, what it hopes to yield is an approach that puts aside those hegemonic discourses such as nationalism and auteurism which historically have weighed on the texts and barred them from multiple, heterodox readings, and to yield instead an approach that embraces some of the very interesting films Fernández made in the 1950s, 1960s and 1970s.

This book hopes to generate new analyses of these other Fernández' films that are critically neglected because they lie beyond the canon of cultural nationalism. These 'forgotten' Fernández films include *The Torch* (1950), a remake of *Enamorada* coproduced with Hollywood, starring Paulette Goddard, Pedro Armendáriz and Gilbert Roland; *La red* (1953), *El rapto* (1953) and *Cita de amor* (1956), films that were made later than the mythic 1940s; *La rosa blanca* (1953) and *Nosotros dos* (1954), films that were made abroad; and *Bugambilia* (1944), *Pepita Jiménez* (1945) and *La Malquerida* (Woman unloved, 1948), films made without evident nationalist sensibility. The recent release on DVD of many of both Fernández' canonical 1940s films and previously unavailable noncanonical post-Golden Age films (particularly *Cita de amor* and *El rapto*) presages a whole new wave of scholarship on his films.

Ultimately it is hoped that this book will help to expand Fernández' cultural legacy by suggesting that there are other possible interpretive

Epilogue: Fernández post the Golden Age

templates for analyzing his work beyond conservative cultural nationalism.

Notes

1 In the few English-language accounts of Mexican and Latin American cinema from the 1950s onward (the 1950s themselves being a marginal era in Mexican and Latin American film history), Fernández and his work is largely absent or marginalized, appearing often only as a counterpoint to Luis Buñuel – and then solely in relation to the canonical films from the 1940s (*María Candelaria, Flor Silvestre*), never to work from the 1950s onward (King, 2000: 130; Acevedo-Muñoz, 2003: 72–3, 151).
2 Toward the end of Alemán's *sexenio* and through the beginning of the repressive, conservative regime of Adolfo Ruíz Cortines (1952–58), the ideological contradictions between the rhetoric of cultural nationalism and Government policy (already evident in the late 1940s *cabaretera* genre and, as I have argued, in *Río Escondido*) could no longer be contained by the national cinema. We could argue that the strong nationalist narratives around which the industry had grown up (e.g. the *comedia ranchera*) were by this point ideologically and filmically exhausted.
3 In August 1968 Government troops opened fire on students and workers protesting in a Mexico City Square, Tlatelolco. Hundreds and some say thousands were killed. The massacre testified to the increasing rift between an authoritarian Government and an alienated populace.

Filmography

21 Grams. Dir. Alejandro González Iñárritu. With Sean Penn, Naomi Watts and Benicio Del Toro. This is That Productions, Y Productions, Mediana Productions Filmgesellshaft, East Coast Films, 2003.
Abandonadas, Las. Dir. Emilio Fernández. With Dolores Del Rio and Pedro Armendáriz. Films Mundiales, 1944.
Adiós Nicanor. Dir. Rafael E. Portas. With Emilio Fernández and Carmen Molina. Producciones Artísticas, 1937.
Ahí está el detalle. Dir. Juan Bustillo Oro. With Mario Moreno (Cantinflas), Joaquín Pardavé and Sara García. Grovas-Oro Films, 1940.
Allá en el Rancho Grande. Dir. Fernando de Fuentes. With Esther Fernández, Tito Guízar and René Cardona. Antonio Díaz Lombardo, 1936.
Almas rebeldes. Dir. Alejandro Galindo. With Raúl de Anda and Emilio Fernández. Producciones Raúl de Anda, 1937.
Amores perros. Dir. Alejandro González Iñárritu. With Gael García Bernal, Vanessa Bauche, Emilio Echeverría and Goya Toledo. Altavista Films and Zeta Films, 2000.
Angelitos negros. Dir. Joselito Rodríguez. With Pedro Infante, Rita Montaner and Emilio Guiú. Producciones Rodríguez Hermanos, 1948.
Angels with Dirty Faces. Dir. Michael Curtiz. With James Cagney, Humphrey Bogart and Pat O'Brien. Warner Bros, 1938.
Automóvil gris, El. Dir. Enrique Rosas. With Joaquín Cros and Juan de Homs. Rosas y Cia and Azteca Films, 1919.
Aventurera. Dir. Alberto Gout. With Ninón Sevilla, Andrea Palma, and Tito Junco. Producciones Calderón, 1949.
Babel. Dir. Alejandro González Iñárritu. With Brad Pitt, Cate Blanchet and Gael García Bernal. Zeta Film, Dune Films, and Central Films, 2006.
Balcón vácio, En el. Dir. Jomí García Ascot. With Alicia Bergua and Martín Bergua. 1964.
Bandida, La. Dir. Roberto Rodríguez. With Emilio Fernández and María Félix. Películas Rodríguez, 1962.
Basic Instinct. Dir. Paul Verhoeven. With Sharon Stone and Michael Douglas. TriStar Pictures, 1992.

Filmography

Battleship Potemkin. Dir. Sergei Eisenstein. With Aleksandr Antonov and Vladimir Barsky. Goskino, 1925.
Beau Geste. Dir. Herbert Brenon. With Ronald Colman and Neil Hamilton. Paramount Pictures, 1926.
Blade II. Dir. Guillermo del Toro. With Wesley Snipes and Kris Kristofferson. New Line Cinema, 2002.
Bring me the Head of Alfredo Garcia. Dir. Sam Peckinpah. With Warren Oates, Isela Vega and Emilio Fernández. United Artists, 1974.
Bringing up Baby. Dir. Howard Hawks. With Cary Grant and Katharine Hepburn. RKO, 1938.
Broken Arrow. Dir. Delmer Daves, With James Stewart and Debra Paget. 20th Century Fox, 1950.
Bugambilia. Dir. Emilio Fernández. With Dolores Del Rio and Pedro Armendáriz. Films Mundiales, 1944.
Castillo de la pureza, El. Dir. Arturo Ripstein. With Claudio Brook, Rita Macedo and Arturo Beristáin. Estudios Churubusco, 1973.
Cat People. Dir. Jacques Tourneur, With Simone Simon and Kent Smith. RKO Radio Pictures, 1942.
Cendrillon. Dir. George Méliès. With Barral and Bleuette Bernon. George Méliès and Star Films, 1899.
Children of Men. Dir. Alfonso Cuarón. With Clive Owen and Julianne Moore. Universal, 2006.
Choca, La. Dir. Emilio Fernández. With Mercedes Carreño, Gregorio Casal and Chano Urueta. Conacite Uno, 1973.
Cita de amor. Una. Dir. Emilio Fernández. With Guillermo Cramer, Agustín Fernández and Jaime Fernández. Cinematográfica Latino Americana y Unipromex, 1956.
Citizen Kane. Dir. Orson Welles. Photog. Gregg Toland. With Orson Welles, Agnes Moorehead and Joseph Cotton. RKO, 1941.
Compadre Mendoza, El. Dir. Fernando de Fuentes, With Alfredo Del Diestro and Carmen Guerrero. CLASA Films, 1935.
Crepúsculo de un dios, El. Dir. Emilio Fernández. With Soledad Acosta and Sonia Amelio. Producciones Centauro, 1968.
Corazón bandolero. Dir. Raphael J. Sevilla. With Domingo Soler, Victoria Blanco and Emilio Fernández. México Films S.A., 1934.
Cronos. Dir. Guillermo del Toro. With Federico Luppi and Ron Perlman. IMCINE and Iguana Producciones, 1993.
Cuando levanta la niebla. Dir. Emilio Fernández. With Arturo de Córdova, Columba Domínguez, María Elena Marqués. Televoz, 1951.
Cuando los hijos se van. Dir. Juan Bustillo Oro. With Fernando Soler, Sara García and Joaquín pardavé. Grovas-Oro Films, 1941.
Cuando los hijos se van. Dir. Julián Soler. With Fernando Soler, Alberto Vázquez and Amparo Rivelles. Filmadora Chapultepec, 1969.
Cucaracha, La. Dir. Ismael Rodríguez. With Emilio Fernández, María Félix, Pedro Armendáriz and Dolores Del Rio. Azteca Films Inc., 1958.

Detour. Dir. Edgar G. Ulmer. With Tom Neal, Anne Savage. Producers Releasing Corporation, 1945.
Día de vida, Un. Dir. Emilio Fernández. With Roberto Cañedo, Fernando Fernández and Columba Domínguez. Cabrera Films, 1950.
Dirty Dancing. Dir. Emile Ardolino. With Patrick Swayze and Jennifer Gray. Vestron Pictures Ltd, 1987.
Distinto amanecer. Dir. Julio Bracho. With Andrea Palma, Pedro Armendáriz and Alberto Galán. Films Mundiales, 1944.
Dorado de Pancho Villa, Un. Dir. Emilio Fernández. With Emilio Fernández and Carlos López Moctezuma. Producciones Centauro, 1966.
Drums of Love. Dir. D. W. Griffith. With Lionel Barrymore and Mary Philbin. Art Cinema Corporation, 1928.
Duelo de pistoleros. Dir. Miguel M. Delgado. With Luis Aguilar, Dacia González and Manuel Capetillo. Cinematográfica Calderón, 1965.
Duelo en El Dorado. Dir. René Cardona. With Luis Aguilar, Crox Alvarado and Lola Beltrán. Cinematográfica Calderón, 1968.
Enamorada. Dir. Emilio Fernández. With María Félix, Pedro Armendáriz and Fernando Fernández. Panamerican Films, 1946.
Enamorado, El. Dir. Miguel Zacarías. With Pedro Infante and Sara Montiel. Producciones Zacarías, 1951.
Entrevista Díaz-Taft, La. Dir. Hermanos Alva. 1909.
Epopeyas de la revolución Dir. Gustavo Carrero. Tláloc Films, 1963.
Erótica. Dir. Emilio Fernández. With Jorge Rivero and Rebeca Silva. Conacite Uno, 1978.
Espinazo del diablo, El. Dir. Guillermo del Toro. With Federico Luppi, Eduardo Noriega and Marisa Paredes. Deseo S.A. and Tequila Gang, 2001.
Este pueblo no hay ladrones, En. Dir. Alberto Isaac. With Luis Buñuel and Alfonso Arau. Grupo Claudio, 1965.
Flor silvestre. Dir. Emilio Fernández. With Dolores Del Rio and Pedro Armendáriz. Films Mundiales, 1943.
Flying Down to Rio. Dir. Thornton Freedland. With Dolores Del Rio and Roger Bond. RKO, 1933.
Fort Apache. Dir. John Ford. With John Wayne, Ward Bond and Henry Fonda. Argosy Pictures, 1948.
From Russia With Love. Dir. Terence Young. With Sean Connery, Daniela Bianci and Pedro Armendáriz. Eon Productions, 1963.
Fugitive, The. Dir. John Ford. With Henry Fonda, Dolores Del Rio, Ward Bond and Pedro Armendáriz. Argosy Pictures, 1947.
Fuoco, Il. Dir. Piero Fosco. With Pina Manicheli and Febo Mari. Itala Films, 1915.
Gaucho, The. Dir. F. Richard Jones. With Douglas Fairbanks and Lupe Vélez. Elton Corporation, 1927.
Girl of the Rio, The. Dir. Herbert Brenon. With Dolores Del Rio and Leo Carillo. RKO, 1932.
Great Expectations. Dir. Alfonso Cuarón. With Gwyneth Paltrow and Ethan Hawke. 20th Century Fox, 1998.

Filmography

Great Train Robbery, The. Dir. Edwin Porter. With Anne Lubin. S. Lubin, 1903.
Harry Potter and the Prisoner of Azkaban. Dir. Alfonso Cuarón. With Daniel Radcliffe, Rupert Grint and Emma Watson. Warner Bros Pictures, 1492 Pictures, Heyday Films and P of A Productions Limited, 2004.
Hellboy. Dir. Guillermo del Toro. With Ron Perlman, Selma Blair and John Hurt. Dark Horse Entertainment and Revolution Studios, 2004.
Hermanos del hierro, Los. Dir. Ismael Rodríguez. With Antonio Aguilar and Julio Alemán. Cinematográfica Filmex, 1961.
Hermanos muerte, Los. Dir. Rafael Baledón. With Emilio Fernández, Lola Beltrán and Fernando Soler. Producciones Sotomayor, 1964.
Holiday. Dir. George Cukor. With Carry Grant and Katharine Hepburn. Columbia Pictures, 1938.
I was a Male War Bride. Dir. Howard Hawks. With Cary Grant and Anne Sheridan. 20th Century Fox, 1949.
Idiots, The. Dir. Lars Von Trier. With Bodil Jørgensen and Jens Albinus. Danish Broadcasting Corporation, 1998.
Impostor, El. Dir. Emilio Fernández. With Pedro Armendáriz. Cinematográfica Latino Americana o CLASA Films, 1956.
In Old Arizona. Dir. Raoul Walsh and Irving Cummings. With Baxter Edmund. Lowe and Dorothy Burgess. Fox Film Corporation, 1928.
Insurrección de México. Dir. Hermanos Alva. 1911.
Isla de pasión, La. Dir. Emilio Fernández. With David Silva, Ema. 1941.
Islas Marías, Las. Dir. Emilio Fernández. With Pedro Infante and Rosaura Revueltas. Rodríguez Hermanos, 1950.
It Happened One Night. Dir. Frank Capra. With Claudette Colbert and Clark Gable. Colombia Pictures, 1934.
Janitzio. Dir. Carlos Novaro. With Emilio Fernández and María Teresa Orozco, Compania Cinematográfica Mexicana, 1934.
Laberinto del fauno, El. Dir. Guillermo del Toro. With Adriana Gil, Ivana Baquero and Maribel Verdú. Warner Bros Pictures and Tequila Gang, 2006.
Lady Eve, The. Dir. Preston Sturges. With Barbara Stanwyck and Henry Fonda. Paramount Pictures, 1941.
Little Princess, A. Dir. Alfonso Cuarón. With Liesel Mathews and Eleanor Bron. Warner Bros. Pictures, 1995.
Lola Casanova. Dir. Matilde Landeta. With Meche Barba and José Baviera. TACMA, 1948.
Loves of Carmen, The. Dir. Raoul Walsh. With Dolores Del Rio and Don Alvarado. Fox Film Corporation, 1927.
Luz, La. Dir. Ezequiel Carrasco. With Ernesto Agüeros and Emma Padilla. México Lux Films S.A., 1917.
Maclovia. Dir. Emilio Fernández. With María Félix, Pedro Armendáriz and Miguel Inclán. Filmex S.A., 1948.
Malquerida, La. Dir. Emilio Fernández. With Dolores Del Rio, Pedro Armendáriz and Columba Domínguez. Francisco P. Cabrera, 1949.
Mancha de sangre, La. Dir. Adolfo Best Maguard. With Heriberto G. Batemberg and José Casal. [No production company], 1937.

María Candelaria. Dir. Emilio Fernández. With Dolores Del Rio and Pedro Armendáriz. Films Mundiales, 1943.
Memorias de un mexicano. Dir. Carmen Toscano and Salvador Toscano. CLASA-Mohme Inc., 1950.
México norte. Dir. Emilio Fernández. With Victor Alcocer, Narciso Busquets and Roberto Cañedo. Conacite Uno, 1977.
Mimic. Dir. Guillermo del Toro. With Mira Sorvino and Jeremy Northam. Miramax, 1997.
Morocco. Dir. Joseph Von Sternberg. With Gary Cooper and Marlene Dietrich. Paramount Pictures, 1930.
Mujer del puerto, La. Dir. Arcady Boytler. With Andrea Palma and Domingo Soler. Eurindia Films, 1934.
Mujer del puerto, La. Dir. Emilio Gómez Muriel. With María Antonieta Pons and Crox Alvarado. Óscar J. Brooks, 1949.
Negra Angustias, La. Dir. Matilde Landeta. With María Elena Marqués, Agustín Isunza and Eduardo Arozamena. TACMA, 1949.
Night of the Iguana, The. Dir. John Huston. With Richard Burton and Ava Gardner. MGM, 1964.
Noche de los Mayas, La. Dir. Chano Urueta. With Arturo de Córdova and Stela Inda. Fama Films, 1939.
Nosotros dos. Dir. Emilio Fernández. With Rossana Podestà, Marco Vicario and Tito Junco. Diana Films, 1954.
Nosotros los pobres. Dir. Ismael Rodríguez. With Pedro Infante, Blanca Estela Pavón and Evita Muñoz. Rodríguez Hermanos, 1947.
Notorious. Dir. Alfred Hitchcock. With Cary Grant, Ingrid Bergman and Claude Rains. RKO Radio Pictures and Vanguard Pictures, 1946.
Olvidados, Los. Dir. Luis Buñuel. With Miguel Inclán, Stela Inda and Roberto Cobo, Ultramar Films, 1950.
On the Town. Dir. Stanley Donen and Gene Kelly. With Gene Kelly and Frank Sinatra. MGM, 1949.
Paloma herida. Dir. Emilio Fernández. With Patricia Conde and Emilio Fernández. Manuel Zeseña, 1962.
Pat Garret and Billy the Kid. Dir. Sam Peckinpah. With James Coburn, Kris Kristofferson and Bob Dylan. MGM, 1973.
Pepita Jiménez. Dir. Emilio Fernández. With Rosita Díaz Gimeno, Ricardo Montalbán and Fortunio Bonavona. Águila Films, 1945.
Perla, La. Dir. Emilio Fernández. With Pedro Armendáriz, María Elena Marqués. Águila Films and RKO, 1945.
Pistolero fantasma, El. Dir. Albert Zugsmith. With Troy Donahue, Sabrina and Emilio Fernández. Famous Players International/Sagitario Films, 1967.
Prisionero trece, El. Dir. Fernando de Fuentes. With Alfredo del Diestre and Luis G. Barriero. Compania Nacional Productora de Películas, 1933.
Pueblerina. Dir. Emilio Fernández. With Roberto Cañedo and Columba Domínguez. Producciones Reforma and Ultramar Films, 1948.

Filmography

Pueblito. Dir. Emilio Fernández. With Columba Domínguez and José Alonso Cano. Producciones Bueno, 1961.
¡Que viva México! Dir. Sergei Eisenstein. Mosfilm, 1932.
Ramona. Dir. Edwin Carewe. With Dolores Del Rio and Warner Baxter. Inspiration Pictures, 1928.
Rapto, El. Dir. Emilio Fernández. With Jorge Negrete and María Félix. Filmadora Atlántida, 1953.
Rebelión de los colgados, La. Dirs. Emilio Fernández and Alfredo B. Crevana. With Pedro Armendáriz and Carlos López Moctezuma, José Kohn, 1954.
Red, La. Dir. Emilio Fernández. With Rossana Podestà, Crox Alvarado and Armando Silvestre. Reforma Films, 1953.
Red Dance, The. Dir. Raoul Walsh. With Charles Farrel and Dolores Del Rio. Fox Film Corporation, 1928.
Redes. Dir. Fred Zimmerman and Emilio Gómez Muriel. Photog. Paul Strand. With Silvio Hernández. Azteca Films, 1934.
Reportaje. Dir. Emilio Fernández. With Roberto Cañedo, Arturo de Córdova, Columba Domínguez. Televoz, 1953.
Resurrection. Dir. Edwin Carewe. With Dolores Del Rio and Rod La Rocque. Edwin Carewe Pictures and Inspiration Pictures, 1927.
Revólver sangriento, El. Dir. Miguel Delgado. With Emilio Fernández, Lola Beltrán and Luis Aguilar. 1963.
Rey del barrio, El. Dir. Gilberto Martínez Solares. With Germán Valdés (Tin Tan) and Silvia Pinal. As Films, 1950.
Rincón de las vírgines, El. Dir. Alberto Isaac. With Emilio Fernández and Alfonso Arau. Estudios Churubusco Azteca, 1972.
Río Escondido. Dir. Emilio Fernández. With María Félix, Fernando Fernández and Carlos López Moctezuma. CLASA Films, 1947.
Rosa blanca, La. Dir. Emilio Fernández. With Roberto Cañedo and Gina Cabrera. Películas Antillas, 1953.
Salón México. Dir. Emilio Fernández. With Marga López, Rodolfo Acosta and Roberto Cañedo. Clasa Films, 1949.
Sangre hermana. Dir. [and also produced by] Hermanos Alva, 1914.
Santa. Dir. Norman Foster. With Esther Fernández, Ricardo Montalbán and José Cibrián. Francisco P. Cabrera, 1943.
Santa. Dir. Antonio Moreno. With Lupita Tovar, Carlos Orellana and Donald Reed. Compania Nacional Productora de Películas, 1931.
Santa. Dir. Luis Peredo. With Elena Sánchez Valenzuela and Alfonso Busson. Ediciones Camus, 1918.
Searchers, The. Dir. John Ford. With John Wayne, Natalie Wood and Henry Brandon. Warner Bros, 1956.
Singin' in the Rain. Dir. Stanley Donen. With Gene Kelly, Donald O'Connor and Debbie Reynolds. MGM, 1952.
Sólo con tu pareja. Dir. Alfonso Cuarón. With Daniel Giménez Cacho and Claudia Ramírez. IMCINE, 1991.

Soy puro mexicano. Dir. Emilio Fernández. With Pedro Armendáriz, Oro Films. 1942.
Strike. Dir. Sergei Eisenstein. With Grigoria Aleksandrov and Aleksandr Antonov. Goskino and Proletkult, 1925.
Superloco, El. Dir. Juan José Segura. With Polo Ortín, Carlos Villarías and Emilio Fernández. Producciones Cinematográficas Exito, 1936.
Tempest. Dir. Sam Taylor. With John Barrymore and Camilla Horn. Joseph M Schenk Productions, 1928.
Ten Commandments, The. Dir. Cecil B. DeMille. With Charlton Heston, Yul Brynner and Anne Baxter. Paramount Pictures, 1956.
Three Godfathers. Dir. John Ford. With John Wayne, Harry Carey Jr. and Pedro Armendáriz. Argosy Pictures, 1948.
Tierra del Fuego se apaga, La. Dir. Emilio Fernández. With Ana María Lynch, Erno Crisa, and Armando Silvestre. Mapol, 1955.
Top Hat. Dir. Mark Sandrich. With Ginger Rodgers and Fred Astaire. RKO Radio Pictures, 1935.
Torch, The. Dir. Emilio Fernández. With Paulette Goddard, Pedro Armendáriz and Gilbert Roland. Eagle-Lion Films, 1950.
Touch of Evil. Dir. Orson Welles. With Charlton Heston, Orson Welles and Janet Leigh. Universal International Pictures, 1958.
Trader Horn. Dir. W.S. Van Dyke. With Harry Carey and Edwina Booth. MGM, 1931.
Trotacalles. Dir. Matilde Landeta. With Miroslava, Ernesto Alonso and Elda Peralta. TACMA, 1951.
Unforgiven, The. Dir. John Huston. With Burt Lancaster, Audrey Hepburn and Lillian Gish. James Production Inc., 1960.
Ustedes los ricos. Dir. Ismael Rodríguez. With Pedro infante, Blanca Estela Pavón and Evita Muñoz. Rodríguez Hermanos, 1948.
¡Vámonos con Pancho Villa! Dir. Fernando de Fuentes. With Domingo Soler and Antonio R. Frausto. CLASA Films. 1935.
Viaje a Yucatán. Dir. [and also produced by] Salvador Toscano. 1906.
Víctimas del pecado. Dir. Emilio Fernández. With Ninón Sevilla, Rodolfo Acosta and Tito Junco. Cinematográfica Calderón, 1950.
Virginian, The. Dir. Victor Fleming. With Gary Cooper and Walter Fleming. Paramount Pictures, 1929.
What Price Glory. Dir. Raoul Walsh. With Dolores Del Rio and Victor McLaglen. Fox Film Corporation, 1926.
Wild Bunch, The. Dir. Sam Peckinpah. With William Holden, Ernest Borgnine and Emilio Fernández. Warner Bros, 1969.
Y tu mamá también. Dir. Alfonso Cuarón. With Gael García Bernal, Maribel Verdú and Diego Luna. Producciones Anhelo and Bésame Mucho Pictures, 2001.
Zona roja. Dir. Emilio Fernández. With Fanny Caso, Armando Silvestre and Victor Junco. Conacite Uno, 1975.

Bibliography

Acevedo-Muñoz, Ernesto R. (2003) *Buñuel and Mexico: The Crisis of National Cinema*, Los Angeles: University of California Press.

Adorno, Theodor and Max Horkheimer. (1999) 'The Culture Industry: Enlightenment as Mass Deception,' in During (ed.), *The Cultural Studies Reader*, 31–41.

Alvarado, Manuel, John King and Ana M. López (eds). (1993) *Mediating Two Worlds: Cinematic Encounters in the Americas*, London: British Film Institute.

Anderson, Benedict. (1991) *Imagined Communities: Reflections on the Origin and Spread of Nationalism*, London: Verso.

Andrew, Dudley. (2000) 'The Unauthorized *Auteur* Today,' in Miller and Stam (eds), *Film and Theory*, 20–29.

Appadurai, Arjun. (1996) *Modernity at Large: Cultural Dimensions of Globalization*, Minneapolis: University of Minnesota Press.

Armes, Roy. (1987) *Third World Film Making and the West*, Berkeley: University of California Press.

Aspden, Peter. (1992) Rev. of *Danzón*, *Sight & Sound* 7: 41.

Ayala Blanco, Jorge. (2004) *La grandeza del cine mexicano*, México: Editorial Oceano.

—— (2001) *La fugacidad del cine mexicano*, México: Editorial Oceano.

—— (1994) *La eficacia del cine mexicano*, México: Editorial Grijalbo.

—— (1993) *La aventura del cine mexicano en la época de oro y después*, México: Editorial Grijalbo.

—— (1991) *La disolvencia del cine mexicano*, México: Editorial Grijalbo.

—— (1986) *La condición del cine mexicano (1973–1985)*. México: Editorial Grijalbo.

—— (1974) *La búsqueda del cine mexicano (1968–1972)*, México: Editorial Grijalbo.

Azuela, Mariano. (1988) *Los de abajo: novela de la revolución mexicana*, México: Fondo de Cultura Económica.

Balderston, Daniel. (1998) 'Poetry, Revolution, Homophobia: Polemics from the Mexican Revolution,' in Sylvia Molloy and Robert McKee (eds) *Hispanisms and Homosexualities*, Durham: Duke University Press, 57–75.
Barnard, Timothy. (1998) 'Book Review of *Mexican Cinema*,' *Studies in Latin American Popular Culture* 17: 255–63.
Bartra, Roger. (1996) *La jaula de la melancolía: identidad y metamorfosis del mexicano*, México: Editorial Grijalbo.
Bazin, André. (1982) *The Cinema of Cruelty: From Buñuel to Hitchcock*, New York: Seaver Books.
Behar, Ruth. (1993) *Translated Woman: Crossing the Border With Esperanza's Story*, Boston: Beacon Press.
Berg, Charles Ramírez. (2000) '*El automóvil gris* and the advent of Mexican Classicism,' in Noriega (ed.), *Visible Nations*, 3–32.
—— (1994) 'The Cinematic Invention of Mexico: The Poetics and Politics of the Fernández-Figueroa Style,' in Noriega and Ricci (eds), *Mexican Cinema Project*, 13–24.
—— (1992) *Cinema of Solitude: A Critical Study of Mexican Film, 1967–1983*. Austin: University of Texas Press.
Bhabha, Homi K. (1994) *Location of Culture*, London and New York: Routledge.
—— (1990) *Nation and Narration*, London and New York: Routledge, 1990.
Bonfil, Guillermo. (1987) *Mexico profundo: una civilización negada*, México: Secretaría de Educación Pública.
Borde, Raymond. (1954) 'Emilio Fernandez,' *Positif* May: 12–20.
Bordwell, David. (1985) *Narration in the Fiction Film*, Madison: University of Wisconsin Press.
—— and Kristin Thompson. (2001) *Film Art: An Introduction*, 6th edn, New York: McGraw Hill.
Brooks, Peter. (1991) 'The Melodramatic Imagination,' in Landy (ed.), *Imitations of Life: A Reader on Film and Television Melodrama*, 50–67.
Buñuel, Luis with Jean-Claude Carrière. (1996) *Mi último suspiro*, Barcelona: Plaza & Janes Editores S.A.
Burch, Noel. (1990) 'A Primitive Mode of Representation?' in Thomas Elsaesser (ed.), *Early Cinema: Space, Frame, Narrative*, London: British Film Institute Publishing, 220–27.
Burton-Carvajal, Julianne. Patricia Torres San Martín and Ángel Miquel (eds). (1998) *Horizontes del segundo siglo: Investigación y pedagogía del cine mexicano, latinoamericano y chicano*, Mexico: Universidad de Guadalajara and IMCINE, 13–27.
Burton-Carvajal, Julianne. (1998a) 'De la pantalla a la página: taxonomía y periodización de la bibliografía sobre cine latinoamericano,' in Burton-Carvajal et al.(eds), *Horizontes del segundo siglo*, 13–27.

Bibliography

—— (1998b) 'A String of Pearls of the Bibliographer's Recompense,' *Studies in Latin American Popular Culture* 17: 233–54.

—— (1992/3) 'Introduction: Changing Gender Perspectives in Latin American Film,' *Journal of Film and Video* 44(3–4): 3–7.

—— (1990) (ed.) *The Social Documentary in Latin America*, Pittsburgh: University of Pittsburgh Press.

Castillo, Debra A. (1998) *Easy Women: Sex and Gender in Modern Mexican Fiction*, Minneapolis: University of Minnesota Press.

Chanady, Amaryll (ed.). (1994) *Latin American Identity and Constructions of Difference*, Minneapolis: University of Minnesota Press.

Chanan, Michael. (2004) *Cuban Cinema*, Bloomington: Indiana University Press.

Colina, Enrique and Daniel Díaz Torres. (1972) 'Ideología del melodrama en el viejo cine latinoamericano,' *Cine Cubano* 74: 14–26.

Cuesta, Jorge. (1991) 'La nacionalidad mexicana,' *Ensayos Críticos de Jorge Cuesta*, Mexico: Universidad Nacional Autónoma de México, 465–9.

Dawson, Alexander S. (1998) 'From Models for the Nation to Model Citizens: Indigenismo and the "Revindication" of the Mexican Indian, 1920–40,' *Journal Latin American Studies* 30: 279–308.

De Certeau, Michel. (1988) *The Practice of Everyday Life*, Berkeley: University of California Press.

De la Mora, Sergio. (2006) *Cinemachismo: Masculinities in Mexican Film*, Austin: University of Texas Press.

—— (1999a) 'Pedro Infante y el Culto al Cuate,' *Archivos de la Filmoteca* 31: 88–104.

—— (1999b) 'Virile Nationalism: Cinema, the State, and the Formation of a National Consciousness in Mexico, 1950–1994.' Ph.D dissertation, University of California, Santa Cruz.

—— (1998) 'Masculinidad y mexicanidad: panorama teórico-bibliográfico,' in Burton-Carvajal et al. (eds), *Horizontes del segundo siglo*, 45–64.

De la Vega Alfaro, Eduardo. (2003) 'Allá en el Rancho Grande/Over there on the Big Ranch,' in Alberto Elena and Marina Díaz López (eds), *The Cinema of Latin America*, London: Wallflower Press, 25–33.

—— (1999) 'The Decline of the Golden Age and the Making of the Crisis,' *Mexico's Cinema: A Century of Film and Filmmakers*, Wilmington: Scholarly Resource Books, 165–92.

—— (1995) 'Origins, Development and Crisis of the Sound Cinema (1929–64),' in Paranaguá (ed.), *Mexican Cinema*, 79–93.

De los Reyes, Aurelio. (1996) *Dolores Del Río*, Ciudad de México: Grupo Condume & Fernández Cueto Editores.

—— (1996a) *Cine y sociedad en México: 1896–1930. Vivir de sueños/Bajo el cielo de México*, México: Universidad Nacional Autónoma de México.

—— (1995) 'The Silent Cinema,' in Paranaguá (ed.), *Mexican Cinema*, 63–77.

—— (1988) *Medio Siglo de cine mexicano 1896–1947*, Mexico City: Editorial Trilla.

Dever, Susan. (2003) *Celluloid Nationalism and Other Melodramas: From Post-Revolutionary Mexico to fin de siglo Mexamérica*, Albany: State University of New York Press.

—— (1994) 'Las de abajo: La Revolución Mexicana de Matilde Landeta,' *Archivos de la Filmoteca* 16: 37–49.

During, Simon. (1999) (ed.) 'Introduction,' *The Cultural Studies Reader*, London and New York: Routledge, 1–28.

Dyer, Richard. (1997) *White*, London and New York: Routledge.

—— (1993) 'And I Seem to Find the Happiness I Seek: Heterosexuality and Dance in the Musical,' in Helen Thomas (ed.), *Dance, Gender and Culture*, London: Macmillan, 49–65.

—— (1992) 'Entertainment and Utopia,' *Only Entertainment*, London and New York: Routledge, 17–34.

—— (1988) 'White,' *Screen* 29(4): 44–64.

Eagan, Linda. (2001) *Carlos Monsiváis: Culture and Chronicle in Contemporary Mexico*, Tucson: University of Arizona Press.

Elsaesser, Thomas. (1991) 'Tales of Sound and Fury: Observations on the Family Melodrama,' in Landy (ed.), *Imitations of Life*, 68–92.

Feder, Elena. (2001) 'Engendering the Nation, Nationalizing the Sacred: Guadalupismo and the Cinematic (Re)Formation of Mexican Consciousness,' in Mercedes F. Durán-Cogan and Antonio Gómez-Moriana (eds), *Hispanic Issues 23 National Identities and Sociopolitical Changes in Latin America*.

Fein, Seth. (2001) 'Myths of Cultural Imperialism and Nationalism in Golden Age Mexican Cinema,' in Joseph et al. (eds), *Fragments of a Golden Age*, 159–98.

—— (1999) 'From Collaboration to Containment: Hollywood and the International Political Economy of Mexican Cinema after the Second World War,' in Hershfield and Maciel (eds), *Mexico's Cinema*, Wilmington: Scholarly Resource Books, 123–63.

—— (1998) 'Transnationalization and Cultural Collaboration: Mexican Film Propaganda during World War II,' *Studies in Popular Latin American Culture* 17: 105–28.

Fernández, Adela. (1986) *El Indio Fernández: vida y mito*, México: Panorama.

—— (1985) *Diccionario ritual de voces nahuas*, Mexico, D.F.: Panorama Editorial.

—— (1983a) *Así vivieron las Mayas*, Mexico, D.F.: Panorama Editorial.

—— (1983b) *Dioses prehispánicos de México: mitos y deidades del panteón náhuatl*, Mexico, D.F.: Panorama Editorial.

—— (1983c) *Mayas: vida, cultura, y arte a través de un personaje de su tiempo*, Mexico, D.F.: Panorama Editorial.

Bibliography

Franco, Jean. (1993) 'High-Tech Primitivism: The Representation of Tribal Societies in Feature Films,' in Alvarado et al. (eds), *Mediating Two Worlds*, 81–94.

—— (1989) *Plotting Women: Gender and Representation in Mexico*, New York: Columbia University Press.

Gamboa, Federico. (2002) *Santa*, Madrid: Catedra.

García Canclini, Néstor. (1997) 'Will there be a Latin American Cinema in the Year 2000? Visual Culture in a Postnational Era,' in Ann-Marie Stock (ed.), *Framing Latin American Cinema: Contemporary Critical Perspectives*, Minneapolis: University of Minnesota Press, 246–58.

—— (1995) *Hybrid Cultures: Strategies for Entering and Leaving Modernity*, trans. Christopher L. Chiappari and Silvia L. López, Minneapolis: University of Minnesota Press.

García Espinosa, Julio. (1997 [1969]) 'For an Imperfect Cinema,' in Martin (ed.), *New Latin American Cinema* Vol. 1, 71–82.

García Riera, Emilio. (1998) *Breve historia del cine mexicano primer siglo 1897–1997*, México: Conaculta/Imcine.

—— (1993a) *Historia documental de cine*, Vol. 1. Mexico: Universidad de Guadalajara.

—— (1993b) *Historia documental de cine*, Vol. 2. Mexico: Universidad de Guadalajara.

—— (1993c) *Historia documental de cine*, Vol. 3. Mexico: Universidad de Guadalajara.

—— (1993d) *Historia documental de cine*, Vol. 4. Mexico: Universidad de Guadalajara.

—— (1987) *Emilio Fernández 1904–1986*. México: Cineteca Nacional de México y Universidad de Guadalajara.

—— (1985) *Historia del cine mexicano*, Mexico City: Secretaria de la Educación Pública.

Gledhill, Christine. (1987) 'The Melodramatic Field: An Investigation,' in her (ed.), *Home is Where The Heart Is: Studies in Melodrama and the Women's Film*, London: British Film Institute, 5–39.

Gruzinski, Serge. (2001) *Images at War: Mexico from Columbus to Blade Runner*, trans. Heather MacLean. Durham: Duke University Press.

Hall, Stuart. (1999) 'Encoding/Decoding,' in During (ed.), *Cultural Studies Reader*, 507–17.

—— (1990) 'The Whites of Their Eyes,' in Manuel Alvarado and John O. Thompson (eds), *The Media Reader*, London: British Film Institute, 8–23.

—— (1981) 'Notes on Deconstructing the "Popular",' in Raphael Samuels (ed.), *People's History and Socialist Theory*, London and New York: Routledge, 227–39.

Hershfield, Joanne. (1999) 'Race and Ethnicity in the Classical Cinema,' in idem and David R. Maciel (eds), *Mexico's Cinema: A Century of Film and Filmmakers*, Wilmington: Scholarly Resource Books, 81–100.

—— (1996) *Mexican Cinema, Mexican Woman 1940–1950*, Austin: University of Texas Press.

Higson, Andrew. (1989) 'The Concept of a National Cinema,' *Screen* 30(4): 36–46.

Hoggart, Richard. (1957) *The Uses of Literacy Aspects of Working-class Life with Special Rreference to Publications and Entertainments*, London: Chatto & Windus.

Huaco-Nuzum, Carmen. (1992) 'Ni de aquí, ni de allá: Indigenous Female Representation in the films of María Elena Velasco,' in Noriega (ed.), *Chicanos and Film*, 127–38.

Irwin, Robert. (1997) 'Los de abajo y los debates sobre la identidad masculina nacional,' in Silvia Elguea Vejar (ed.), *La otredad*, Mexico City: Universidad Autónoma Metropolitana, 71–82.

Isaac, Alberto. (1993) *Conversaciones con Gabriel Figueroa*, Mexico: CIEC, Universidad de Guadalajara.

Joseph, Gilbert, Anne Rubenstein and Eric Zolov (eds). (2001) 'Assembling the Fragments: Writing a Cultural History of Mexico since 1940,' in *Fragments of a Golden Age: The Politics of Culture in Mexico since 1940*, Durham: Duke University Press, 3–22.

King, John. (2000) *Magical Reels: A History of Cinema in Latin America* Rev. edn. London: Verso, 2000.

Kraniauskas, John (trans.). (1997) 'Critical Closeness: The Chronicle Essays of Carlos Monsiváis,' in Monsiváis, *Mexican Postcards*, London: Verso, ix–xxii.

Landy, Marcia (ed.) (1991) Introduction. *Imitations of Life: A Reader on Film and Television Melodrama*, Detroit: Wayne State University Press, 13–30.

Larsen, Neil. (1995) *Reading North by South: On Latin American Literature, Culture and Politics*, Minneapolis: University of Minnesota Press.

Lent, Tina Olsin. (1995) 'Romantic Love and Friendship: The Redefinition of Gender Relations in Screwball Comedy,' in Kristine Brunouske Karnick and Henry Jenkins (eds), *Classical Hollywood Comedy*, London and New York: Routledge, 314–30.

Levi, Heather. (2001) 'Masked Media: The Adventures of Lucha Libre on the Small Screen,' in Joseph et al., *Fragments of a Golden Age*, 330–72.

Lomitz Adler, Claudio. (1992) *Exits from the Labyrinth: Culture and Ideology in the Mexican National Space*, Berkeley: University of California Press.

López, Ana M. (2002) 'Early Cinema and Modernity in Latin America,' *Cinema Journal* 40(1): 48–78.

—— (2000a) 'Crossing Nations and Genres: Travelling Filmmakers,' in Noriega, *Visible Nations*, 33–50.

—— (2000b) 'Facing up to Hollywood,' in Christine Gledhill and Linda Williams (eds), *Reinventing Film Studies*, New York: Arnold/Oxford University Press, 419–37.

Bibliography

—— (2000c) 'Fernández, Emilio ('El Indio'),' in idem, Dan Balderston and Mike Gonzalez (eds), *Encyclopedia of Caribbean and Latin American Cultures*, London and New York: Routledge, 560.

—— (1998) 'From Hollywood and Back: Dolores Del Rio, A Trans(National) Star,' *Studies in Latin American Popular Culture* 17: 5–32.

—— (1997) 'Of Rhythms and Borders,' in Celeste Fraser Delgado and José Esteban Muñoz (eds), *Every Nightlife: Culture and Dance in Latin/o America*, Durham: Duke University Press, 310–40.

—— and Chon A. Noriega (eds). (1996) *The Ethnic Eye: Latino Media Arts*, Minneapolis: Minnesota University Press.

—— (1994) 'A Cinema for a Continent,' in Noriega and Ricci (eds), *The Mexican Cinema Project*, 7–12.

—— (1993a) 'Tears and Desire: Women and Melodrama in the "Old" Mexican Cinema,' in Alvarado et al., *Mediating Two Worlds*, 147–64.

—— (1993b) 'Are all Latins From Manhattan? Hollywood, Ethnography and Cultural Colonialism,' in idem, Alvarado and King (eds), *Mediating Two Worlds*, 67–80.

—— (1991) 'The Melodrama in Latin America: films, telenovelas and the currency of a Popular Form,' in Landy (ed.), *Imitations of Life*, 596–606.

Machlachlan, Colin M, and William Beezley. (1999) *El Gran Pueblo: A History of Greater Mexico*, 2nd edn. Upper Saddle River, N.J.: Prentice Hall.

Magdaleno, Mauricio. (1937 [1929]) *El resplandor*. Mexico: Ediciones Bota.

Martí, José. (1977) *Nuestra América*, Caracas: Biblioteca Ayacucho.

Martin, Michael T. (1997) *New Latin American Cinema*, Vol. 1: *Theory, Practices and Transcontinental Articulations*, Detroit: Wayne State University Press.

Martín Barbero, Jesús. (1998) *De los medios a las mediaciones: Comunicación, cultura y hegemonia*, Mexico: Ediciones Gili.

—— (1995) 'Memory and Form in the Latin American soap-opera,' in Robert C. Allen (ed.), *To be Continued... Soap Operas around the World*, London and New York: Routledge, 276–85.

Martínez, Rubén. 'Corazón del Rocanrol,' in Joseph et al., *Fragments of a Golden Age*, 373–89.

Miller, Michael Nelson. (1998) *Red, White, and Green: The Maturing of Mexicanidad 1940–1960*, El Paso: Texas Western Press.

Miller, Toby and Robert Stam. (2000) *Film And Theory: An Anthology*, Boston: Blackwell.

Miquel, Ángel. (1998) 'Reseña bibliográfica de la historia reciente del cine en México,' in Burton-Carvajal et al. (eds), *Horizontes del segundo siglo*, 28–38.

Monsiváis, Carlos. (2000) *Aires de familia: cultura y sociedad en América Latina*, Barcelona: Editorial Anagrama.

—— (1997) *Mexican Postcards*, trans. John Kraniauskas. London: Verso, 88–105.

—— (1995a) 'All the People Came and Did Not Fit Onto the Screen: Notes on the Cinema Audience in Mexico,' in Paranaguá (ed.), *Mexican Cinema*, 145–51.

—— (1995b) *Los rituales del caos*, Mexico City: Biblioteca Era.

—— (1995c) 'Mythologies,' in Paranaguá (ed.), *Mexican Cinema*, 117–127.

—— (1994a) and Carlos Bonfil *A través del espejo: el cine mexicano y su público*, México: Ediciones el Milagro.

—— (1994b) 'Se sufre pero se aprende: el melodrama y las reglas de la falta de límites,' *Archivos de la filmoteca* 16: 7–19.

—— (1993) 'Mexican Cinema: Of Myths and Demythifications,' in Alvarado et al. (eds), *Mediating Two Worlds*, 139–46.

—— (1992) 'Emilio Fernández, El Indio: Los sueños de la nación engendran símbolos,' *Intermedios* 11 (March), 28–39.

—— (1988a) *Escenas de pudor y liviandad*, Mexico City: Grijalbo, 1988.

—— (1988b) 'Gabriel Figueroa: Establishing Point of View,' *Artes de México* 2: 93–5.

—— (1985) '"Landscape, I've got the Drop on You." (On the Fiftieth Anniversary of sound Film in Mexico),' *Studies in Latin American Popular Culture* 4: 236–47.

—— (1977) 'Salvador Novo: Los que tenemos unas manos que no nos pertenecen,' *Amor perdido*, Mexico City: Biblioteca Era, 265–96.

—— (1976) 'Notas sobre la cultura mexicana en el siglo XX,' in Daniel Cosío Villegas (ed.), *Historia general de México*,Vol. 4. México: El Colegio de México. 305–476.

Mora, Carl J. (1989) *Mexican Cinema: Reflections of a Society, 1896–1988*, Berkeley: University of California Press.

Morris, Meaghan. (1990) 'Banality in Cultural Studies,' in Patricia Mellencamp (ed.), *Logics of Television*, Bloomington: Indiana University Press, 14–43.

Mraz, John. (2001) 'Today, Tomorrow, and Always: The Golden Age of Illustrated Magazines in Mexico, 1937–1960,' in Joseph et al. (eds), *Fragments of a Golden Age*, 116–57.

Mulvey, Laura. (1990) 'Visual Pleasure and Narrative Cinema,' in Patricia Erens (ed.), *Issues in Feminist Film Criticism*, Bloomington: Indiana University Press, 28–40.

Musser, Charles. (1990) *The Emergence of Cinema: The American Screen to 1907*, New York: Charles Scribner's Sons.

Naremore, James. (1993) *The Films of Vincente Minnelli*, Cambridge: Cambridge University Press.

—— (1990) 'Authorship and the Cultural Politics of Film Criticism,' *Film Quarterly* 44(1): 14–22.

—— (1988) *Acting in the Cinema*, London: University of California Press.

Bibliography

Nason, Richard W. (1984) 'Mexican on the Move: Pedro Armendariz is Discovering that All the World is a Sound Stage,' *New York Times Encyclopedia of Film 1952–57*, New York: New York Times Books.
Nava, Mica. (1987) 'Consumerism and Its Contradictions,' *Cultural Studies* 1(2): 204–10.
Noble, Andrea. (2005) *Mexican National Cinema*, London and New York: Routledge.
—— (2001) 'If Looks Could Kill: Image Wars in *María Candelaria*,' *Screen* 42: 77–91.
Noriega, Chon A. (2000) (ed.) Introduction. *Visible Nations: Latin American Cinema and Video* Minneapolis: Minnesota University Press. xi–xxv.
—— (ed.) (1992) *Chicanos and Film: Representation and Resistance*, Minneapolis: Minnesota University Press.
—— and Steven Ricci (eds).(1994) *Mexican Cinema Project*, Los Angeles: UCLA Film and Television Archive.
Nowell Smith, Geoffrey. (1987) 'Minnelli and Melodrama,' in Gledhill (ed.), *Home is Where the Heart Is*, 70–4.
O'Connor, Alan. (1991) 'The Emergence of Cultural Studies in Latin America,' *Critical Studies in Mass Communication* 8: 60–73.
O'Malley, Ilene V. (1986) *The Myth of the Revolution: Hero Cults and the Institutionalization of the Mexican State, 1920–1940*, New York: Greenwood Press.
Paranaguá, Paulo Antonio. (1998) 'Of Periodizations and Paradigms: The Fifties in Comparative Perspective,' *Nuevo Texto Critico* 11(21–22): 31–43.
—— (ed.). (1995) 'Ten Reasons to Love or Hate Mexican Cinema,' *Mexican Cinema*, London: British Film Institute, 1–13.
Paz, Octavio. (1997 [1951]) *El laberinto de la soledad*, Mexico: Fondo de Cultural Económica.
Peredo Castro, Francisco.(2004) *Cine y propaganda para Latinoamérica: México y Estados Unidos en la encrucijada de los años cuarenta*, México: Universidad Nacional Autónoma de México.
Perkins, Victor. (1990) 'Film Authorship: The Premature Burial,' *CineAction* Summer/Fall: 57–63.
Pick, Zuzana M. (2006) *Transnational Formations: Imagery of the Mexican Revolution*, manuscript.
—— (1993) *The New Latin American Cinema: A Continental Project*, Austin: Texas University Press.
Pilcher, Jeffrey M. (2001) 'Mexico's Pepsi Challenge: Cooking, Mass Consumptions and National Identity,' in Joseph et al., *Fragments of a Golden Age*, 71–90.
Podalsky, Laura. (1993a) 'Disjointed Frames: Melodrama, Nationalism and Representation in 1940s Mexico,' *Studies in Latin American Popular Culture* 12: 57–73.
—— (1993b) 'Patterns of the Primitive: Sergei Eisenstein's ¡*Que viva México!*' in Alvarado et al., *Mediating Two Worlds*, 25–40.

Ramos, Julio. (2001) *Divergent Modernities: Culture and Politics in Nineteenth-century Latin America*, Durham: Duke University Press.
Ramos, Samuel. (1972) *Profile of Man and Culture in Mexico*, trans. Peter G. Earle, Austin: University of Texas Press.
Rashkin, Elissa J. (2001) *Woman Filmmakers in Mexico: The Country of Which We Dream*, Austin: University of Texas Press.
Rozado, Alejandro. (1991) *Cine y realidad social en México: Una lectura de la obra de Emilio Fernández*, Mexico: Universidad de Guadalajara.
Schatz, Thomas. (1988) *The Genius of the System: Hollywood Filmmaking in the Studio Era*, New York: Pantheon Books.
Schmidt, Arthur. (2001) 'Making It Real Compared to What? Reconceptualizing Mexican History since 1940,' in Joseph et al. (eds), *Fragments of a Golden Age*, 23–68.
Shakespeare, William. (2000) *The Taming of the Shrew*, New York: Applause.
Shea, Maureen. (1993) 'Latin American Women and the Oral Tradition: Giving Voice to the Voiceless,' *Critique* 34(3): 139–53.
Shohat, Ella. (1991) 'Ethnicities in Relation: Toward a Multicultural Reading of American Cinema,' in Lester D. Friedman (ed.), *Unspeakable Images: Ethnicity and the American Cinema*, Urbana: University of Illinois Press, 215–50.
Smith, Paul Julian. (2003) *Amores Perros*, British Film Institute Modern Classic, London: British Film Institute.
Solanas, Fernando and Octavio Getino. (1997 [1970]) 'Towards a Third Cinema,' in Martin, *New Latin American Cinema*, Vol. 1, 33–58.
Sommer, Doris. (1991) *Foundational Fictions: The National Romances of Latin America*, Berkeley: University of California Press.
Spence, Louise and Robert Stam. (1999) 'Colonialism, Racism and Representation,' in Leo Braudy and Marshall Cohen (eds), *Film Theory and Criticism: Introductory Readings* 5th edn, Oxford: Oxford University Press, 235–49.
Spivak, Gayatri. (1995) 'Can the Subaltern Speak?' in Bill Ashcroft, Gareth Griffiths and Helen Tiffin (eds), *The Post-Colonial Studies Reader*, London and New York: Routledge, 24–8.
Stam, Robert. (2000) *Film and Theory*, Oxford: Blackwell Publishers.
Steinbeck, John. (1975) *The Pearl*, New York: Bantam Books.
Syder, Andrew, and Dolores Tierney. (2005) 'Mexploitation /Exploitation: or How a Crime-fighting, Vampire-slaying Mexican Wrestler almost Found himself in a Sword-and-sandals Epic,' in Stephen Jay Schneider and Tony Williams (eds), *Horror International*, Detroit: Wayne State University Press, 33–55.
Taibo, Paco Ignacio. (1986) *El Indio Fernández: El cine por mis pistolas*, Mexico: Planeta.
Tasker, Yvonne. (1993) *Spectacular Bodies: Genre, Gender and the Action Cinema*, London and New York: Routledge.

Bibliography

Tierney, Dolores. (2003) 'Gender Relations and Mexican Cultural Nationalism in Emilio Fernández' *Enamorada*/Woman in Love,' *Quarterly Review of Film and Video* 20(3): 225–36.

—— (1997) 'Silver Sling-Backs and Mexican Melodrama: *Salón México* and *Danzón*,' *Screen* 38(4): 360–72.

Torres San Martín, Patricia. (1999) 'Adela Sequeyro and Matilde Landeta: Two Pioneer Women Directors,' in Hershfield and Maciel (eds), *Mexico's Cinema*, 37–48.

—— (1998) 'La investigación sobre el cine de mujeres en México,' Burton-Carvajal et al. (eds), *Horizontes del segundo siglo*, 39–64.

—— and Eduardo de la Vega Alfaro. (1997) *Adela Sequeyro*, Mexico: Universidad de Guadalajara.

Tuñón, Julia. (2003) '*María Candelaria*,' in Elena Alberto and Marina Díaz López (eds), *The Cinema of Latin America*, London: Wallflower Press, 45–51.

—— (2000) *Los rostros de un mito: Personajes femeninos en las películas de Emilio Indio Fernández*, Mexico: Conaculta and Imcine.

—— (1997) *Mujeres de luz y sombra en el cine mexicano: la construcción de una imagen 1939–1952*. Mexico: Instituto Mexicano de Cinematografía.

—— (1995) 'Emilio Fernández: A Look Behind Bars,' Paranaguá (ed.), *Mexican Cinema*, 179–92.

—— (1993) 'Between the Nation and Utopia: The Image of Mexico in the Films of Emilio "Indio" Fernández,' *Studies in Popular Culture* 12: 159–74.

—— (1988) *En su propio espejo (Entrevista con Emilio 'El Indio' Fernández)*, México: Universidad Autónoma Metropolitana.

Vargas, Juan Carlos. (2002) 'Mexican post-industrial cinema (1990–2002)' *El ojo que piensa* online magazine, www.elojoquepiensa.udg.mx/ingles/revis_03/secciones/codex/artic_02.pdf, accessed 10 March 2006.

Vasconcelos, José. (1999) *La raza cósmica*, Mexico: Colección Austral.

West, Dennis. (1999) 'South American Cinema: A Critical Filmography, 1915–1994,' Book Review, *Cineaste* 25(1): 61.

Willemen, Paul. (1994) *Looks and Frictions: Essays in Cultural Studies and Film Theory*, London: British Film Institute.

Wolfe, Bertram David. (2000) *The Fabulous Life of Diego Rivera*, New York: Cooper Square Press.

Woll, Allen L. (1980) *The Latin Image in American Film*, Los Angeles: UCLA Latin American Center Publications, University of California Press.

Wollen, Peter. (1970) *Signs and Meaning in the Cinema*, London: British Film Institute.

Wu, Harmony. (2000) 'Consuming Tacos and Enchiladas: Gender and Nation in *Como Agua Para Chocolate*,' in Chon Noriega (ed.), *Visible Nations*, 174–93.

Zolov, Eric. (1999) *Refried Elvis: The Rise of the Mexican Counter Culture*, Berkeley: University of California Press.

Index

Note: 'n' after a page reference indicates the number of a note on that page. Page numbers in *italic* refer to illustrations and numbers in **bold** refer to the main discussion of that film/genre.

abandonadas, Las 2–3, 8, 20, 54, 63, 107, 121–3, **137–9**, 142, 169
Academia Mexicana de Ciencias y Artes Cinematográficas, La 25
Acevedo-Muñoz, Ernesto 12–13, 144, 148, 150–1, 154–5, 159n.9
Acosta, Rodolfo 122, 139
Adiós Nicanor 65
Adorno, Theodor 33
Afro-Mexican 135–6, 142–3n.4
Alemán, Miguel 2–3, 28, 34, 52, 143, 145–6, 148, 150–3, 159n.9, 160, 171n.2
alemanista 34, 145, 150
Almas rebeldes 65
Alva brothers 19
  Entrevista Díaz-Taft, La 19
  Insurrección de México 19
Amores perros 13, 46n.6
Anderson, Benedict 37
Andrew, Dudley 71
Angels With Dirty Faces 119n.1
Appadurai, Arjun 31
Ariel award 25, 161–2, 165
Dr Arlt 55
Armendáriz, Pedro 1, 65, 81, 84–9, 95, 97–8, *99*, 108, 112, 119n.2, 137, 169–70
Armes, Roy 12, 48, 55

auteur criticism 12, 48, 50, 162
auteurism 5, 7, 9, 50–2, 54–5, 57, 60, 71, 75, 163, 170
Ávila Camacho, Manuel 2–3, 23–4, 26–8, 34, 52
avilacamachista 34
Ayala Blanco, Jorge 9, 11, 74, 124, 126, 143, 148
Azuela, Mariano 102n.7
  Los de abajo 102n.7, 105

Balderston, Daniel 105
Baledón, Rafael 164
  hermanos muerte, Los 164
Banco Cinematográfico 10, 27, 146
Bandida, La 164, 167
Bartra, Roger 42, 49, 106–7
Basic Instinct 114
Bazin, André 5, 71
Behar, Ruth 68
Benjamin, Walter 11
Berg, Charles Ramírez 2–5, 7, 12–16n.7, 20, 29, 43, 46n.3, 47n.11, 48, 55–7, 63, 71, 74, 85–6, 90, 145, 153–4, 160, 165–6
Bernal, Manuel 148, 150 159n.9
Best Maguard, Adolfo 22
  mancha de sangre, La 22
Bhabha, Homi 11, 35, 75, 133, 143n.2

Index

bolero 22–3, 129 *see also* Agustín Lara
Bon, C.F. 18
Bonfil, Carlos 11
Bonfil, Guillermo 49
Borde, Raymond 3, 53–5
Bordwell, David 89, 156
Boytler, Arcady 22, 122
  mujer del puerto, La (1934) 22, 122–3, 126
Bracho, Julio 11, 42, 60, 121, 164–5
  Distinto amanecer 121, 123
Brandon, Henry 86
Bring Me the Head of Alfredo García see Peckinpah, Sam
Broken Arrow 86, 102n.9
Brooks, Peter 35, 125
Bugambilia 63, 67, 170
Buñuel, Luis 12–13, 16n.9, 48, 70–1, 151, 155, 159n.9
  olvidados, Los 16n.9, 151, 155–6, 162
  Nazarín 159n.11
  Mi último suspiro 70–1
Burton-Carvajal, Julianne 10
Busquets, Narciso 69, 104
Bustillo Oro, Juan 34, 165
  Ahí está el detalle 34–5
  Cuando los hijos se van (1941) 165

cabaretera see film genres
Cahiers du cinéma 5, 54
Campana de Dolores 146, 159n.4
Cañedo, Roberto 65, 98, 122
Cannes Film Festival 1, 25, 53, 84, 161–2, 166
Cantinflas (Mario Moreno) 34–5, 84, 163
Cárdenas, Lázaro 22–4, 26, 47n.8, 52, 78, 83, 103n.16, 116, 148
  cardenismo 26, 83, 153
  cardenist 79
Cardona, René 3, 164
  Duelo en el Dorado 164
Carranza, Venustiano 4, 20, 63
Castillo, Debra 46n.7, 123
Ceballos, Margarita 139

Centro de Investigación y Estudios Cinematográficos (CIEC) 10–11
Chanan, Michael 46n.5
chingada, la 106–7
chingón, el 105–6, 167
Choca, La 66, 165
churros 42, 161–2, 165, 168
Churubusco Studios 3, 166
cita de amor, Una 162, 170
Cineteca Nacional 71
CLASA films 25–6
Colina, Enrique 30, 38, 125
comedia ranchera see film genres
Contemporáneos 102n.10, 105
contradanza 136
Corazón bandolero 65
Cortés, Busi 14
Cortés, Hernán 41, 73, 106
Cosío Villegas, Daniel 148, 151
crepúsculo de un dios, El 164
Crevana, Alfredo B. 162
Cuando levanta la niebla 161
Cuarón, Alfonso 46n.6
Cuba 30, 161
Cuban 135–6, 140
  Afro-Cuban 135–6, 140, 143n.6, 169
  market 162
  revolution 162
cucaracha, La see Ismael Rodríguez
Cuesta, Jorge 102n.10
cultural nationalism 2
  classical Mexican cinema and 2, 26–7, 32, 39, 44–5, 51, 166, 169
  Eisenstein and 78, 107
  Fernández and 4, 6–9, 12, 16n.8, 18, 33–5, 44, 57, 71, 144–5, 155, 168, 170–1
  gender, sexuality and 108–119, 122–3, 130–1, 134–5, 137, 139, 141
  Government and 28, 148, 151–2
  indigenismo and 79–80, 87, 94
  race and 135, 141

danzón 122, 130, 132–6, 140–1
Davison, Tito 3

Dawson, Alexander 75
De Certeau, Michel 28, 31, 37, 50
de Fuentes, Fernando 1, 22–3, 42, 52, 60
  Allá en el Rancho Grande 23, 28, 47n.8
  compadre Mendoza, El 22, 39
  prisionero trece, El 22
  ¡Vámonos con Pancho Villa! 22, 26, 52
de la Huerta, Adolfo 63–4
de la Mora, Sergio 13–14, 119n.2, 161
de la Vega Alfaro, Eduardo 2, 11, 26–7, 47n.8, 143, 160–1
Delgado, Miguel 164
  Duelo de pistoleros 164
  revólver sangriento, El 164
de los Reyes, Aurelio 9–11, 18–21, 74, 78–9, 84, 88, 102n.6, 102n.10, 169
del Rio, Dolores 1, 10–11, 14–15, 15n.2, 64–5, 74, 81, 84–91, 94, 102n.4, 102n.6, 137, 169
  as María Candelaria 89, 92-3
del Toro, Guillermo 46n.6
Derba, Mimi 122
Derbez, Silvia 122
Dever, Susan 12–14, 16n.8, 83, 102n.5, 151–2
día de vida, Un 66, 161
Díaz, Porfirio 4, 18–19, 26
  Porfirian 4, 105, 117
  Porfiriato 26, 73
Díaz Conde, Antonio 65
Díaz Torres, Daniel 30, 38, 125
Dirty Dancing 130
Dogme '95 43
Domínguez, Columba 65, 97, 154
Domínguez, Francisco 65
Dondé, Manuel 97
dorado de Pancho Villa, Un 164
Dracula (George Melford, 1931) 21
During, Simon 31
Dyer, Richard 60, 80, 86–7, 90–2, 94, 103 n.12, 128–30

Eagan, Linda 11–12
Echeverría, Luis 165
Eisenstein, Sergei 8, 16n.7, 33–4, 47n.9, 55, 64, 77–8
  Eisensteinian 79–80, 82, 153, 155, 159n.11
  see also ¡Que viva México!
Elsaesser, Thomas 126–7
Enamorada 2–3, 6, 8, 16n.8–9, 25, 57, 63, **104**, **107–22**, 121–2, 124, 153, 169, 170
Enamorado, El 119n.2
Erótica 166
Estridentistas 105

Feder, Elena 12
Fein, Seth 14, 24–5, 52–3, 117, 151–2, 157–8n.1, 159n.9, 159n.9, 160
Fernández, Adela 12, 48, 62–3, 69, 72n.2–6, 106
Fernández, Emilio 61
  life story 63–7
  films, as extra 16n.6
  films acted in 65, 162, 164–5
  see also Baledón, Rafael; Cardona, René; *Flor Silvestre*; Huston, John; Jurado, Peckinpah, Sam; Rodríguez, Ismael
Fernández, Fernando 56, 144
fichera 122–3, 130–1, 139–41
Figueroa, Gabriel 1–2, 12, 25, 29, 47n.9–48, 54–7, 65, 111, 118–19, 145, 159n.11, 162, 170
Film genres
  action adventure 6, 109, 112–13
  cabaretera 14, 22, 36, 44, 54–5, **121–43**, 171n.2
  chili-western 164, 167
  comedia ranchera 22–3, 28, 35, 171n.2
  melodrama 5–6, 8, 13–14, 22, 30–1, 35–6, 38, 44–5, 104, 108, 110, 112, 117–19, 121, **124–9**, 136, 157
  musicals 128, 130
  screwball comedy (in *Enamorada*) 6, 8, 29, 57, 104, 107–8, **112–18**, 169

Index

western 33, 56, 85, 102n.9, 124, 149
women's films 8, 29, 127, 130–1, **139–40**, 143n.1, 169
Fiske, John 38
Flor Silvestre 27, 34, 60, 65, 107, 149, 153, **156–7**, 162, 171n.1
Ford, John 5, 16n.7, 55, 86, 88
  Fort Apache 88
  Fugitive, The 88
  Searchers, The 86
  Three Godfathers 88
Foster, Norman see *Santa* (1943)
Fox, Vicente 49
Franco, Jean 16n.9, 63, 106, 108, 110, 115–17
Frankfurt School 30–1, 38

Galán, Alberto 80
Galindo, Alejandro 1, 42, 60, 165
  Almas rebeldes 65
Gamboa, Federico 21, 123
  Santa 46n.7, 123
García Ascot, Jomí 163
  balcón vácio, En el 163
García Canclini, Néstor 29, 32, 51, 58, 71, 168–9
García Espinosa, Julio 42, 50
García Márquez, Gabriel 163
García Riera, Emilio 3, 8–12, 15n.1-n.5, 23, 25, 27, 29, 42, 48, 53–4, 63–4, 69–71, 74, 94–5, 98, 102n.3, 104, 120n.4–21, 132, 138, 149, 159n.4, 160–7
Gavaldón, Roberto 1, 3, 64, 165
Getino, Octavio 50, 159n.10
Gledhill, Christine 35, 110, 127, 140, 143n.1
Goddard, Paulette 170
Gómez Muriel, Emilio 22, 78, 143n.3
  mujer del puerto, La (1949) 143n.3
  Redes 22, 26, 52, 74, 78
Gout, Alberto 122
  Aventurera 122, 129–30, 137, 139, 142
Gramsci, Antonio 50
Gramscian 32

Grant, Cary 113
  Bringing up Baby 113–14
  I was a Male War Bride 113
  Holiday 117
Grey Car Gang 139
  see also *abandonadas, Las*
Gruzinski, Serge 83
Gutiérrez Alea, Tomás 49

Hall, Stuart
  'Encoding/Decoding' 5, 43–5, 119
  'Notes on Deconstructing the Popular' 31, 37; 47n.10
  'Whites of Their Eyes' 62
Hayek, Salma 46n.6
hermanos del hierro, Los 164
Hershfield, Joanne 13, 16n.9, 74, 121, 123–4, 132, 134–6, 143n.4, 151, 159n.9
Heston, Charlton 91
Hidalgo, Padre Miguel 146, 158n.2
Higson, Andrew 51–3
Hitchcock, Alfred 5, 49, 103n.16
  Notorious 103n.16
Hoggart, Richard 30
Holiday see Grant, Cary
Hollywood 50, 52–5, 80
  and classical Mexican cinema 17, 39–43, 168
  collaboration with and containment of Mexican film industry 24–5, 160–1
  depiction and image of Mexicans 85–8, 102n.8, 167, 169
  Fernández 'in' 3, 16n.6, 64–6, 103n.15, 162, 164–5, 170
  Fernández' borrowings from 6, 8, 29, 57, 75, 82, 169
Hispanic cinema 21–2
melodrama see Film genres
musicals see Film genres
screwball comedy see Film genres
share of Mexican market, 15n.1, 29
Horkheimer, Max 33
Huaco-Nuzum, Carmen 74, 84
Huerta, Victoriano 20

Huston, John
 Unforgiven, The 162
 Night of the Iguana, The 164
Hybridity 8, 38, 73, 75, 94-5, 169

Impostor, El (1936) 65
Impostor, El (1956) 66, 162
Iñárritu, Alejandro González 46n.6
Inclán, Miguel 65, 81, 95, 122
Indigenismo (indigenism) 4, 8, 33, 67, 73-91, 94-101, 167, 170
 indigenista (indigenist) 8, 58-9, 73-5, 77-84, 96, 98-100
Infante, Pedro 14, 119n.2
 see also Rodríguez, Ismael
Institutional Revolutionary Party (PRI) 28, 49, 51-2
Irwin, Robert 105
Isaac, Alberto 163, 165
 En este pueblo no hay ladrones 163
 rincón de las vírgenes, El 165
 isla de pasión, La 65
 Islas Marías, Las 66, 161
 It Happened One Night 113-15, 117, 119n.3

Janitzio **58-61**, *61* 65, 74, 78-80, 82, 95-8
jarabe tapatío 23
Jenkins, William 160-1
Joseph, Gilbert 4, 28, 52, 62, 148
Juárez, Benito 146, 153, 158-n.3
Junco, Tito 139
Junco, Victor 137

Kahlo, Frida 27, 146
King, John 26, 51, 155, 159n.11, 161, 171n.1
Kohn, José 162
Kraniauskas, John 119, 124

Lady Eve, The 114
Landeta, Matilde 12, 14, 16n.8, 16n.10, 34, 131, 143n.4
 Lola Casanova 16n.8

Trotacalles **131-2**
 negra Angustias, La 16n.8, 34, 143n.4
Landy, Marcia 125
Lara, Agustín 22, 127, 129
Larsen, Neil 51
Lent, Tina Olsin 113
Levi, Heather 28, 58
Lomitz Adler, Claudio 8, 49, 53, 58, 66, 73, 86, 95, 135
López, Ana M. 13-15n.1, 29, 32, 35, 43-4, 72n.5, 125, 127-9, 133, 136
López, Marga 65, 122
López Moctezuma, Carlos 65, 95, 144
López Portillo, José 165-6
López Portillo, Margarita 166
Lucha libre 28

machismo 66, 106-9, 112, 118, 127
 'lo macho' 8, 104, 106-8, 118
Machlachlan, Colin M 158n.3
Maciel, David R 13
Maclovia 2-3, 8, 25, 34, 59, 74-5, **95-8**, 100, 153, 155, 169
Madero, Francisco 4
Magdaleno, Mauricio 54, 65, 102n.7
Malinche, La 41, 73, 105-7, 123
 malinchismo 8, 73
 malinchista 102n.1
Malquerida, La 170
María Candelaria 1-3, 8, 15n.3, 25, 27, 34, 54, 59, **73-5**, **79-97**, *89*, 92-93, 100, 102n.10, 107, 125, 149-50, 153, 155-7, 169-71n.1
marimacha 34
Marqués, María Elena 65, 98
Martí, José 63
Martin, Michael T 159n.10
Martín Barbero, Jesús 28-32, 35-8, 40, 44, 50, 83, 125, 168
Martínez, Rubén 28
Martínez Solares, Gilberto 3, 34
 see also Tin Tan
Mary, Virgin 91-2, *93*
Menchú, Rigoberta 68

Index

Méndez, Leopoldo 149
  cacique issuing orders (engraving) *149*
  raised torch (engraving) *152*
mestizaje 62, 73
mestizo 58–60, 69–70, 74, 81, 85–6, 97, 135, 141
Mexican cinema
  audience of 32, 35–8
  criticism on 6–15, 39–43
  history of 18–26, 160–8
  the State and, 27, 32–3, 52
Mexicanness 1, 33, 42, 94, 104–7, 127, 155
mexicanidad 2, 4–5, 12, 33, 73, 77
mexicano, lo 1, 28, 80, 152, 168–9
Mexican revolution 1, 4, 19
  crisis of 148
  gender and 104–43
  institutionalization of/the myth of 2, 49, 145
México norte 166
Miller, Michael Nelson 26–8, 77, 83
Miller, Toby 50
Miquel, Ángel 10
Monsiváis, Carlos 6–9, 11–12, 26, 28–9
  analysis of Emilio Fernández 44, 48–50, 53, 59, 63, 66–7, 69, 72n.4
  on classical Mexican cinema 32–42, 44, 168–9
  gender, the Revolution, *Enamorada* and 104–7, 111, 113
  on melodrama, *bolero*, the cabaret 125–6, 129, 133
  Nuevo Cine group and 163
Montaner, Rita 140, 143n.6
Mora, Carl J 13, 74, 155, 159n.9, 161
Morris, Meaghan 37–8, 47n.10
Morocco 120n.4
modernity 6, 8, 18–19, 32–3, 39, 45n.1, 83–5, 90, 95, 129, 142, 144, 150, 155, 157, 169
modernization 2–3, 27–8, 33, 83, 96–7, 168
Moreno, Antonio *see Santa* (1931)

Mraz, John 28, 102n.2
Mulvey, Laura 110–11
Musser, Charles 46n.5
Mutual Film Company 20

Naremore, James 43, 50, 85
Nason, Richard 88
National Action Party (PAN) *see* Fox, Vicente
national cinema 7, 9, 14, 29, 42, 51
National Palace Murals *see* Rivera, Diego
Nava, Mica 47n.10
New (Latin American) Cinema 12, 30, 42–3, 50, 54, 124, 153, 159n.10
Noble, Andrea 12–13, 34, 45n.2, 80, 91, 94, 167
Noriega, Chon 15, 51
North American Free Trade Agreement (NAFTA) 169
Nosotros dos 161, 170
Novaro, María 14
Nowell-Smith, Geoffrey 126–7
Nuevo cine 163
Nuevo cine 163, 166

Obregón, Álvaro 21, 26, 46n.4, 77
O'Connor, Alan 30
Office of the Coordinator for Inter-American Affairs 24
O'Malley, Ilene 4, 76, 106, 146, 159n.6
On the Town 130
Orozco, José Clemente 8, 77, 82
Orozco, María Teresa 58

pachuco 34, 73
Paget, Debra 86
Palacio Nacional 146, 159n.2
Palma, Andrea 142
Paloma herida 164
Paranaguá, Paulo Antonio 13, 15n.1, 23, 39, 71, 85, 102n.8, 161, 168
Pardavé, Joaquín 34
Paz, Octavio 8, 41, 49, 66, 73, 105–7, 124

Peckinpah, Sam 62, 164–5
  Bring Me The Head of Alfredo Garcia 62, 165
  Wild Bunch, The 62, 66, 164
  Pat Garret and Billy the Kid 165
pelado 34–5
  see also Cantinflas
Pepita Jiménez 67, 167
Peredo Castro, Francisco 24, 103n.16, 146, 153
perla, La 2–3, 8, 25, 59, 74–5, **98–102n.3**, 103n.15, 154–5, 169, 99
Perkins, Victor, 55–6
Pick, Zuzana M 46n.4
Pilcher, Jeffrey M. 28
Podalsky, Laura 12, 78, 82, 94, 103n.14, 125, 148, 157
Pons, María Antonieta, 135, 143n.3
popular culture 6–7, 17, 28–32, 37, 40, 58–9
Posada, José Guadalupe 55, 78, 107, 153
Positif 54
Positivism 45n.1, 45n.3, 76
  Positivist 19
Pueblerina 166
Pueblito 66, 163

¡Que viva México! 47n.9, 64, 77–8, 82, 153

Radio, Televisión y Cinematografía (RTC) 166
Ramos, Julio 76
Ramos, Samuel 35, 41, 49, 66, 167
rapto, El 161, 170
Rashkin, Elissa 13–14
rebelión de los colgados, La 162, 167
red, La 61, 66, 161, 166, 170
Reportaje 161
Reyes, Alfonso 66
Río Escondido 2–3, 8, 16n.8, 25, 34, 54, 56, **144–59**, *147*, *149*, *152*, 160, 163, 169, 171n.2
Ripstein, Arturo 11, 165
  castillo de la pureza, El 165

Ripstein, Arturo Snr. 162
Rivera, Diego 8, 27, 53–4, 74, 77, 82, 107, 146–8, 159n.6
  National Palace Mural *maestras rurales* 147
  National Palace Mural *campesinos* held at gunpoint 147
rosa blanca, La 161, 170
RKO 98
Rocha, Glauber 50
Rodríguez, Ismael 1–3, 66, 104, 119, 162, 164
  cucaracha, La 66, 104, 162
  hermanos del hierro, Los 164
  Nosotros los pobres 2
  Ustedes los ricos 119n.2
Rodríguez, Joselito 22, 143n.4
  Angelitos negros 143n.4
Rodríguez, Roberto 22, see also *La Bandida*
Roland, Gilbert 170
Rooner, Charles 100
Rosas, Enrique 14, 20, 46n.3
  El automóvil gris 14, 20, 32, 46n.3
Rotberg, Dana 14
Rozado, Alejandro 2–3, 12, 48, 153–5
Ruíz Cortines, Adolfo 160, 171n.2
rumba 133–4, 136
rumbera 129–30, 134–5, 139–41
  see also Sevilla, Ninón; Pons, María Antonieta

Sadoul, George 1, 3, 53, 84
Salazar Bondy, Agusto 107
Salón México 2–3, 8, 54, **121–36**, 137–43n.6, 169
Sandino, Augusto César 64
Santa (1918) 21, 46n.3
Santa (1931) 21–3, 29, 122–3, 126–7
Santa (1943) 122–3
Schatz, Thomas 49
Schmidt, Arthur 156
Schoeman, Gloria 54
Schyfter, Guita 14
screwball comedy *see* film genres
Second World War 23–5, 52, 65, 103n.16, 122, 160

Index

antifascism and, 100, 103n.16
  see also Hitchcock, Alfred,
    Notorious
  see also perla, La
Secretaría de Educación Pública (SEP)
  77–8
Sequeyro, Adela 14, 16n.10
Sevilla, Ninón 129, 135, 139
Shakespeare, William 108
Shea, Maureen 68
Shohat, Ella 60
Singin' in the Rain 56
Siqueiros, David Alfaro 55, 82
Sirk, Douglas 125
Sistach, Maryse 14
Smith, Paul Julian 13
Solanas, Fernando 50, 159n.10
Soler, Domingo 144
Soler, Fernando 164
Soler, Julián 165
  Cuando los hijos se van (1969) 165
Sommer, Doris 46n.7
Soto Rangel, Arturo 139
Soy puro mexicano 65–7
Spanish-American War (1898) 46n.5
Spence, Louise 21, 75
Spivak, Gayatri 68
Stam, Robert 21, 50, 71, 75
Steinbeck, John 98, 100
Strand, Paul 22, 52, 74, 78
  Redes see Emilio Gómez Muriel
superloco, El 65
Syder, Andrew 168

Taibo, Paco Ignacio 12, 15, 48–9, 53, 57, 59–64, 66, 69–72n.3–4, 161–2
Tasker, Yvonne 109
telenovela 31, 125
testimonio 67–9
Tierra del Fuego se apaga, La 161–2
Tin Tan (Germán Valdés) 34, 73, 102n.2
  rey del barrio, El 34
Tissé, Edouard 77
Tlatelolco massacre 165, 171n.3
Toland, Gregg 29, 55

Top Hat 130
Torch, The 170
Torres San Martín, Patricia 14, 16n.10
Toscano, Salvador 10, 19, 45n.2
Toscano, Carmen 10, 45n.2
  Memorias de un mexicano 10, 19, 45n.2
Tovar, Lupita 21–2
Trader Horn 80
Tuñón, Julia
  classical Mexican cinema 33–7, 40–2, 44, 132, 142
  on Fernández 1, 3–4, 7, 12, 15n.3, 48–9, 53–4, 58–9, 63–4, 66–71, 74, 83, 101, 104, 106–7, 116, 123, 133, 137, 153–4, 167
  images of women 14–16n.10

Urueta, Chano 3, 64, 80
La noche de los Mayas 80

Valentino, Rudolf 48, 64
Vargas, Juan Carlos 46n.6
Vargas, Pedro 129
Vasconcelos, José
  murals and 77, 102n.5
  raza cósmica, La 63, 76
  state support of culture and 26–7, 41
Venice Film Festival 25
Veyre, Gabriel 18
Víctimas del pecado 2–3, 8, 16n.8, 54, 66, 107, 121–3, 127, **138–42**, 143n.6, 160–1, 169
Villa, Pancho 4, 20, 63, 106
villista 106, 151
Villarías, Carlos 21
Villarutia, Xavier 53
Virgin of Guadalupe 11, 91, 103n.11, 107, 123
Von Trier, Lars 43
  Idiots, The 43

Wagner, Fernando 100
Wallerstein, Gregorio 162
Welles, Orson 29, 42, 87, 91
  Touch of Evil 91
Willemen, Paul 55

Williams, Raymond 11
Wollen, Peter 55–6
women's films *see* film genres

Zapata, Emiliano 4, 106
   zapatista 108
Zea, Leopoldo 107

Zinneman, Fred 22, 78
   Redes see Gómez Muriel, Emilio
Zolov, Eric 2
Zona roja 66, 165
Zugsmith, Albert 164
   Pistolero fantasma, El 164

EU authorised representative for GPSR:
Easy Access System Europe, Mustamäe tee 50,
10621 Tallinn, Estonia
gpsr.requests@easproject.com